The Legacies of a Hawaiian Generation

The Legacies of
a Hawaiian Generation

From Territorial Subject to American Citizen

Judith Schachter

berghahn
NEW YORK · OXFORD
www.berghahnbooks.com

Published in 2013 by

Berghahn Books

www.berghahnbooks.com

© 2013, 2016 Judith Schachter
First paperback edition published in 2016

Library of Congress Cataloging-in-Publication Data

Schachter, Judith, 1941-
  The legacies of a Hawaiian generation : from territorial subject to American citizen /
Judith Schachter.
       pages cm
  Includes bibliographical references and index.
    ISBN 978-1-78238-011-5 (hardback) — ISBN 978-1-78533-204-3 (paperback) —
ISBN 978-1-78238-012-2 (book)
    1. Hawaiians—Kinship. 2. Hawaiians—Ethnic identity. 3. Hawaiians—Government
relations. 4. Social values—Hawaii. 5. Statehood (American politics)—History.
6. Imperialism—United States—History. 7. United States—Politics and government.
8. United States—Race relations. I. Title.
  DU624.65.S32 2013
  305.899'42073—dc23

                                                                        2013005542

British Library Cataloguing in Publication Data

A catalogue record for this book is available from the British Library

ISBN: 978-1-78238-011-5 hardback
ISBN: 978-1-78533-204-3 paperback
ISBN: 978-1-78238-012-2 ebook

For John, for Eleanor
"Another story to tell"

Contents

Preface and Acknowledgments   viii

Introduction. A Perspective on Hawai'i–US Relations   1

Chapter 1. Living on the Land: *Mālama ʻāina* from Past to Present   16

Chapter 2. "Educating the Polynesian American": Two Worlds of Learning   52

Chapter 3. Work, War, and Loyalty: The Impact of World War II   85

Chapter 4. Making a Way, Building a Family: Preserving ʻOhana in an American State   118

Chapter 5. "Stand Fast and Continue": Homestead Generations and the Future   158

Epilogue   199

Glossary of Selected Terms   211

Bibliography   213

Index   222

Preface and Acknowledgments

The story of my engagement with Hawai`i is long and somewhat meandering. I went in the first instance to investigate a particular topic—the persistence of customary adoption (hānai) under an American legal system. I imagined I could draw boundaries—chronological and theoretical—around the topic. I quickly discovered that the presumption simplified a tangled history of American presence in the archipelago, the simplification that still characterizes depictions of the islands as "paradise." My initial inquiry into adoption and hānai brought polite but baffled responses, and those reactions prompted my subsequent interest in everyday interpretations of American imperial presence in Hawai`i. I ended up returning, for two decades, to follow out threads in the conversations I had.

I was fortunate in my earliest conversations. Colleagues at the University of Hawai`i provided introductions to individuals and to associations whose roles in the state of Hawai`i varied and whose identification as "Native Hawaiian" covered a wide array of interpretations. In every case I entered as an anthropologist, clearly a stranger and not a resident of the state. My times in Hawai`i were limited, and my immersion in local events constrained by the necessity of returning to the mainland. I accepted these limitations, and do not in my book speak as a local person, or describe "Hawaiian culture" or represent sources of Native Hawaiian identity that I cannot share. Rather, I let the conversations I had structure an analysis of the impact of American policy on individuals who in myriad ways enact their attachment to an indigenous culture.

Good luck came to me in other ways. John Simeona and his sister Eleanor Ahuna began by teaching me the lessons they thought a haole should know and ended by bringing me into the `ohana of which each was senior member. Their children and grandchildren accorded me the title of "Auntie" and then simply greeted me with affection. The younger generation followed in the footsteps of the elders, and they too offered me stories of their experiences. In both households, I was given meals, invited to celebrations, taken to hula classes, and expected to pull my weight ("you can move off the couch," John's sister Winona said to me, when I politely asked for a glass of water). It was assumed that I would watch children when no one else was around, send gifts on the right occasions, and, most importantly, "come home" to the homesteads of Waimānalo and Keaukaha regularly.

Along the way, I met other homestead residents, as well as individuals in social service agencies, in health clinics, in the courts and law offices I visited, and through a spreading network of contacts. In Waimānalo, Helene and Gordon became advisors, guides, and close friends; we talked of the intimate as well as the public domains of life. Sensitive to the problems created by a history of marginalization and discrimination, they searched for modes of empowering the young and the old, the male and the female, the keiki of the next generation of Native Hawaiians. Gordon's mother was a further inspiration, as she marched up and down the hilly homestead streets to work in Blanche Pope, the homestead elementary school.

Many individuals will remain anonymous, by their choice or my decision. They are voices that represent diverse viewpoints about custom and tradition, about the history of American presence in Hawai`i, and about the particular accommodations a person will make to the conflict between "native" and "foreign" ways of being. They taught me through the gift of their mo`olelo, the talk-stories that form a backbone of my book, and through the behaviors to which I became—or tried to—a silent observer. Always I had to keep John's first lesson in mind: don't ask questions, don't be nosy, just listen and watch.

In the spring of 1989, Cathie Jordan and Paula Levin arranged for me to spend several months at the Kamehameha Schools. Then director, Richard N. Roberts offered me a position as adjunct researcher with the Center for Development of Early Education. I worked at the schools for three months, observing the preschool programs spread around O`ahu. Teachers and parents participated generously in my project. A summer later, I received permission from a Honolulu social service agency to attend an anger management group for men and a domestic violence group for women, both on the Leeward Coast of O`ahu. The facilitators of those groups continued with the set agenda, sometimes letting my presence fade and other times insisting that I tell my own stories of relationships and family. I made close friends with several women in the group, and they introduced me to their friends and family. I spent time in Nanakuli, Mā`ili, and Wai`anae talking with individuals whose concern and whose work focused on problems of health, child care, unemployment, and homelessness on the Leeward Coast.

I did not speak pidgin (Hawaiian Creole English) with the people I met, and I don't use pidgin in my book. When a conversation occurred partly in pidgin, I transcribe the sentences into English; I translate from a language I do not speak into one that I do. Most of the people I met used pidgin sparingly, acknowledging my malihini status.

John and Eleanor used English in their conversations with me. The writings they gave me, too, are primarily in English, as are the numerous letters

John sent over the eight years of our friendship. Late in our friendship, John incorporated pidgin into his letters, and in quotations I let those phrases stand just as he wrote them. Eleanor used Hawaiian words in the documents she gave me; those were the words that captured the spirit of what she needed to say. John was not fluent and rarely did I hear a Hawaiian word in his stories. In my book, I leave unchanged both Eleanor's spelling of Hawaiian words and her translations of Hawaiian terms. Similarly, I leave in its original form the English each one used in writing.

I use the ʻokina and the kahakō, now considered part of the Hawaiian alphabet, in my interpretive sections, so that, for example, John's Waimanalo is "Waimānalo" in analytic passages. Similarly, scholarly works before the 1970s omit the ʻokina and the kahakō. In all quotations from sources I leave the original spelling. I italicize and define Hawaiian words in my text only in the first usage, unless a definition is later necessary for clarification.

A more problematic issue concerns the designation of "Hawaiians." In the following chapters, I use *Native Hawaiian* to refer to individuals who identified themselves that way, regardless of blood quantum (in official state agencies, "native Hawaiian" with a small *n* refers to individuals with 50 percent or more Hawaiian blood; "Native" with a capital *N* refers to those with some Hawaiian ancestry). I also use the term *kānaka maoli* (real or true people) to reflect the changing patterns of identification in the late twentieth century, when that term came into use to displace the blood- (and race-) based definition instituted by an American regime. The choice of terms is complicated for individuals I met, and the choice of kanaka maoli or ʻōiwi or kanaka ʻōiwi places a person in relation to the debates that continue to occur over sovereignty, indigenous rights, and cultural autonomy. John and Eleanor used "Native Hawaiian" and "Hawaiian" for the people with whom they identified; when "Hawaiian" refers to residents of the state or territory, that is clear in context.

I owe a debt of gratitude and special thanks to Grace K. Mamoaliʻiokalani Bezilla, Eleanor's granddaughter. Grace is a student and teacher of the Hawaiian language at a time when that language is coming to prominence—and achieving acceptance—throughout the state of Hawaiʻi. She read through my whole manuscript, correcting and re-translating Hawaiian words. She made suggestions about my interpretations of her grandmother's writings, and she offered guidance on some of my general interpretive points. When I had doubts and sent her an urgent email message, she answered quickly—despite her own very busy life.

In Waimānalo, John's daughter Carla and her husband Michael Hare kept the doors open for me, and their four daughters—Nohea, Ana, Christeen, and Chelsea, have been equally welcoming; I thank the whole ʻohana. In Keaukaha, Eleanor's children assumed the kuleana she gave them, and kept me close to the changes in their lives. Thanks to Kihei and Bev Ahuna, to Alberta Nicolas, and especially to Aloha and George Bezilla, and their children and mo`opuna. Throughout the extended `ohana in O`ahu and on the Big Island, individuals I do not name granted me their trust and welcome.

I benefited from close reading of the manuscript by several persons: Ty P. Kāwika Tengan read the whole manuscript with a fine-tooth comb; Alan Howard and Jan Rensel read and commented on several earlier articles and drafts; Karen Sinclair gave pointed and detailed criticisms, as did Mac Marshall. Participants in several workshops at meetings of the Association for Social Anthropology in Oceania provided critical comments and advice on aspects of my inquiry. John and Eleanor read earlier pieces of mine, and commented on the interpretations in those accounts.

In the 1970s, when I attended the University of Pennsylvania, Bill Davenport took me under his wing, and to him and his wisdom I owe my interest in Hawai`i in the first place. Not only did he school me in things Hawaiian and Pacific, he gave me his library of Hawaiian material when he moved on to other research interests. He encouraged me in this project all along the way.

In Hawai`i, Stephen Boggs brought me to the meetings in Waimānalo where I first met John, and then Helene. Meda Chesney-Lind, on my second trip to Hawai`i, cautioned me against simplifying the "story." Jane Silverman shared her knowledge of the Hawaiian judiciary system (and her apartment). Ho`ipo De Cambra invited me to a woman's group on the Wai`anae Coast. There I met Odetta Medeiros with whom, over the years, I have spent many hours talking story. Eric Enos, Puanani Burgess, Father Gigi, and others involved with Hawaiian culture and education projects were generous with their time. There are more individuals than I can possibly list, who, across the places I visited, offered time, thoughtfulness, and engagement with my work. Unnamed, they are all crucial to the book, though none is responsible for the final story, which is my own.

Librarians and archivists to whom I owe appreciation include staff in the Hawaiian and Pacific Collections, the University of Hawai`i, Mānoa; the Hawaiian Mission Houses Historic Site and Archives, Honolulu; the Library of the Ethnological Museum, Berlin; Hunt Library at Carnegie Mellon University, Pittsburgh. I received financial support for the project from the Fulbright Program and two Carnegie Mellon University Faculty Development Grants.

Students in my classes on Hawai`i: Mark Rau, Kristina Izumi, Tara Sakauye, Randy Wong, Michelle Spitzer, and Scotty Ah Sam Wright—all residents of Hawai`i and unfailingly assiduous in correcting my stories (and my pronunciation) in class. Becky Kluchin and I talked about various modes of doing "life history," and Jeff Suzik commented on my account of the CCC from his own expertise on that American organization. Professor Rubie Watson and Professor Keith Brown encouraged me to pursue—and expand—my project in Hawai`i after I gave a talk at the University of Pittsburgh. My Carnegie Mellon colleague, Richard Tucker, talked with me about the role of Standard English in schooling in the Pacific. Roger Rouse, Paul Eiss, and Richard Maddox, anthropologists in the History Department with me, read and commented on drafts of earlier pieces. In addition, our informal conversations provide essential support for the interdisciplinarity we share.

I owe particular thanks to friends who stayed with this project for all its years: Eugene Ogan, whose guidance began when I was a graduate student at the University of Minnesota and continued in Hawai`i; Bill Chismar, who facilitated my "beach crossings"; and, Jane Bernstein who commented on parts of the book from her own experience as a writer. Albrecht Funk, who read more drafts than either of us are willing to count, deserves particular gratitude.

A Perspective on Hawai`i–US Relations

In 1988, I went to Hawai`i for the first time. As part of a study of American adoption policy and practices, I intended to include a chapter on Polynesian customs in the fiftieth state.[1] My initial contacts with social workers and lawyers soon led to an expansion of the subject, as did three months of fieldwork a year later.

Adoption, I realized, was not a bounded subject; or, to put it differently, the boundaries reflected a conception based on a North American legal transaction. Court-approved transactions concerning a child were accompanied by nineteenth-century intrusion into the public and the private lives of an indigenous people. This was, then, one mode through which the United States colonized the archipelago. The complementary, intensifying, and subtle ways in which the US defined the lives of a "native" people expanded the original focus of my research into adoption.

I met John Simeona when I returned to Hawai`i the next year. In May 1989, a colleague brought me to a meeting of the Waimānalo Senior Citizens Association.[2] John stood at the front of the room, his back to the group, leading the pledge of allegiance to the stars and stripes hanging on the wall. A rendition of "Aloha `Oe" followed, the seniors joining in song as assiduously as they had recited the pledge.[3] John ran the meeting, and introduced me at the end. I spoke of my research, still focusing on adoption as an approach to Hawai`i–US relations. The seniors responded with indifference. As president of the group, John took on the responsibility of communicating my message in their words. She is interested in Hawaiian *custom*, he said, and the "ways of old." Then, after the meeting ended, he spent forty-five minutes talking story into my tape recorder.

So began a friendship that is crucial to the form and approach of *The Legacies of a Hawaiian Generation*. Several years after we met, John added a typed document to the stories he had already provided in hours of talk, in tape recordings, and in letters. The "book," as he described it, was called *Life Story of a Native Hawaiian*, and the subtitle read "100 percent Hawaiian."[4] John's reference to a percentage both recalls and rejects the US government's categorization of Native Hawaiians as a racial group, with blood quantum taken as the measure. By referring to the loaded percentage notion, John acknowledged the power of an imposed racial definition in his life. By claiming "100 percent," he asserted that being Hawaiian, acting Hawaiian, and practicing Hawaiian "ways" meant something radically different from the bureaucratically inscribed blood quantum.[5]

The subtitle of *Life Story of a Native Hawaiian* connects the percentage to the names of his father and his mother, which appear on the lines above: "Kaheekai Kuakahela Simeona and Sarah Kealohapauole." The phrase equally points forward, to thirty-two chapters in which he describes the customs, behaviors, and attitudes that comprise his identification of himself as a Native Hawaiian man.[6]

The process of identification through an enactment of Hawaiian values persisted even as he engaged—involuntarily and then voluntarily—in the institutions established by an American colonial regime. From his childhood in the Hawaiian Homestead of Keaukaha, on the Big Island, to the last years of his life in the Waimānalo Homestead on Oʻahu, John brought the lessons of his ancestors to bear on practices and injustices that are the outcome of US governance. In a phrase he would not have used, John *negotiated* his Hawaiian and his American identities until the end of his life. He died in June 1996.

After his death, his sister Eleanor took me under her wing, assuming her responsibility as the *hānau mua*, eldest living member of the family, the accepted source of wisdom, and the keeper of tradition.[7] She carried on the relationship between Native Hawaiian and outsider that John had begun. Through the years of our friendship, John and Eleanor influenced my approach as a cultural anthropologist.[8] From them, I learned the significance of writing with commitment, of avoiding the neutral voice conventionally prescribed in academic disciplines, and of including bonds of attachment as a form of data.

John offered advice on the book about Hawaiʻi and the United States he expected me to write. Although he told the seniors in Waimānalo I was studying "Hawaiian custom," his subsequent interactions with me conveyed a different subject, one closer to his own efforts to sustain Hawaiian values within an American milieu. Over the years, he shared his changing interpretations of the past in the face of developments in the present he called *modern times*. His interpretations of custom reflected his perspective on my work. At first he viewed me as the researcher, an anthropologist visiting the senior citizens group. I was a *malihini*, a stranger who came to the shores of Hawaiʻi to pursue my project. In time, my work established my genealogy and accorded me a place, without erasing my origins: a *haole* from the mainland—pale and citified. John did not solidify those identities, any more than he held one position regarding his own identity. He would, he teased, "brown" me in the sun, fatten me on Hawaiian foods, and, most importantly, socialize me in proper Hawaiian manners. Through acting right, I might achieve understanding. In a letter about my work, he jested: now you are becoming *"hapa Hawaiian."*

Hapa is crucial to the chapters in this book. *Hapa* translates as "half," and the common usage in Hawai`i is *hapa haole*: residents of the islands whose background is half Caucasian and half Hawaiian. Over time, the term *hapa* grew to include other locals, thereby shedding the one-dimensional racial significance of whiteness.[9] Stretching from a dichotomous categorization, the change softened the colonial impact of the designation, placing hapa along a complex continuum of difference.

Critics claim that hapa haole resembles "Hawaiian at heart" with its superficial embrace of Hawaiian culture.[10] For John, however, hapa was positive, a sign of flexible identities. When he called me "hapa Hawaiian," he reversed the negative attributions of hapa by assuming I could learn the processes that produce identification as a Native Hawaiian person.[11] For him, hapa represented an active and respectful apprenticeship to experts in culture teaching. I could learn to act according to Hawaiian cultural norms by listening to the elders, by observing behaviors, and by keeping my mouth shut. "Be quiet," he instructed, "and wait for the stories." In granting me the possibility of moving between identities, from malihini anthropologist to familiar pupil, he mimicked his own life story. For over seventy years, he had worked at juxtaposing the behaviors that represented *being Hawaiian* with those that demonstrated his acquisition of American teachings; he learned how to practice the right culture at the right time. Hapa was no more a portion or fraction than was 100 percent a fixed totality. As individuals judge and measure Native Hawaiian and American influences in their everyday lives, the components are inevitably in flux, reflecting shifting relationships.

Relationships are at the core of this book. My relationship with John, moving from friendship to collaboration—he called the project "ours"—has primary place as inspiration and as ligament for the following five chapters. We were culture learners together, he said, crossing geographical, historical, and cultural boundaries in our many conversations. Hapa shifted for John, too, as he prepared his writings for my students, colleagues, and an audience entranced by tourist images of Hawai`i. "Your students don't know Hawaiian culture," he told me. He had brought his learning to the `ohana in his *Life Story,* and he adjusted the presentation—and the meanings of being Hawaiian—for a project that through me entered another arena.

Eleanor was my other teacher, and she participated in the project less as a partner than as a *kupuna* (elder) and expert. She also extended her interpretations of Hawaiian identity through conversations about my work, my role as pupil, and my perspective on a place she revered.

Beach Crossings

I have always admired the work of Greg Dening and I particularly like the title of his 2004 book *Beach Crossings*, contemplating fifty years of writing about Oceania. I like the title because it resonates with my relationship with John. I can think of our partnership as a mutual beach crossing: he pulled me toward Hawaiian ways when he corrected my "manners" and I pulled him toward my side of the beach when he placed his writings in an academic context.

"This wet stretch between land and sea is the true beach, the true in-between space," writes Dening, who continues: "it is a sacred, a *tapu* space, an unresolved space where things can happen, where things can be made to happen. It is a space of transformation. It is a space of crossings."[12] John and I sat at his favorite Waimānalo Beach for hours, talking story. We sat in between, under casuarina trees that separated dry land from the sea. Eventually we crossed the highway—named after Prince Jonah Kūhiō Kalaniana'ole—that separated the beach park from homestead lots.[13] I met his daughter, her husband, and the four children I was to watch grow up. I met John's sister Winona, who painted his kitchen cabinets black, and I met his sister Eleanor, second oldest in the family. Winona moved away, but my relationship with Eleanor evolved and developed its own character, just as her negotiation between being Hawaiian and being American differed from her brother's. She was the political actor in the family, participant in the cultural renaissance in the 1970s, Department of Hawaiian Home Lands commissioner in the 1980s, and self-defined activist in the 1990s. Auntie Eleanor died in December 2008.

She was "Auntie" but John was never "Uncle" for me. He had initially defined our relationship as reciprocal, an equal exchange of information; we were, in his words, first partners, then collaborators, and finally good friends. "Aloha Pumehana," he began his letters, that means "greetings with affection," he explained. The first self-reference he offered me persisted throughout the years I knew him. When I met Eleanor, I was already pupil, learner, and *familiar*; "Auntie" suited our relationship from the start.

John and Eleanor opened a space in the whole 'ohana for me. In different ways, each member of the family welcomed the visiting anthropologist who "came home" every summer.[14] Yet while other anthropologists have described themselves as "kin" in a family—sister or child—a fixed relational category does not fit either my experience or the notion of kinship in an 'ohana. I was welcomed home and I did, in a fashion, belong to the 'ohana, but I also slipped back and forth across boundaries: I went home to Pittsburgh every year. John kept these crossings in our minds when he used the term *hapa*. To belong, in the Native Hawaiian cultural context, means acting with concern, generosity, and involvement, not the kind of inherent connection my own culture suggests. I was both in and out of the ʻohana, a crossing that did not contradict the understandings of relationship I learned in Hawaiʻi.

Over a decade and a half, I formed other relationships, with individuals who became colleagues and friends. In 1989, I was granted an office in the Kamehameha Schools, on Kapalama Heights behind Honolulu. I spent hours talking with parents of children in the preschool program. Sitting in parks and playgrounds, these parents talked about education in Hawaiʻi, about their ambitions for the children, and about the implications of private schooling reserved for children of Native Hawaiian ancestry in an American state.[15] Teachers at Kamehameha talked with me about the same issues, struggling with the meaning of Princess Bernice Pauahi Bishop's bequest in the context of scarce resources and an increasingly vocal sovereignty movement.

A year later, in 1990, an anthropologist, Stephen Boggs, introduced me to teachers and social workers in Waimānalo. I met Helene, and she and her husband Gordon became my close friends. After they married, they had moved into the homestead, where they raised three children and five *moʻopuna* (grandchildren). Throughout the 1990s and into the new century, each devoted hours to the improvement of conditions on the homestead—particularly the education of a younger generation. Helene died in September 2008. Gordon is still a friend, a colleague, and a wise advisor for my project.

In 1990, too, I participated in two groups on the Waiʻanae Coast—an anger management group for men and a domestic violence group for women. I made friends there, too, with both men and women, and they expanded my circles of contact. I sat on Nanakuli Beach, I watched Odetta paddle into Waiʻanae Bay with her canoe team, and I attended meetings at the Waiʻanae Health Center. For some people I remained the inquiring anthropologist, and those individuals kindly provided information on the persistence of custom in a modern state. For others I became pupil, a person who could learn Hawaiian ways of life by listening and watching—no longer a complete stranger.

John and Eleanor also gave me "writings." In addition to *Life Story of a Native Hawaiian*, John wrote two books for me: a *Work History* and a *Family History*.[16] Eleanor gave me her four books on Hawaiian grammar written for the language revitalization project in Hilo, a book of Hawaiian recipes, and letters she had written as president of a homestead *hui,* or association. A 2009 collection of women's stories includes her memoir of her mother.[17] Both siblings used the word *writings* to refer to stories prepared for a "mixed" audience—outsiders to Native Hawaiian culture as well as intimates within that culture. These stories differ in style, though not consistently, from the moʻolelo recorded on tape and in the many conversations the two contributed to my book.

And alongside these stories were the hundreds of letters John sent to me over eight years. Sometimes he wrote every day and sometimes only when he could spare time from his other projects. These letters addressed my life and my family, my work and my visits to Hawai`i, and they provided lessons couched in advice, sympathy, and understanding. John's handwritten letters offer invaluable reflections on his life, on conditions in the state of Hawai`i, and on the future for Native Hawaiians in a twenty-first-century world.

Stories and Histories

Different relationships with me produced different stories—some cautious about the role of the United States in Hawai`i, and others deeply, frankly, critical of a nation that had stolen land and suppressed the language of an indigenous people. The composite provided a picture of American colonialism full of subtexts, modifications, and intersecting themes. Without minimizing the injustice and the illegality of the American takeover, my account emphasizes the fluidity of the relationship between Hawai`i and the United States—and points to the possibility of change in the twenty-first century.

John welcomed me into his `ohana, a stranger from the nation that had taken over an existing *lāhui* (nation), seized acres of land, and subdued the voices of the people. Our conversations crossed over this intersecting history, and we exchanged interpretations of the role of the US in Hawai`i. John interpreted American presence through the lens of a public school education, his time in the Army, and his job at the Pearl Harbor Naval Shipyard. In the mid-1990s, he sent me letters carefully assessing the sovereignty movement in terms of timing, responsibility to the people, and the debt the United States owed Native Hawaiians.[18] Eleanor was more directly critical in her talk, sharply appraising the outcome of the federal government's Hawaiian Homes Commission Act, recalling her protests against military appropriation of acreage, and arguing for revisions in the American judiciary system in Hawai`i.

Like John, Eleanor, and others I met, I am critical of the role the US plays in Hawai`i, and I indicate the continuation of colonial practices from earliest contact, through the territorial period, and into statehood. My book, however, is not a history of American colonialism. Nor is it a study of Native Hawaiian culture under US domination. Rather, I tell a story of relationships between an often overwhelming, arrogant, and appropriative nation and the people whose ancestry stretches to the eras before James Cook introduced the Western world to Hawai`i.[19] I write about members of a generation who identified strongly with Native Hawaiian culture despite the insistent efforts of the United States to assimilate and deny them identity as an indigenous people. This is a generation, too, that grew critical of the benefits offered by the federal and, after 1959, the state government, that warned their children and grandchildren about the "superficiality" in American construction of the islands, and that worked to counteract a spreading consumerism by practicing/teaching values drawn from "the people of old."[20] Yet, as John and Eleanor conveyed, a given relationship with the United States offered opportunity; both insisted, for instance, on Standard English as a route "to the future." The stories I heard from them deny the simplicity of a historical narrative propelled by colonial intrusion and indigenous opposition.

In this book, I shun theoretical approaches that exceptionalize American imperialism as benevolent assimilation and limit the resilience of Native Hawaiians to nostalgic traditionalism.[21] I have an equally skeptical attitude toward approaches in which resistance becomes the exclusive strategy that allows indigenous people to regain their cultural autonomy and sovereignty, and to shed the legacies of colonialism.[22] While insisting on the fact of American conquest, I try in the following chapters to capture the complexities of Hawaiian history through the lens of the many and diverse accounts that contest and subvert the dichotomous narratives of colonization and resistance.[23]

These accounts emerge from stories exchanged on diverse occasions. In interviews, conversations, and casual kitchen-table chat, the individuals I met told stories, adapting the exemplary Native Hawaiian–style discourse. "When you come, we can *talk stories* about everything," John wrote to me in 1994.[24] Digressive, anecdotal, and meandering, talk-story captures a person's perspective and stance in the world.[25] "These stories are all mo`olelo," the Hawaiian historian Jonathan Osorio explains, "whether they tell of mythic beings, of 'real' individuals whose power and influence affected the society in which they lived, of personal occurrences and family stories, and whether remembered in the mind or committed to writing." Such stories are a form of recounting and assessing experience, as well as placing personal reflections into a wider context. Such stories are history, no less (and no more) factual, true, or neutral than the "disciplined" history of the conventionally trained Western scholar. Osorio points to another dimension: mo`olelo, he continues, are a "form of assertive scholarship," meant to persuade, motivate, and call the reader to action.[26] As Auntie Eleanor put it, a person writes in order to cause change. "'Ōlelo': 'word' or 'speech' was far more than a means of communicating.... The word was itself a force."[27]

Writing alters the power of the word, freeing expression from the constraints of oral communication and opening the way to an assertion of individual viewpoint.[28] Eleanor put it clearly one afternoon: "all books are a person's opinion." She referred to the book she knew I was planning to write—a warning, perhaps, or more likely a lesson. And she presented a challenge: to assert a point of view without making oneself the central subject of the story.

Writing Lives

In one of his early morning phone calls, John asked me, "When will you finish my biography?" I was startled by the question. I had not thought of our interactions that way. I had not considered the outcome of my research in Hawai`i to be the account of an individual life. I have mulled over his question ever since. Why, when John's writings, talk-stories, and gestures of incorporation are crucial to my experience of Hawai`i, did I not write his biography? His *Life Story of a Native Hawaiian* provides part of the answer.

John wrote *Life Story* in 1982 and he gave it to me a few years after we met. The sixty-four-page document, typed by a daughter, traces his life from childhood through adulthood. Chronology, however, serves to organize a wealth of digressions, anecdotes, and assertive points of view. Talk-story style, John's *Life Story* is a mo`olelo, a tale of *being Hawaiian* under the hegemonic rule of the United States. It is also a mo`olelo in that the writer calls a younger generation to action, insisting on the importance of custom as a strategic response to the policies enforced by state and federal governments. His five-page list of medicinal "Hawaiian Herb plants," for instance, precedes a list of the teachers in his American public school—a comment on the juxtapositions he managed all his life. In thirty-two chapters, the writer offers instruction on combining the arts of *ka po`e kahiko* (the people of old) with the techniques necessary for success in the "modern" world. Consequently, the person—the presumptive hero of autobiography (or biography, for that matter)—is conveyed through the process of managing identities, negotiating cultures, histories, and opportunities. John's portrayal blends Native Hawaiian notions of self as embedded in social relations with American-style emphasis on individual agency and responsibility.

John wrote *Life Story* to instruct his children and grandchildren in his knowledge, his "learning," and his experience.[29] He wrote in English, the language he had learned—and initially resisted—in American public schools. By the time he sat down to do his writing, the language of the conqueror served the purpose of the conquered or, at least, provided John with a wider audience. The daughter who typed the manuscript occasionally edited, crossing out pidgin (Hawaiian Creole English) and inserting English: *uncle-them* becomes "my uncle and his family." When he gave the document to me, he turned me into pupil—and into a messenger for principles to which he was committed and values he brought from the past.

Over the years, John gave me more of his writings. He sent hundreds of letters, and with the passing of time, he used pidgin to express strong emotions and forceful opinions. Letters that tell the story of the Second World War, for instance, are sprinkled with pidgin, and pidgin phrases appear in the two accounts he wrote especially for me, the *Work History* and the *Family History*.[30] Work and family were, for him, the core of his identity—and the arc along which he negotiated between acting "100 percent Hawaiian" and being an American citizen. In return for his writings, he asked for mine—for my books and articles, in addition to the letters I sent from Pittsburgh. I gave him my biography of Ruth Benedict, and he responded with a letter full of comments. "It is hard," he said, "to write about another person." It takes work, he continued, to put everything down in words. The biography of Benedict appealed to him—the writing of mine he most evidently appreciated.[31] Because, I learned, the biography absorbed my "knowledge," and he generously treated it like my mo'olelo—a perspective on the world through the story of a life.

I have not written a biography, as John suggested on that early spring morning.[32] Instead, I accepted a lesson about writing lives from his *Life Story*. His is not an account of a single individual, but rather his intent emerges as pedagogical: his mo'olelo is the story of transmitting knowledge and learning to future generations. Biography, in its conventional definition, does not suit the "life" John gave me in numerous talk-stories, on beaches, at home, and through letters. His way of telling lives provides a template for the wider story I tell of a fluid, complicated, and often inequitable relationship between Hawai'i and the United States.

Guided by John and by Eleanor, my story reflects the knowledge/learning of a particular generation. Throughout the following chapters, the term *generation* has several meanings. In the context of kinship, it represents not only elders by age—a grandparental generation—but also kūpuna, "elderlys" (in John's word) who possess special wisdom. These kūpuna play a crucial role in the "transmission of cultural heritage" for Native Hawaiians. At the same time John and Eleanor are part of a social generation, individuals exposed to the same historical events and the same intrusions by the United States into their everyday lives.

Born in the 1920s and 1930s, members of the generation shared a process of Americanization that influenced negotiations of identity as they moved into adulthood. Two decades old, territorial status seemed to lock the fate of Hawai'i to the United States. The Great Depression further toppled the self-sustaining economy their parents and grandparents struggled to maintain. And the continued dominance of a haole elite—complemented by the melting-pot ideology of American citizenship—restricted the expression of indigenous language and custom.

Such common experiences did not result in an individualized, passive, and silent cohort of territorial subjects. Not simply docile or compliant with a colonial regime, this generation exchanged mo'olelo—as John and Eleanor did—in order to preserve, pass on, and perform the values of the past. They were a generation "in actuality," as Karl Mannheim put it, vigorously determining the "common destiny" of the Native Hawaiian people.[33]

John initially introduced me to members of this generation, the siblings and cousins he recommended as "experts" on Native Hawaiian culture. I was neither the first nor the last pupil. The elderlys to whom John attributed wisdom accepted a burden, a *kuleana* or responsibility to the youth who would inherit new stories and altered social contexts. Defined by a relationship to predecessors and to successors, not by kinship or age, ʻōpio (youth) turned to the elders when, in the 1970s, historical circumstances gave birth to a Hawaiian cultural renaissance. The experiences, the "generational consciousness" of kūpuna, provided essential resources for a movement whose outcome neither John nor Eleanor prescribed when they urged action on "those who come after."

John's *Life Story* ends: "I love everybody in our surroundings, my family, my friends and our good Lord for giving me this privilege to put all I know about my livelihood, my knowledge, my learning, my good attitude and all the good things I know from my past and from my present experiences. I hope that my family will do the same for their families, when they get as old as I am." In my book, I try to fulfill the task John gave his ʻohana and that his generation gave the next.

Organization

The chapters are roughly chronological, following the life span of John and of Eleanor. From the 1920s, when John was born, to the first decade of the twenty-first century, when Eleanor died, I delineate major strands in the history of Hawaiʻi through the eyes of a generation that negotiated identity as Native Hawaiian against the grain of Americanization. In a culture of oral remembering, in stories, chants, and song, the telling of experience at once interprets and domesticates—brings into generational relations—the core values of the past. Moreover, ʻōlelo (the word) has a force, and constitutes the doing/learning nexus that transmits Hawaiian cultural traditions. The "elderly" generation worked to exemplify custom for a younger generation, exposed to the forces of an American way of life.

Inasmuch as my account depends on the moʻolelo I heard, I refrain from burdening those stories with the paraphernalia of my own academic background. Rather, I weave material from relevant anthropological and historical literature into the stories told by "ordinary" people—the main spokespersons in this book.[34] In this effort, recent works by Native Hawaiian scholars play a crucial role. These writings uncover aspects of the relation between kānaka maoli and the United States that alter the way this relation has been seen by primarily Western or Western-trained scholars. In the following five chapters, I demonstrate how an intersection between everyday moʻolelo and Native Hawaiian scholarship can revise theoretical and methodological approaches to colonialism, to indigeneity, and to movements for self-determination.

Each chapter moves between present and past, combining memories, comments on current conditions in Hawaiʻi, and projections into the future for the state and its heterogeneous population. Like the stories I heard, the chapters are organized around the subjects that most forcefully bring US colonial policies and practices into the realm of personal experience. I depict the impact of relations of power on individuals who strenuously and steadfastly redesign that impact every day of their lives.

The book begins where John and Eleanor spent their childhood: on the homestead called Keaukaha, five miles from Hilo, Hawai`i's second largest city. Chapter 1, "Living on the Land," examines the significance of a Congressional act, the Hawaiian Homes Commission Act, for the way individuals interpret Hawaiian values and the impact of a colonial government on those values. The chapter moves between the viewpoints of John and Eleanor, and the background in policies of land distribution that haole advisors initiated in the mid–nineteenth century and that remain under dispute today. For John and Eleanor, Keaukaha connected past and present, represented the virtues of Hawaiian culture, and demonstrated the possibilities for future economic development on the part of Native Hawaiians. The chapter ends with Eleanor's script for improving the lives of Native Hawaiians, and her vision of Hawai`i in an international arena.

In 1930, John and, three years later, Eleanor walked the half-mile from home to Keaukaha Elementary School. Chapter 2, "'Educating the Polynesian American,'" describes two worlds of learning, strikingly at odds with one another. The practical, experiential learning through which John and Eleanor acquired "arts and skills" contrasted with American teacher-centered instruction in an alien language. In the chapter, I show how American public school perpetuates the civilizing mission of nineteenth-century settlers, with their ideas of work, virtue, and character. A Department of Public Instruction policy that followed the dictates of a plantation economy and reiterated the racism of US colonial practices tracked the children of the territory into place. At sixteen, John quit school and joined the Civilian Conservation Corps. The chapter concludes with a reappraisal of colonial practices through John's appreciation of a 1930s US federal work program for its preservation of Hawaiian-style *mālama `āina* (care for the land).

Pearl Harbor, 7 December 1941, transformed the economic, political, and social structures of the territory. A rush of newcomers, wartime jobs, and service in the military reconfigured the relationship between Hawai`i and the United States. Through his writings, John provides a unique perspective on the importance of World War II for a Native Hawaiian man, and chapter 3, "Work, War, and Loyalty," closely follows his accounts. In *Life Story, Work History, Family History,* and numerous letters, John reflected on the manipulation of race by an American government at war: the discriminatory division of labor in defense industries; the designation of enemy aliens at home; the treatment of the enemy abroad; and, the contradiction between US propaganda and administrative practice. Returning to Hawai`i for John, as for thousands of others, exposed the two sides of US rule: new opportunities in a post-war economy were bound to visible and demonstrated loyalty to an American way of life.

John's return to Honolulu coincided with the post-war years of prosperity in the islands. In Chapter 4, "Making a Way, Building a Family," John's search for work and for housing in a competitive environment tells a larger story of the increasing Americanization of Hawai'i, formalized by statehood in 1959. But, the chapter shows, Americanization did not overpower indigenous Hawaiian culture. For John and Eleanor, the privileges of US citizenship became resources for maintaining values associated with homestead life. The chapter depicts a turn in Native Hawaiian reactions to colonial history, as individuals like John and Eleanor increasingly used US law and ideals of democracy in order to maintain Hawaiian-style kinship and relationship with the land. At the same time, class differences, the changing worth of property, and federal programs intruded further into the lives of Native Hawaiians.

Chapter 5, "'Stand Fast and Continue,'" concludes my book. By the end of the century, John and Eleanor assumed the role of hānau mua, wise elders and caretakers of custom. The role carried a *luhi*—the burden of serving the people. This chapter draws on the activities (and the writings) of John and Eleanor to examine the impact of grassroots associations on the federal and state agencies that regulate Native Hawaiian lives. At meetings and in casual conversations, as well as in documents and public statements, individuals I knew on homesteads and elsewhere in the state condemned the United States for its failures to compensate an indigenous people for the loss of land and nationhood. Talk-stories spell out those failures, in anecdotes that define the problems faced by individuals in their everyday lives. These stories reveal a profound opposition to the categories, divisions, and institutions mandated by a federal government still negotiating its responsibilities in terms of race. For John and for Eleanor, poverty and dispossession justify demands against the US, and provide a designation of *Native Hawaiian* based on history and not on race. These are the stories that count. Told by the generation John and Eleanor represent, hānau mua in an American state, the stories convert the past into a vital template for the future.

Notes

1. Robert Levy's inquiries into adoption on Tahiti—Polynesian custom under the impact of French law—influenced my original research idea. See Levy, *The Tahitians: Mind and Experience in the Society Islands*.
2. My thanks to Stephen Boggs for this contact.
3. Composed by Queen Lili'uokalani, "Aloha 'Oe" is often sung to represent the spirit of Hawai'i.

4. John called *Life Story* a book, when he referred to its role in my project. The copy I have is a 64-page typed document.
5. John did qualify for a home lands plot, with the over 50 percent blood that program requires; see chapter 1.
6. According to the Office of Hawaiian Affairs *Native Hawaiian Data Book,* "Native Hawaiian" refers to people with Hawaiian ancestry, while "native Hawaiian" refers to individuals who possess 50 percent or more Hawaiian blood (Appendix, 44). I use the capital *N* inasmuch as my friends and contacts identified as Hawaiian based on genealogy and culture.
7. Mary Kawena Pukui, E. W. Haertig, and Catherine A. Lee, *Nānā I Ke Kumu* (I), 126.
8. As kūpuna and teachers, John and Eleanor pushed me to consider the anthropology in which I had been trained, and most especially the strictures on writing in that discipline. The last decades of the twentieth century witnessed a good deal of self-examination among cultural anthropologists in particular about "how we write," sometimes with a view to the audience for whom we write and sometimes with an eye on a discipline caught in a long history of colonial relationships in the places we work. I have borne those critiques in mind in composing the chapters in *The Legacies of a Hawaiian Generation.* While theoretical perspectives and methodological considerations in anthropology inform my research and my writing, I do not include those in the text itself. I have discussed how my approach fits into contemporary discussions in anthropology in a recent article (Schachter, "One Hundred Percent"). I have listened as carefully, I hope, as John instructed me to, and read through the documents he and Eleanor provided for the book. In addition, I draw on a wealth of archival and secondary sources in the process of interpreting the many stories I was told. These sources, too, are noted in endnotes so that the opinions, the mo'olelo, and the experiences the people I met shared with me are not overwhelmed with scholarly paraphernalia.
9. Judy Rohrer points out that hapa has positive connotations for residents of the islands who use it to refer to mixed identities of any sort—a marker of racial harmony; Rohrer, *Haoles in Hawai'i,* 46.
10. In her 2005 article "'Hawaiian at Heart,'" Lisa Kahaleole Hall uses the phrase to refer to individuals who "assume that knowing and appreciating Hawaiian culture is enough to transform them into being Hawaiian," 410.
11. See Karen L. Ito, *Lady Friends,* 4–5.
12. Greg Dening, *Beach Crossings,* 16–17.
13. Prince Kūhiō was responsible for the passage of the 1921 Hawaiian Homes Commission Act, granting homestead lots to native Hawaiians; see chapter 1.
14. Being welcomed "home," as I was after a while, was a phrase I regarded as a sign of the acceptance I had generously been accorded by the Simeona, Hare, and Ahuna families.
15. See chapter 2 , on education.
16. He occasionally used the word *book* to describe two packets of yellow-lined paper, each about 20 pages long.
17. Eleanor Ahuna, "Mama," 12–17.
18. Neither John nor Eleanor used the terms current in political discourse: kanaka maoli; 'ōiwi; 'ōiwi maoli. The word *Hawaiian* represented the people whose culture they shared; when the word indicates residents of the state, that is clear in context.
19. See Gary Y. Okihiro, *Island World,* 206; Rohrer, *Haoles in Hawai'i,* 14.
20. From the Hawaiian nineteenth-century writer Samuel Kamakau, *Ka Po'e Kahiko: The People of Old.*

21. The story of American exceptionalism lies deep in the national ideology that dominates history textbooks until today. Arthur Schlesinger's account of the annexation of Hawai`i as an accidental accession to power is exemplary: "It took half a century of argument before we annexed Hawaii, and this might not have taken place had it not been for the war with Spain. … We did annex the Philippines but set them free 40 years later. And by 1960 Alaska and Hawaii were states, not colonial possessions. … In short, the imperial dream had encountered consistent indifference and recurrent resistance through American history. … Americans, unlike the Romans, the British, and the French, are not colonizers of remote, and exotic places." Arthur Schlesinger, "The American empire?" 45. See, for an extensive discussion of American exceptionalism, Julian Go, *The Provinciality of American Empire,* and Bernard Porter, *Empire,* chapter 2.
22. Relying on Franz Fanon's vision of resistance to and liberation from colonialism, Hawaiian nationalists argue that Native Hawaiians can cleanse their culture of the destructive influence of American and Asian settler colonialism only if they obtain "native sovereignty controlled by natives." Haunani-Kay Trask, "Settlers of Color," 53. And as Momiala Kamahele adds in the same volume, "no matter how strong the resistance to the colonizers, Native culture will always be subjected to and subordinated by the state interests and needs. Native culture is still subject to the settler's rule." Kamahele, "`Īlio`ulaokalani," 87. See, in addition, the essays of Haunani-Kay Trask in *From a Native Daughter* that influenced a subsequent generation of Hawaiian scholars.
23. *The Legacies of a Hawaiian Generation* enters a dialogue (occasionally acrimonious) between Western and Hawaiian scholars that influences contemporary literature on Hawai`i. In the past four decades, Hawaiian scholars have successfully challenged the hegemony of Western anthropological and historical accounts of the islands. Lilikalā Kame`eleihiwa reanalyzed the story of land distribution by drawing on Hawaiian records in *Native Lands and Foreign Desires,* while Davianna Pōmaika`i McGregor describes the significance of these policies for contemporary Native Hawaiians in *Nā Kua`āina.* Historian Jonathan Osorio provides the background to contemporary movements in *Dismembering Lāhui* and Noenoe Silva, *Aloha Betrayed,* draws on Hawaiian-language newspapers to depict the resistance to American takeover, a phenomenon that has been underestimated. In *Hawaiian Blood,* J. Kēhaulani Kauanui examines the context, the content, and the consequences of the debates that culminated in the 1921 Hawaiian Homes Commission Act. Through a participatory and analytic study of a men's group, in *Native Men Remade,* Ty P. Kāwika Tengan links notions of masculinity to US colonial policies, Hawaiian cultural revitalization, and current nationalist movements.
24. John Simeona to the author, 7 June 1994.
25. Stephen Boggs, Karen Watson-Gegeo, and Georgia McMillen, *Speaking, Relating, and Learning;* Ito, *Lady Friends,* 12–13.
26. Jonathan Kay Kamakawiwo`ole Osorio, "'What Kine Hawaiian Are You?'" 360.
27. Pukui, Haertig, and Lee, *Nānā I Ke Kumu* (II), 124.
28. I thank Karen Sinclair for pointing to the difference between the spoken and the written word. She remarks on the similarity with Maori *korero:* "the conventions of korero mean it is not and cannot be opinion; writing, more individual and not so controlled, can be more readily reduced to opinion"—though I would replace "reduced to" with "enhanced by."
29. For John, learning was always an active and ongoing process—a verb and not a noun.
30. I do not add [*sic*] to either John's or Eleanor's writings, inasmuch as the change would imply a correct Standard English form.

31. I also gave him my book on Homestead, Pennsylvania, a former steel town, and the articles I published from my fieldwork in Hawai'i; see bibliography.
32. For a longer discussion of my approach to life history, biography, and "conversations" in the field in the context of evolving anthropological theory and method, see Schachter "One Hundred Percent."
33. According to Karl Mannheim in his 1932 essay "The Problem of Generations," people are significantly influenced by the socio-historical environment, forming on that basis a shared "generational consciousness" that provides the foundation for social action and agency.
34. Historical and anthropological materials form a background for my interpretations, and those are cited in endnotes. I have consulted standard accounts of Hawaiian history (e.g., Ralph Simpson Kuykendall, *The Hawaiian Kingdom;* Gavan Daws, *Shoal of Time;* Lawrence H. Fuchs, *Hawaii Pono*) as well as contemporary works that revise the arguments and approaches in these histories. In addition, I address the controversial subject of American imperialism in the Pacific by taking a close look at its manifestation in everyday lives. The writings of Paul Kramer, *The Blood of Government,* George Steinmetz, *The Devil's Handwriting,* Ann Laura Stoler, *Haunted by Empire,* Nicholas Thomas, *Colonialism's Culture,* and Margaret Jolly and Martha MacIntyre, *Family and Gender in the Pacific,* among others, establish a framework for analyzing the extent of colonial intervention that I apply to US presence in twentieth century Hawai'i. And while seminal critiques of anthropological theory and method appeared in the 1980s and 1990s (e.g., Marcus and Fischer, *Anthropology as Cultural Critique;* Clifford, *The Predicament of Culture*), self-consciousness about disciplinary conventions still merits attention. In its blurring of genres, *The Legacies of a Hawaiian Generation* advances the critique.

    My book also refers to earlier anthropological approaches to Hawaiian culture and history. These include: theoretical contributions, like William Davenport's classic analysis in "The 'Hawaiian Cultural Revolution,'" and Marshall Sahlins's provocative account in *Islands of History* of the encounter between "outsiders" and the indigenous people who greeted them; ethnographic inquiries like Alan Howard's *Ain't No Big Thing* and Jocelyn Linnekin's *Children of the Land;* and, specialized studies like Boggs, Watson-Gegeo, and McMillen on talk-story in *Speaking, Relating, and Learning.* In 2000, Sally Engle Merry's *Colonizing Hawai'i: The Cultural Power of Law* appeared, detailing the impact of colonialism through the laws imposed on an occupied nation. In recent decades, Bruce Cumings, *Dominion from Sea to Sea,* Eric T. L. Love, *Race over Empire,* and other Western scholarly works have begun to confront the role of the United States, placing Hawai'i in the context of American imperialism. Critical histories interpret the long past of Hawai'i–US relations through a focus on the devastating impact of US dominance over economic, political, and educational institutions (Coffman, *Nation Within a Nation;* Kent, *Hawaii: Islands under the Influence;* Okihiro, *Island World*).

    It would be impossible to focus on the relationship between Hawai'i and the US, as I do, without consulting the literature on land by Western scholars whose work complements that of Hawaiian scholars (e.g., King and Roth, *Broken Trust;* Linnekin, *Children of the Land;* Parker, *Native American Estate;* Van Dyke, *Who Owns the Crown Lands of Hawai'i?*). These works break down the dichotomy between "Hawaiian" and "Western," demonstrating that careful scholarship can override nationalist agendas, whatever their content and origin.

1

Living on the Land
Mālama ʻāina from Past to Present

On a spring day in June 1996, Auntie Eleanor gave a eulogy for her brother John. She sat at the front of a memorial chapel in downtown Honolulu in her wheelchair, facing a gathering of kin, friends, and neighbors. Eleanor was now the oldest living member of the ʻohana, and in her role as hānau mua she recited the experiences she and John shared, offering these to the mourners.[1] In her stories, she touched expansively on the childhood the two had spent together in a homestead called Keaukaha, just outside of Hilo, on the Big Island of Hawaii.

She was talking about a place they grew up in, where they were raised Hawaiian on land allotted by the US government. These were more than reminiscences: Keaukaha played a large role in the way John and Eleanor constructed their lives as Native Hawaiians in an American territory and state. The homestead epitomized the core of Hawaiian values—the 100 percent Hawaiian that is the subtitle of John's *Life Story*—and a source of responses to an increasingly Americanized society. The word *aloha* came up in these stories of a homestead, evoking the generosity and sharing that constituted true living on the land. In the eulogy, Eleanor conveyed the nuanced meanings of aloha when she described the teaching of arts and skills by kūpuna who were wise in Hawaiian history and culture. She talked of the ʻohana, an inclusive group of kin, and of John's role as *hiapo*, the first-born child in a family. She described the exchanges—fish from the sea for taro from the mountainsides—that extended the customs of the past into the present. Behind her words lay an interpretation of land: the ʻāina people honored as the source of sustenance and continuity over generations.

In 1921, the US Congress passed the Hawaiian Homes Commission Act, which promised to "save" the indigenous residents of an American territory by returning them to the land. Keaukaha was the second homestead established under the act and observers quickly arrived to gauge the success of the proposed rehabilitation. Virtually all visitors praised Keaukaha as a model community, reporting on the peaceful and harmonious lives of residents. Representatives from federal and territorial agencies describe "orderly and productive natives," implicitly endorsing an imperial policy of managing a population by prescribing a mode of subsistence. US government insistence on the well-being of natives obscured both the failure of its manifest agenda and the unintended success of the policy. Not planned and not projected, the 1921 Act provided space that became a place of preservation, of self-sufficiency, and of cultural sovereignty.

Eleanor's eulogy for John provides a counter-narrative to histories of American homesteading in Hawai`i. She talks of *caring for* the land, and of the people's *relationship* with the land. Her memories of life in Keaukaha constitute an interpretation of "home lands" that links congressional debates to the efforts of an *ali`i*, Prince Jonah Kūhiō Kalaniana`ole, to restore "life" to his people. There were other mo`olelo, constructed by her and by her brother over their lifetimes. Filled with anecdotes, digressions, and *kaona* (hidden meanings), these accounts transform the notion of land-as-property promulgated by an American Congress into the ancestral being portrayed in *mele,* ancient chants.

Land, with its diverse meanings and varied uses, constitutes an essential strand in the histories of two nations, knitting together the actions and the words of politicians, leaders, kānaka maoli, the people, and *kama`āina,* children of the land.

For John and Eleanor, the mo`olelo begin in Keaukaha. Eleanor lived in the homestead all her life, and John returned there regularly for family reunions, gatherings of former residents, and celebrations of birthdays, weddings, and graduations. I came to know Keaukaha after John's death, when Eleanor assumed the role of hānau mua and took me on as "learner." When I visited her, we drove through Keaukaha and into the companion homestead, Pana`ewa. The houses and yards in both places formed the background for her evolving commentary on the outcome of a congressional decision. In Keaukaha, the residential homestead, small bungalows lined straight, crisscrossing streets; a public school, American and Hawaiian flags flying, occupied a substantial central space. The houses in the agricultural homestead, Pana`ewa, also lay along a grid but the spaces between them were larger: the allotment for a farm. Juxtaposed, the residential and agricultural home lands Eleanor showed me expose a vacillating, uncertain, and murky American policy.

This chapter traces almost one hundred years of entanglement—beyond the span of John's life and a testimony to the force of Eleanor's critique of homestead policy. An American ideal of "good governance" for indigenous peoples intertwines with the struggles of Native Hawaiians to build their lives on parcels of land assigned as "leased plots." The Hawaiian Home Lands proposed by the US as a reservation for an indigenous people turned out to guarantee the resilience of an ancient culture.

To Save a Dying Race

For fifteen years, from 1905 to 1920, Prince Kūhiō brought the plight of his people to the United States Congress in his role as elected delegate from the territory. He argued for rehabilitating the Native Hawaiians, a people he described in language that make concession to the prevalent imperial racism in Congress. Hawaiians, the prince asserted, are a "dying race." And he proposed a route to rehabilitation through returning Hawaiians to the land. In the fall of 1920, he made a final effort to persuade his reluctant colleagues. "If conditions remain as they are today, it will only be a matter of a short space of time when this race of people, my people, renowned for their physique, their courage, their sense of justice, their straightforwardness, and their hospitality, will be a matter of history."[2] He argued that agricultural subsistence would restore the health, the well-being, and the stamina of kānaka maoli, the native people.

An heir to the throne and a favorite of Queen Lili`uokalani, Prince Kūhiō showed himself to be a consummate politician. When the powerful Republican Party recruited him as candidate, he deemed the position of congressional delegate the "best" route for helping his people.[3] He won election ten times, from 1902 until his death in 1922. Throughout, his positions in Congress steered a course between attending to his political supporters and acting on the responsibility he had to the "race" whose interests he championed—ali`i as much as politician. The haole elite had one set of interests, the kānaka maoli another, and both groups made their voices heard, in different ways and with different agendas. Members of the haole elite were not interested in the rehabilitation project; their interests lay in protecting plantation land. And they acted in full awareness of the economic and political power that gave them a veto position in negotiations in Honolulu and in Washington. For the Native Hawaiians, Prince Kūhiō's proposals provided an opportunity to articulate their political interests for the first time in the territorial regime the haole elite had imposed on them.

"On November 13, 1914, 200 Hawaiians attended a meeting at the Waikiki residence of Prince Jonah Kuhio Kalaniana`ole and agreed to form the Ahahui Pu`uhonua O Na Hawai`i (Hawaiian Protective Association)," writes Davianna Pōmaika`i McGregor.[4] Discussions in Ahahui Pu`uhonua covered a number of issues pertinent to the condition of Native Hawaiians, from poverty to population decline—a decrease of over 90 percent in a century.[5] At the heart of proposed responses lay the importance of land, the `āina that provided spiritual and material sustenance. Prince Kūhiō took the lesson of meetings to heart, and in 1918 he supported the establishment of Hawaiian Civic Clubs in order to further the participation of his people in the decisions the federal government might make. These clubs, whose members were by and large middle- and upper-class Hawaiians, stood behind Kūhiō in arguments he made to the Territorial Legislature and the US Congress. Different in membership, the Civic Clubs and Ahahui Puʻuhonua equally stressed the importance of "return" to the land to rescue a people who had been forced out of traditional modes of subsistence.

Joining the pleas of his people to an American tradition, Prince Kūhiō and his allies proposed homesteading as the way to rehabilitate the Native Hawaiian.[6] Debates in Congress complicated the proposal, veering between obedience to the oligarchy in Hawaiʻi and the appeal of "rural living" for rescuing an indigenous people. Negotiations and compromises ensued until at last the fractious Congress approved the Hawaiian Rehabilitation Bill; final approval occurred five days after American Independence Day, on 9 July 1921.[7] The Hawaiian Homes Commission Act (HHCA) established a commission to supervise the distribution of land to qualified applicants. At first glance, the similarity between "homes" and "homesteads" suggests that Congress had agreed on a practice the United States first instituted in the mid-nineteenth century: settling a country and domesticating a people by giving them land to farm.

In 1862, President Abraham Lincoln signed a Homestead Act that gave "freehold title" to individuals willing to establish farms on lands west of the Mississippi.[8] Six decades later the HHCA put a similar emphasis on the significance of farming, but the 1921 Act instituted a regime with quite other implications for its subjects. In many ways the HHCA looked more like the General Allotment Act of 1887, better known as the Dawes Act after its senatorial sponsor in Congress.

The Dawes Act was designed to "break up tribal organizations and Indian communities," and as a result to defuse the threat posed by the existence of autonomous Indian nations.[9] Under the rubric of granting economic opportunity, the Dawes Act allotted plots to individuals to be used for farming; recipients gained proprietary title to the plots. The congressional decision accomplished its underlying goal: by privatizing land once communally held, the 1887 Act destroyed a primary foundation for tribal autonomy. Dawes disrupted existing modes of subsistence, destroyed a way of life, and, not incidentally, freed thousands of acres to be bought by the highest bidder.[10]

The HHCA both resembles and differs from its predecessor in the approach to an indigenous people. Like the Dawes Act, the HHCA perpetuates the ideal of yeoman farmer, who becomes a self-sufficient American citizen by working the land. Yet the implementation distinguished the Native American from the Native Hawaiian. Confronting the "tribal mass," Dawes proposed a breakup of collective lands and an individualization of property through ownership rights granted to each recipient. By contrast, the HHCA kept the land in trust for the Native Hawaiian people. The 1921 Act did acknowledge the rights of Native Hawaiians to land the US defined as *public,* shy of the word *Crown* that appeared in the 1848 distribution.[11] The Act did not grant ownership rights but accorded leases to a successful applicant.[12] The goal of the Dawes Act was assimilation through the privatization of property. The goal of the HHCA was to rescue a "race" the United States had already assimilated through informal and then formal incorporation. Both the 1887 and the 1921 Acts, however, established the basis for competing narratives about justice, self-determination, and identity that continue to this day.

Prince Kūhiō's pleas before Congress achieved a delicate balance between the needs of his people and the demands of his Republican supporters at home, framed within a respected federal policy. Implementation of the act, however, placed the Native Hawaiian in a vulnerable and dependent position. Ultimately the HHCA proposed and simultaneously undercut the transformation of Native Hawaiian into the yeoman farmer so deeply embedded in American ideology. The size of the plots designated for agriculture fell way below the 160 acres granted to pioneers and, as well, to qualified American Indians. The Native Hawaiian received 10 acres, on land that was arid, rocky, and cut off from sources of water.[13] The terms of the act exempted land that was already under cultivation, not by chance the land held by large sugar and pineapple plantations. "The sugar barons won out," Eleanor told me. In a 1993 account of Keaukaha, she wrote: "Lands were leased to the sugar cane industry from which funds became available for a very frugal subsistence for the pioneer homesteaders"—using the American concept of pioneer in her complaint against the congressional decision.[14] The "funds" to which she refers are the taxes from plantation lands, which were supposed to be turned back to the homesteads for building infrastructure and making improvements.

The prince had faced an almost impossible task—a luhi or heavy burden, according to Eleanor. His people were dying. In 1920, the number of persons with Hawaiian blood had declined to 23,000 from nearly 500,000 a century earlier.[15] Disease, dispossession, and demoralization threatened the survival of kānaka maoli—intensified by the narrowing of economic opportunities. Deprived of sustenance from the land, Hawaiians migrated into cities, primarily Honolulu, where conditions were poor, crowded, and unhealthy. Kūhiō's plea acknowledged the damage urbanization wreaked on a people whose lives were tied to the ʻāina. Yet he owed an obligation to the plantation-based elite who supported his role as congressional delegate. And members of the elite insisted that he protect the thousands of profitable cultivated acres that upheld their positions in the territory.

The group known as the Big Five constituted an oligarchy based on five "factors" or business enterprises: Castle and Cooke, C. Brewer, American Factors, Theo H. Davies, and Alexander and Baldwin. "The elite controlled a diverse empire consisting of plantations, banks, insurance companies, shipping lines, trust companies, railroads, and retail and wholesale outlets."[16] And it was obvious that no bill would be passed that infringed on the vested interests of the Big Five by taking away the land crucial for a plantation economy. The final form of the 1921 Act satisfied the merchants at home and quieted the congressional representatives in Washington who worried that a homesteading policy would open a floodgate of claimants.

The "gift" from the federal government of lands already designated for the Native Hawaiians under the 1900 Organic Act came tied in tape. The most severe restriction involved the category of rightful claimant. Acknowledging the concerns about "unbridled" claims, Prince Kūhiō accepted the necessity of establishing criteria for applicants. Had his position been unfettered, he might have succeeded in inserting genealogical reckoning into the act, following kanaka maoli modes of calculating identity through ancestry.[17] However, in a Congress thoroughly imbued with imperial ideologies, a bill using a customary rather than an administrative criterion would not have passed. As in the Dawes Act of three decades earlier, the US government imposed a "true" legal identity on an indigenous people that was based on race. The 1921 Congress inserted the same criterion as predecessors had in 1887: *blood* identified an individual as genuinely Native Hawaiian.[18]

The prince bowed to congressional demands for a fixed definition while acknowledging the mixed backgrounds of a majority of his people, the chop suey ancestry Eleanor described one afternoon. But the 1/32 blood quantum he initially proposed was not restrictive enough, either for US politicians or for the oligarchy at home. In the ensuing debates, blood remained an unmistakable measure of worth, expediently narrowed. Eleanor named the victors: "The Sugar Planters lost us our declaration of native Hawaiians as being 1/32. … Why was this done? Was it to keep the Native Hawaiian away from this rewards? Definitely!"[19] The bill passed with the same quotient as in the Dawes Act: 50 percent or more Hawaiian blood qualified an applicant.[20] The designation of *native,* with a lowercase *n,* underlined the special status of these Hawaiian beneficiaries.

Over the decades, the list of applicants for plots grew longer and the restrictive criterion excluded an increasing number of indigenous Hawaiians. With a growing population of part-Hawaiians, debate over the blood quantum as a form of identification intensified. When John talked of being Hawaiian, he used the phrase "100 percent" to refer to his assertion of values—the significance of aloha and mālama`āina—and not to a quantum of blood. That he qualified for a home lands plot because he possessed the needed 50 percent did not contradict his articulation of Hawaiian identity.[21] Eleanor shared his interpretation of being Hawaiian, and a "customary" understanding prompted her protest against a legal criterion that shortchanged beneficiaries. But she did not ignore the efforts Prince Kūhiō made to reconcile federal requirements and kanaka maoli custom. Her writings hold to the proposal of 1/32 blood quantum as the qualifying criterion for applicants, and she turned her objection elsewhere—to the tedious accumulation of paperwork required to "prove" blood quantum.[22] For many potential applicants, written documents were not available. Eleanor did not mince words: "This discrimination greatly stresses and depresses beneficiaries."[23]

In the meantime, the original allotment of 203,000 acres diminished as the US took land for public purposes, mainly defense and a few national parks. Prince Kūhiō's program for self-sufficiency through small-scale farming succumbed to the dominant political and economic interests in the territory. Wage labor superseded yeoman farming as a primary mode of subsistence, and in 1923 Congress added "residential lots" to the Homes Commission Act. Near major industries, residential lots immediately took precedence over farm lots in the applications submitted by kānaka maoli, and they still do.

The Sugar Barons, Eleanor continued in her commentary, "lost us ... our lease life of 999 years."[24] She is referring to a lease program in the Land Act of 1895 that granted 999-year leases to applicants for land in the territory.[25] Never a large number, the 999-year leases disappeared from public discussion of land, except in cases of dispute over succession.[26] Eleanor's reference to a minor program accords a particular interpretation to a lease—the arrangement is virtually endless. This was not what legislators had in mind when they included a lease provision in the HHCA. The 1921 Act prescribed a 99-year lease as the term on a homestead award. The decision marked a radical reinterpretation of *lease*: from a holding in perpetuity to a limited contract. A lease and not ownership, Congress rationalized, would protect the Native Hawaiians from further loss by preventing the "alienation of land set aside under this Act." Held in trust, the land could not be bought, sold, or, as it turned out, simply willed to a successor.

Congress handed the Hawaiian Homes Commission a complicated charge. Ostensibly established for the benefit of Native Hawaiians, the HHC was first of all a federal agency that regulated individual applications, distributed the plots, and supervised homestead governance. In 1959, when Hawai`i became a state, Congress transferred administration of the program from a federal to a new state agency, the Department of Hawaiian Home Lands (DHHL). Initially a predominantly haole institution, the Department increasingly co-opted Native Hawaiians into service. The Hawaiian Homes Commission, which oversees DHHL, now includes members who must be qualified by blood quantum. Yet regardless of the extent to which commissioners and staff of DHHL accept responsibility to the Hawaiian people, the agency remains an institution of the state of Hawai`i. The governor appoints the executive board of the DHHL, the home lands commissioners, and each appointment requires the approval of the Hawaiian Senate. Kānaka maoli remain the beneficiaries of a trust.

Even with all the restrictions and control, the act grants space on which residents can adapt traditional modes of subsistence, organize action, and practice the "arts and skills" John ascribes to life in Keaukaha.[27] And once the act was in place that is exactly what happened. Leaning on custom and on history, residents organized into various associations, *hui,* to take protection of the land into their own hands. These grassroots associations have no formal relationship to the DHHL; rather, groups of residents act together to mālama`āina—and on that foundation to develop strategies for confronting the failures in the state's management of home lands.

These hui keep the significance of `āina just ahead of the transformation of land into private property, maintaining an interpretation of sustenance that depends on *relationship with* and not *exploitation of* land. The writers of the act "returned" Hawaiians to the land. Residents of the homesteads return the land to meanings that are not anticipated by the formal, stilted provisions of a congressional decision.

Keaukaha: A Homestead near Hilo

Congress gave its final approval to the Hawaiian Rehabilitation Bill, and then proceeded with caution. The first homestead was an "experiment." Legislators selected land on Moloka`i, the least populated island in the archipelago, and made ten-acre farm plots available to petitioners. Arriving on the plots, successful applicants encountered the stingy and unyielding acres the government allotted to natives. Owners of large pineapple plantations, their land exempted by the act, commandeered water supplies for a crop that was central to the territory's economy. The first group of Hawaiian homesteaders adopted the best available option and sub-leased their plots to the plantation owners. And so the beneficiaries of a "return to the land" lived on income from rent.[28] Nevertheless, legislators in Washington, DC, deemed the experiment a success and they soon designated another homestead. This was Keaukaha, on the Big Island.

Implicitly acknowledging the problems of agricultural homesteads, Congress altered the policy. On 15 December 1924 the federal body accorded Keaukaha the status of a *residential* homestead and opened the area to petitioners. An expanding economy provided the justification for residential lots, linked to urban industries. The mid-1920s were good years in the territory. A government report noted: "Yet again is Hawaii privileged to record a year of uninterrupted prosperity and material progress, confirming the view of its being a highly favored land."[29] In Keaukaha, 5 miles from Hilo, each successful applicant received approximately one acre, enough for a house and a small yard. Simultaneously, persisting in the idea of turning *native* into *yeoman farmer*, Congress designated a nearby agricultural homestead. Successful applicants received 10 acres each in Pana`ewa, and were expected to live on the land in the way the original act anticipated. But the land in Pana`ewa was not much better than the farm lots in Moloka`i, and this experiment in small-scale farming was doomed to fail.

Forty families already lived in Keaukaha, "upstanding citizens" of a US territory. They were descendants of the initial subjects of American missionary conversion, their ancestors schooled in Christianity by Titus Coan and his wife. The Coans bequeathed to the people with whom they lived not only Congregationalism, but also the literacy and the demeanor that justified American presence to authorities for decades to come. In the 1920s, the men of Keaukaha worked on Hilo's docks, in sugar refineries, and in civil service positions; the women engaged in domestic tasks. In the eyes of the American Congress, these natives were model citizens, steady workers and reliable wage earners. With the granting of homestead status, more families moved into the area. John and Eleanor's grandfather Waipa Kealohapau`ole was an early resident. He was, John writes in *Life Story*, "a huge man, standing about 6'5" tall and built like an ox. He was very strong, intelligent and was a dedicated Police Officer."[30] John and Eleanor grew up in Keaukaha with kin who filled the roles of stevedores, store clerks, and sheriffs.

Keaukaha's approximately 700 native Hawaiian residents in the 1920s constituted a small proportion of the island's total population of 65,000. For territorial and US officials, however, Keaukaha played a large role, demonstrating the success of "rehabilitation." No need to create farmers: the residents of Keaukaha proved the irrelevance of the act's original goal. Keaukaha, not the farm lots in Pana`ewa, held the star role in US government documents.

A year and a half after Keaukaha's founding, the Executive Secretary of the Homes Commission visited the homestead. "Though the homes are not palatial residences, they are good homes for them and all are busy and happy. They are developing little gardens about their homes and are thus able to be in the open and live the kind of life they enjoy."[31] His extensive description of contented, hardworking homesteaders reassured federal and territorial officials who had, in 1920, witnessed bitter strikes spreading through the plantations on the islands.[32] Led by Japanese and Filipino workers, these work stoppages threatened the economic stability of Hawai`i, and fear of their recurrence lay not far beneath the surface in governmental reports on the territory. A visit to Keaukaha presented in glowing terms provided an antidote, and an alternative interpretation of a regime that subordinated natives and subjected aliens to surveillance.

In 1928, the United States Department of the Interior sent its own observer to Keaukaha. He shared the enthusiasm of his territorial predecessor. "At Keaukaha, Waiakea, near the town of Hilo, on the island of Hawaii, there is a home settlement that is an unqualified success. There the purpose was to give an acre of land and a house to Hawaiians who work for wages in the city of Hilo, or in adjacent industries. The manner in which these lots are being improved, the neatness of the homes and the enjoyment which the dwellers in these homes have in their mode of life, show that it is accomplishing every purpose for which the act was designed." He did not disguise his appreciation of the discipline a homestead policy imposed on the native population. "Inquiries showed that men who were subject to temptation, becoming dissipated in town, were leading orderly, sober lives and giving their spare time to the development of their homes when they move out of the city."[33] Titus Coan would have nodded his approval.

I found the reports in a booklet called *Ku'u Home I Keaukaha*. A Hilo High School project, the 1975 booklet celebrates the fiftieth anniversary of the homestead. Its stated purpose is to strengthen "the realization that the Hawaiians were an important cog in the community of mankind."[34] The booklet contains a mélange of intersecting and diverging mo'olelo, a mirror of the tangled histories that comprise US–Hawai'i relations.

The fiftieth anniversary celebrated a coming-together of residents and of migrants invited back *home*. In *Ku'u Home*, kūpuna recall the "good old days" in phrases that subvert the implications of order and harmony in government reports by giving those concepts their Hawaiian meanings. These are mo'olelo whose superficial similarities to the juxtaposed government reports undercut the condescending tone of those reports—exploiting the subtle nuances, the kaona, an outsider misses. Eleanor contributes her mo'olelo, and the details are resonant with what she would review twenty years later at her brother's funeral. In the 1975 account, she states: "I think that my childhood way of living was really like the way the old Hawaiians lived, in that they lived close to nature and off nature."[35]

Ku'u Home commemorates a reunion, a community of present and past residents. The booklet comes at a time of cultural renaissance, and takes its place as part of a resurgence of Hawaiian custom. In its celebration of Keaukaha, *Ku'u Home* points to the importance of homesteads as the material basis for the unfolding of a renaissance. Eleanor's interview is not nostalgia; her expression of opinion is a call to action. "As far as Hawaiian Homes youngsters are concerned, never forget your Hawaiian ancestry. … Know the positive and negatives so you know where to stand."[36]

The call to action in Eleanor's oral history propels her writings and similarly prompts John's various accounts of his life. Keaukaha, claims the introduction to *Ku'u Home,* means the time of writing. "Keau meaning the 'time' or 'era' and kaha meaning 'to write.'"[37] The booklet celebrates, and the oral histories support, a positive picture, not of *reservation* (American Indian style) but of preservation, Hawaiian style, through reiterations of significant values, convictions, and interpretations. Writings, for John and Eleanor, carry custom into the present—not a frozen archive but a living, meandering, changing body of knowledge. For both, writings become a "weapon" not so much of the "weak" as a tool appropriate for commentary in a context where *pepa*, texts, and documents dominate the relations between the US and kānaka maoli.

Mixing English, pidgin, and, in Eleanor's case, Hawaiian, the writings draw on personal experiences in order to convey an "opinion" of Hawaiian culture. While John titled his writing, *Life Story of a Native Hawaiian,* the subtitle indicates the meaning of the *life* in his account. He adds, in capital letters: "BIRTH PLACE—KEAUKAHA, HILO, HAWAII. PARENTS—FATHER—KAIHE'EKAI KUAKAHELA SIMEONA. MOTHER—SARAH KEALOHA-PAU'OLE. 100 percent HAWAIIAN."[38] Belying the Western interpretation of life story, John depicts an individual life through the connection to place and to kin. Eleanor even more clearly attached her life to the genealogical reckoning of Hawaiian tradition and to the places that provide "roots" for the growth of personal identity.[39]

John begins his *Life Story:* "I was born in Keaukaha, a Hawaiian Homestead land." He provides the place and not the date of his birth—which I did not learn until later. "Yes, there's lots of questions you want to know of me. First you may not understand my birthday—03-09-25. But I was born Feb. 22-25 [1925]. Yes, that's my regular age."[40] The confusion makes an implicit reference to the disconnection between his birth and the official papers that documented the event. In any case, the date only came to matter under particular circumstances, when, for instance, he shaved off a year in order to join the Civilian Conservation Corps. More dominant, in *Life Story,* were the arts he acquired, the places in which he learned those, and the commitment to Hawaiian values he offered members of his 'ohana through his writing.

Eleanor composed her life story in the genealogical records she kept over the years. She showed me these records, in composition books and on the loose sheets of paper on which she noted new members of the 'ohana. And she supplemented this written life story when we drove through the homesteads, onto dirt roads of former cane fields, and into the hilly land behind Hilo. The genealogy was straightforward: "John Ione Simeona, the eldest; Eleanor Kalawai'akamali'iwahineli'ili'i, the next oldest; Winona Leina'ala, and Priscilla L. Kealohapau'ole." She did not include two boys, who died in childhood. It was very sad, John writes, that the boys "did not grow up to see what life was."[41]

In *Ku'u Home,* Eleanor expands the genealogy for an audience beyond the boundaries of the 'ohana. "My father's name was John Kaihe'ekai Kimona and his father's name was Kuakahela. My mother's name was Sarah Kahaulelio Waipa Kealohapau`ole."[42] This is a story, too, of shifts between Americanization and Hawaiianization of names: Kimona turns "Simon" into a Hawaiian sounding name; later, in another phase of Anglicization, Kimona became Simeona, the name passed down in John's `ohana.[43] After Eleanor died, I visited the place where she was buried. Sarah's grave is marked "Sarah K. Pakele" and it is right next to the grave of Eleanor and John's stepfather, Thomas Kanelunamokuhunakaleikamoku Pakele. The father John commemorated, Kaihe`ekai Kuakahela Simeona, is buried some distance away.

Names are the tangible chart of a life history. In presenting their lives this way, neither John nor Eleanor explained the meanings of a name to me and both alternated between American and Hawaiian names in addressing kin.[44] When we knew each other better, John increasingly used *Ione* rather than *John* in his letters. These shifts are as thoroughly political as they are personal. Eleanor wrote her own name differently, depending on the purpose of her writings. In a memoir she wrote about her mother, looking back to the past in Keaukaha, she extends her Hawaiian name: Eleanor Kalawai`akamali`iwahineli`ili `i Simeona Ahuna. In letters she sent to bureaucrats addressing homestead issues, she signs: "E. Ahuna, President." Unelaborated and official—her married name superseding the Hawaiian—the signature speaks to an Americanized political setting. Eleanor's names are an alternate genealogy, tracing the positions she takes as a Native Hawaiian, active in an American territory and state.

The memoir of Sarah is a story of arts and skills, much like the pages in John's *Life Story*. The prose of the memoir evokes a chant: "I remember Mama teaching hula.... I remember Mama and her slack key guitar music at night to lull us to sleep.... I remember Mama weaving lauhala (pandanus leaf) mats for the floor." And at the end: "I'm happy to share my mother's knowledge to help others today."[45] Sarah emerges through the work she did, the lessons she taught, and the customs she practiced, and so does the significance of the "old" days for the new. In the sixty-four-page *Life Story,* John devotes fourteen pages to a thickly detailed account of the tasks he learned from the elders in Keaukaha: "those old days were wonderful because I got to learn more of my Hawaiian culture."[46]

Keaukaha is unmistakably at the heart of the writings both siblings did throughout their lifetimes. The place grounds a continual process of interpreting and enacting Native Hawaiian identity, and represents the strong source of a critique of American policy, of the Americanization of society, and of the values perpetuated by American institutions. Our drives through Pana`ewa offered, dramatically, the visual background to the comments Eleanor made in her writings.

Filled with abandoned cars and overgrown yards, the *agricultural* homestead exposed the failures of the 1921 Act. A physical setting spoke of decline and demoralization. Encroaching American enterprises thwarted the practice of mālama`āina: the Mauna Loa Macadamia Nut Company took acres for its flourishing orchards and Hilo County authorities ran sewer lines through the backyards of homestead houses. And in a forceful reminder of the experiment on Moloka`i, where a pineapple crop absorbed the best land, residents of Pana`ewa gave up agriculture for other sources of income. Abandoned houses told the story of evictions, and of the outcome of a home lands policy in homelessness. Eleanor explained that residents who did not meet DHHL standards were "thrown out," and jeopardized the claims on land by future generations in the family. She wrote about this abuse of beneficiary rights on the farm lots, and she ended with a demand: "The Commission Must Stop This!!!" [47]

Together, Eleanor's and John's writings tell a story of land that is missing from the 1921 Act and from subsequent rulings composed first by a federal and then by a state agency. They present the views of kānaka maoli, whose experiences on a particular homestead, Keaukaha, underline the links between place, genealogy, and the construction of Hawaiian identity. Throughout their writings, representations of life on Keaukaha demonstrate Hawaiian resilience, not regrets for a bygone past. The mo`olelo uphold the vision of Hawaiian `āina, without which the allotted land becomes a simple piece of fungible property—land, in the American sense.

"Harmonious and Nurturing Relationships": The Ahupua`a Model

Congress returned Hawaiians to the land through a distribution of carefully surveyed lots. The spatial layout of a homestead reinforces a concept of the effective use of resources, predicated on individual initiative, enterprise, and prudence. Through the terms of the act, Congress imposed the virtues of thrift and industry haole had long preached to the islanders. On the homesteads themselves, life on the land proceeded according to a different plan.

"They would go out to sea in their canoes and they would catch fishes like akule, ōpelu, `ahi, kalekale, kumu, and many more different fishes," John writes in the second paragraph of his *Life Story*. "When they returned with their catches the surrounding communities would meet them at the beach and they would exchange fish for other commodities."[48] John's sentences recreate an *ahupua`a*, the division of land that provided sustenance for the people of Hawai`i before outsiders interfered. Each division ran from mountain to ocean, giving it a characteristic wedge shape, like a slice of pie. [49] John evokes the traditional subsistence pattern: residents on the shore exchanged resources of the ocean for the crops cultivated along the sides of mountains. The exchange formed and sustained "harmonious and nurturing relationships."[50]

What John tried to convey in different ways was his vision of a "community of love," inserting *aloha* into his account of living on the land. "I know the families and neighbors that we had known lived in a community of love. Everyone was close."[51] On the homesteads, generosity, and not income-generating activity, sustained the people. Speaking to American legislators, Prince Kūhiō downplayed the Hawaiian version of a return to the land. The *aloha* John remembers from his childhood does not appear in the prose of a congressional act, which ultimately aims to create sober, orderly, and hardworking citizens for an American territory. The amendment to the act adding residential lots to the original farm lots reflected the fact that more and more Native Hawaiians were drawn into the expanding labor market of the territory, filling the positions in an infrastructure crucial for a plantation economy—building roads rather than working fields. As wage workers, homesteaders succumbed, inevitably, to the disaster of the 1930s Great Depression.

John was born in 1925, and his memories of the ways of life preserved in Keaukaha gain significance against the background of the precipitous economic decline that coincided with his childhood. "Money was scarce," writes John in a paragraph in which he describes the fishing skills of his grandfather and his uncles. He went out with his kin, diving for the resources the family exchanged for cultivated crops from further inland. The legislators did not intend to revive exchange-based subsistence in the homesteads, nor could they anticipate the worth of this revival a decade after they passed the Homes Commission Act. The Depression toppled the islands from the prosperity under which Congress had agreed to the prince's plan. On allotted homestead lands, residents confronted the economic crisis by invigorating a mode of subsistence distinct from the market and disconnected from precarious territorial enterprises.

Soon after Eleanor's birth in 1928, John Kaiheʻekai Kimona died. Sarah moved the family across the island, into the Kimona ʻohana and onto the coffee plantations of Kailua-Kona. But coffee prices were falling and John describes the further distancing of the family from dependency on the American economy. "Then we were told that our family was going to Honokahau, the Fish Pond, to stay for a little while." This move took them even more thoroughly away from wage labor. "During our stay in Honokahau there were no jobs, only fishing, hunting, and also exchanging other goodies with Kailua's community."[52] The stay at Honokahau proved to be temporary as well.

Sarah returned to Keaukaha, and eventually moved in with Thomas Pakele. Not long afterward, he lost his job as a stevedore on Hilo's docks, and he never got the work back again. "To get one of these jobs," John writes, "you would have to wait until someone got fired or died, to get in."[53] Pakele's brother did better in the American economy. "He was a Deputy Sheriff in Hilo, a Colonel in the Hawaii National Guard, 298th Infantry Regiment, a Defense Co-ordinator and held many civic positions."[54] The status of the older did not help the younger brother, who drifted through the Depression, tempted away from sobriety. John's mother went to work, selling leis to the tourists who managed to take vacations despite the economic crisis.

John described Sarah Kealohapau`ole as tiny, feisty, and authoritarian. Early in the mornings, the sky still dark, she woke the children and assigned their tasks. Both John and Eleanor recalled these 4 AM interruptions of sleep, a pattern that continued even when they went to school. They followed their mother into the hills beyond Keaukaha, gathering the flowers she needed. "My young sister and I would help Mom pick up all kinds of flowers and Mom would string them up and sell the leis down at the pier, when the ships came in, or in town during special activities in the evening. Mom was one of the original lei sellers in Hilo."[55] John describes another activity that contributed to the household economy, one that was more fun than pre-dawn trips to the forests. "When the ship is ready to leave with all its passengers, I would jump in the water with the other boys, to dive for coins. The passengers would throw lots of coins in the water and we would retrieve it."[56] In her mo`olelo, Eleanor told of diving "for pennies thrown by the tourists" who leaned over the decks of luxury liners that entered Hilo Harbor.

In documents of the Depression, images of Hawaiian children diving for pennies thrown by rich tourists are far less prevalent than photographs of dust bowl migrants, men on bread lines, and tramps on the rails. The extensive and poignant visual record of a country in dire straits dramatized the conditions to which Franklin Roosevelt responded in his New Deal initiative. He instituted programs across the forty-eight states, and he did not neglect the overseas territories, which he considered crucial to national security and defense. Territorial authorities in Hawai`i implemented New Deal programs, confronting rates of unemployment that struck at every racial group in the archipelago. "There were NRA and PWA jobs for people out of work," John writes, referring to the National Recovery Act and the Public Works Administration. "The people working for NRA or PWA, worked two and a half days out of the week." Then he adds: "Luckily my grandfather had a good job. He worked as an overseer and being a policeman."[57]

John's account of the Great Depression focuses less on the programs that came from Washington, DC, than on the day-to-day strategies adopted by homestead residents. The American citizen whose Hawaiian culture persisted had a different set of options than the wage laborer on the mainland or the farmer on the Great Plains. On residential homesteads, men and women who lost their jobs were able to take up the skills their ancestors had practiced and to maintain a collective way of life at the margins of the colonial-capitalist economy. The dust bowl tragedy of sweeping displacements from hearth and home in the Midwest did not cross the Pacific. That catastrophe had occurred before, when land acts facilitated the seizing of a resource by non-Hawaiians. In the 1930s, Native Hawaiians drew on the mālama'āina that had sustained a people through scarcity and suppression for a century. Crowded squatter camps on the west coast, bread lines on the east coast, and tramps riding the rails were distant images of crisis, content of a newsreel and not the visual landscape of the archipelago.

During the Depression, the significance of a Hawaiian home lands policy extended beyond the "rescue" for which the prince argued. On the periphery of dominant industries in the territory, residents of homesteads exemplified a mode of survival that the script of the 1921 Act did not include. Nor did this unintended consequence of the HHCA end with the Depression or with the Second World War hard on its heels; the meanings of *living on the land* expanded in the post-war context of a cultural renaissance and bids for sovereignty.[58] The conceptualization of "sustenance" in the late twentieth century has grounding in responses to the economic crisis of the 1930s. The practices of that decade motivate understandings of *being Hawaiian* enacted not only by residents of homesteads, but also by dwellers in crowded urban centers and suburban housing tracts.[59]

In 1991, John introduced me to his cousin and contemporary, Henrietta. We met, to talk story, at her favorite beach on the Windward Coast of O'ahu. She told stories of growing up on the Big Island, and she showed me the black and white composition books in which she recorded genealogies. Henrietta did not grow up on a homestead, but her memories of childhood in the 1930s bear striking similarities to the talk-stories of John and Eleanor. Like the siblings, she remembered with particular vividness being awakened "before dawn" to help with household tasks. In the darkness, she told me, her grandmother brought the children out to gather "ginger and hibiscus." Like Sarah Kealohapau'ole, Auntie Etta's grandmother kept the family going by participating in the tourist industry, making the leis "rich visitors" carried home from their trips. Etta described her grandmother as tiny, the same word John used when he referred to his mother. Small and hardworking, these figures resist Western stereotypes of the indulgently sensual Polynesian woman.

Henrietta learned lei making from her grandmother. Fifty years later, she grew ginger and hibiscus on the land she called her farm. I visited her at home only after many conversations on the beach. The drive took me along the coast, from Honolulu toward the northern tip of the island. Auntie Etta's house sat at the edge of open fields, surrounded by thick foliage. Inside the yard were chickens, a cow, two dogs, and other small animals I could not identify. During our visit, Henrietta made it clear that these were pets: she did not sell either the animals or the plants that grew in such abundance. Yet she consistently applied the word *farm* to the place on which she lived, as if deliberately exposing the misunderstandings encoded in American laws and conventions. She owned her land free and clear, and on this property she practiced the Hawaiian way of life the prince had advocated in his speeches to Congress.

Mr. Ōʻili even more deliberately scrambled the meanings of farm, teasing the understandings of a non-Hawaiian. A slight, sinewy man, Mr. Ōʻili lived behind a small shop on the highway that ran along the dry leeward side of Oʻahu. His farm abutted the store, which catered to neighbors and to the few tourists who traveled around that side of the island. Mr. Ōʻili grew crops on land that, not designated as a homestead, was as unyielding as any the US government provided to applicants. Behind the house, we walked together through a conglomeration of bushes, coconut trees, and flowering plants. Mr. Ōʻili attached his stories to the flora we passed.

Picking a berry here, a leaf there, he asked me to "try them." This herb, he said, will cure that ailment, and he waited for me to swallow what he offered. We were surrounded, hidden from the road, and enclosed in a flourishing space. Chickens occupied the space with us, and the smell they produced diffused over the plants. The smell connected Ōʻili to his neighbors and to the American authorities: his neighbors, he told me, complained about the chickens and caused the Honolulu County zoning board to deny the legality of his farm. He asserted the right he had to farm the area around his house, protested against the zoning board, and complained that his neighbors had become "haolified." The only way to "rescue" Hawaiian culture, he continued, was to put "all Native Hawaiians on a cruise ship." The ship, he went on, would sail around the islands, stopping in ports only to gather the resources that would permit self-sustainability.

His story presented a multi-level parable of relations between Hawaiians and the haole who governed them. Mr. Ōʻili linked the infusion of white values into "Hawaiian farming" to the presence of cruise ships that, in fact, sustained the economy of island life. His story also commented on a homestead policy, in which Hawaiians were separated into enclaves—not "floating," but certainly bounded off from surrounding neighborhoods. Intricate and ambiguous, the moʻolelo Mr. Ōʻili told was a call to action, phrased in the digressive, contradictory, and meandering style of talk-story.

Claiming Space in a Segregated Honolulu

The HHCA established the first homesteads in rural areas or, like Keaukaha, at a convenient distance from urban centers. Behind the choice of location lay the conclusions of policymakers and of scholars that Native Hawaiians did not thrive in a dense city environment. But there they were: from the late nineteenth century on, Hawaiians migrated in large numbers to the island's growing cities—Honolulu primarily.[60] Hawaiians joined Japanese and Chinese families, who left the plantations, incoming haole, and an expanding military population. Already in 1930, the population of Honolulu was 137,582, up from 81,820 in the 1920 census.[61]

From the debates over annexation to later government reports, Hawai`i appears as the epitome of racial harmony. Against the background of bitter racial divides in mainland cities, Honolulu represented the possibility of peaceful coexistence among "diverse cultures." These images obscured the intensifying racial tensions in the territory, exacerbated by the 1931–32 Massie case.[62] In that infamous case, a Naval officer's wife, Thalia Massie, accused five non-white boys of raping her one night after a party. She had little evidence to support her accusation and a jury acquitted the boys. Lieutenant J. G. Thomas Massie and Thalia's mother, Grace Fortescue, were outraged and demanded justice. Failing an official response, they organized a kidnapping, with the result that one of the boys, the Native Hawaiian Joseph Kahahawai, was murdered.[63] Gaining further publicity for the racism permeating the case, Massie and Fortescue brought a well-known lawyer from the mainland, Clarence Darrow, to defend their actions. He held forth, but without total success. The Massie-Fortescue group was judged guilty of manslaughter, and ultimately subjected to punishment: "one day to be served in the custody of the High Sheriff."[64] This symbolic punishment provoked protests across the islands, fresh evidence of the power whites had to control the territorial justice system. Media reports exacerbated the situation, either condemning the mock sentence insisted on by haole or defending the "honor killing" committed by a mother and a husband.

The Massie case brought the full impact of American racism into the territory, undermining the code that had long preserved class and ethnic relations.[65] Moreover, the outcome of the Massie case coincided with an increasing influx of strangers, whose racial stereotyping added fuel to a simmering fire. Thousands of US military personnel arrived in the islands in the 1930s, importing ideas about dark-skinned people. Beach boys and surfers, once a tourist attraction, came to seem dangerous: the native male whose color and bearing struck high chords of suspicion and fear. If name calling and fighting were more common than murder, still the possibility of fateful aggression always existed. In the words of anthropologist Ty P. Kāwika Tengan, "Hawaiian and local Asian men embodied the 'black peril,' a trope readily deployed in colonial settings throughout the Pacific."[66] As the decade passed, individuals with Asian features experienced even greater risk of hostility, caught in media alarm about the rise of Japanese power in the Pacific.[67]

In the urban center of Honolulu, the touted harmonious integration of a diverse population depended on residential segregation. While based on economic disparities, the pattern ended up creating ethnic enclaves that reinforced the racist distinctions of a colonial regime. Successful Japanese and Chinese occupied the better housing in the city, while Caucasians moved out of the center—the wealthiest into the luxurious Nuʻuanu Valley where the royal family had maintained a summer palace. At the low end of the economic scale, Native Hawaiians shared crowded spaces, a version of ʻohana living forced upon them by stringent circumstances, discrimination, and a sharp disconnection between the competitive ethos of urban life and Hawaiian kuleana.[68]

Already in the 1920s, territorial newspapers were crying "foul" about urban neighborhoods, overcrowded, noisy, and unsightly. The attack focused on a small corner of Honolulu called Papakōlea, occupied mainly by Native Hawaiians. In 1923, the territorial authorities took advantage of perceived "slum conditions" to put the land up for sale.[69] The property had high value in a growing city, and there was no way the residents could pay the proposed price for a lot. But the citizens of Papakōlea did not sit passively by: they formed a group to protest against the blatant destruction of a way of life. The Papakōlea Association ignored the territorial legislature and petitioned the federal government for homestead status. The hoped-for congressional mandate could offer protection against the greed and aggressive practices of local authorities. Homestead status would, presumably, keep land out of the hands of real estate developers and commercial enterprises as well as individual buyers.

Seventy years later, a homestead website tells the story: "In 1923, the lifestyle of the settlers was again threatened by a notice of sale of these lands by public auction at 10 cent a square foot. The settlers were well aware of their inability to buy what had been their home and way of life for many years. In a fashion that has never changed to this day, they organized and went to the legislature for aid, which resulted in the Commission [of] Public Lands immediately canceling the notice. It was the beginning of an initiative by Hawaiians to secure their land."[70]

Congress was slow to grant the request. Eleven years went by before US legislators granted homestead status to Papakōlea. That was 1934, the same year Congress passed the Indian Reorganization Act, which accorded American Indian tribes the collective ownership and self-determination the Dawes Act had eliminated. In 1934, too, President Roosevelt visited Hawaiʻi. He praised the "neatness and cleanliness in the homes" all over the islands—a more pleasing sight to the eye than American Indian conditions. Under the extension of "beneficent" programs to upstanding indigenous peoples, Congress granted homestead status to the Native Hawaiians living in Honolulu.[71]

Unlike the first homesteads, Papakōlea lies in the midst of an urban center. Where subsistence depends solely on a market economy, the model of the ahupuaʻa must be stretched and remolded in order to endure.[72] Residents of homesteads on Molokaʻi and the Big Island had "gardens" that permitted replication of customary modes of exchange. Yet residents of Papakōlea describe their lives in much the same language, emphasizing sharing, giving generously, and, above all, gathering and working together. "The story of the Papakōlea,

Kewalo and Kalawahine community is one of strength in the face of over-whelming adversity, of courage and determination, and of aloha and family. It is a success story proving what can happen when a community comes together to heal, rebuild, and continue to be a source of positive change."[73]

The story of Papakōlea, Kewalo and Kalawahine, appears on a website created to mark the seventieth anniversary of homestead status. The 2004 text refers to the time of victory in the 1930s and, less directly, to the impact of political movements in the 1990s. "Their 1930s victory continues to affect the lives of Hawaiians to this day while their determination to keep their culture alive is told by the few surviving elders."[74] A reference to the past intertwines with an accent on the present, reiterated in the regular gathering of residents old and young, local and diasporic. On the "modern" medium of the Internet, Papakōlea's reunion organizers stress the importance of the elders, the kūpuna who keep culture in contemporary activism.

"Enriching All Who Come"

A kupuna when we met, John often talked about the reunions he organized—the gatherings of the "children" of Keaukaha. "Excuse me for not answering your letter earlier, cause I spent two weeks in Hilo, Hawaii making ready for a grand Homestead Reunion. This was for a 65th anniversary and the reunited reunion of all people who had moved out of the Hawaiian Homestead land and living elsewhere in the world."[75] In a letter he sent two weeks later, he provided more details. "Everyday we had a special occasion. We had workshops in Hawaiian culture, Lei Haku, Weaving of mats, hats, some small items, quilting blankets, Hawaiian Language, music beginning, music learning, Hawaiian herbs." And last but not least he described the food: "We had donations of three steers, about 10 pigs and everything that goes for the whole week."

The 1989 Keaukaha reunion included Hilo County ranchers, plantation owners, shopkeepers, and downtown businessmen. The event ended with a motorcade through Keaukaha, led by the mayor of Hilo in his black limousine. Participants from Keaukaha-Pana`ewa, and those who traveled from other islands and from the mainland, observed a line of cars carrying the Hilo County officials who legislated the "right" use of land. The reunion countered this visual presentation of power with performances by kānaka maoli and tables full of items that testified to the vigor of culture learning.

"I wish you were here," John wrote from Hilo, "I would introduce you to many old time Hawaiians, then you would get a true story of Native Hawaiians and their surroundings."[76] In our conversations, John reminded me again that reunions present the true story, untangling the history of competitive claims to the life-giving resource of Hawai`i. Embedded in the reunions was a larger dimension of life on the homestead, the working together or *laulima* John re-membered: "They would gather for anything that needed to be done." A col-lective ethos contrasted with the individualism in classic American tales, and the cooperation for which John used the Hawaiian word constituted a litmus test he used in all domains.

Laulima materializes in the consensual decision making a kupuna pro-motes within an ʻohana and outside its boundaries in the place people and ʻāina share. Not always successful, still laulima constitutes a model for effec-tive action within the institutions imposed by the United States.

When Keaukaha held its sixty-fifth reunion in 1989, Eleanor was president of a newly formed homestead association. Hui Hoʻomau O Keaukaha-Panaʻewa represented the residential and the agricultural lots, and the reunions brought people together whose concerns might conflict at formal association meetings. During the reunions, Eleanor was one of several kūpuna who told stories to the younger generation. At meetings of the hui, she was president, bent on keeping order and crafting a unified agenda. She acknowledged, however, that the one could not be separated from the other, and that gathering in a commu-nity setting established the foundation for a coherent political strategy. With her brother, at a vast reunion—so big they were held sometimes on space bor-rowed from the Hilo Airport—she played her role as hānau mua. She acted in her cultural status, if not unencumbered by American politics at least offering a different slant on those politics.

Following the anniversary reunion, Eleanor developed new interpretations of the laulima that reunions demonstrate. The Hawaiian values represented in those gatherings could, she claimed, be a "source of positive change." And looking for ways in which Hawaiian culture could be an agent of change be-came Eleanor's main task in the 1990s.

A decade earlier, in 1980, Governor George Ariyoshi had appointed her to the Hawaiian Homes Commission, executive board of the Department of Ha-waiian Home Lands. Eleanor represented the interests of Big Island Hawaiian homesteads at meetings across the state, and Commission minutes indicate that she generally cooperated with the majority in decisions.[77] Later she said: "I learned politics." She learned the virtues, and the difficulties, of compromis-ing. And she brought the lessons home. Her daughter remembered strenuous discussions in the evenings, as Eleanor replayed—and reviewed—the battles of a commission meeting. Her term as commissioner ended in 1989.

Released from the pressures of cooperating with her fellow commissioners, Eleanor turned her energies to the homestead association she had helped cre-ate. As president, she focused her energies on remedying the conditions un-der which homestead residents lived, developing programs in areas where the state and federal governments failed the Native Hawaiian. During her term, which lasted until 1995, she wrote letters to officials describing the plight of her people and pleading for redress in very specific terms. The letters delineate a plan for the self-improvement of her neighbors, friends, and kin. The plan was concrete, addressed to an array of needs she perceived on the homesteads. The plan also evoked a memory she had of childhood in Keaukaha in the 1930s, and the bases for community-generated subsistence. These several strands came together in an impassioned proposal for the construction of a Hawaiian Cultural Center on acres reserved for the Hawaiian people.

Iterations of the plan reveal how much the Center incorporated, bearing a weight it could not carry in late twentieth-century Hawai`i. The Center incorporated elements from the past, referred to the dominant tourism industry in the state, addressed the impoverishment of Native Hawaiians, and represented the unique value of Hawaiian culture. Ambitious and dedicated, Eleanor took on the burden she attributed to Prince Kūhiō and she outlined a modern plan for rehabilitation.

Eleanor initiated her campaign for a Cultural Center early in her tenure as president of Hui Ho`omau. In 1997, she showed me a letter she had written in 1992, addressed to the "Honorable Trustees, Kamehameha Schools/Bernice Pauahi Bishop Estates." The largest landowning corporation in the state, with 350,000 acres of land held in trust for the Hawaiian people, the Estate trustees had come under fire for failing to disclose their investment strategies.[78] In response, the trustees published a financial accounting in Hawai`i's main newspaper. There, Eleanor read the details of an investment strategy, and she took advantage of the opportunity to pursue her own plan.

Her September letter begins: "Dear Honorable Trustees—Aloha," and continues: "I have just read your Investment Philosophy explanation in your 'Legacy' series in today's Honolulu Advertiser and thank you so much for that because it impressed me to write and relate my concerns and desire to you." The plan for a Hawaiian Cultural Center, she explained, originated in 1990 and had not proceeded smoothly. "Several requests for use of the lands were made but not granted. So now, he [DHHL administrator] says, we need to get our financial supporters." She turned to the trustees for advice, she wrote, because they were local.[79] The Cultural Center was a Native Hawaiian project, centered on Keaukaha and Pana`ewa. "Because it is planned to be entirely Hawaiian in concept and being, I hesitate to seek Federal or State funds, and because I feel it should be profit making to give our people a real outlook on ownership and earning."

Her neighbors did not take to the "outlook" she proposed. She described the difficulty to the businessmen who ran the Trust. "In my writings, I tried to encourage our homesteaders to be the owners, as investors, but have found it does not go favorably with them. We have a real opportunity to begin to become self-sufficient, but I must acknowledge the reality of all that is involved— the economy, the attitude and divisions of thought—however, I do not wish to lose this opportunity for our children and their children, for surely this is their future."[80] Auntie Eleanor set the bar for the homesteaders very high. She asked them not only to endorse but also to *own* the Center, in the dual sense of the word: to contribute financially and to possess the Center as a cultural project. And she repeatedly failed to gather her neighbors to act as entrepreneurs and as culture producers. Consequently, she was on her own in efforts to address potential funding organizations. These organizations, however, ignored her. Whether other events intervened or the trustees were reluctant to engage in a local endeavor whose difficulties were clear, meetings she hoped for did not occur.

Eleanor was not daunted. Her years on the Department of Hawaiian Home Lands Commission and her familiarity with local politics taught the lesson of persistence in the name of her hui: hoʻomau, which translates as *to stand fast and continue.*

Six months later, on 31 January 1993, Eleanor wrote to a long list of recipients: "Hawaii County Administration and Council; Hawaii State Legislators; United States Congress (Hawaii members); Office of Hawaiian Affairs" and trustees of "Hawaiian Homes Commission; Kamehameha Schools/Bishop Estate; Alu Like, Inc.; Queen Liliʻuokalani Children's Center; Lunalilo Home; Hawaii Visitors Bureau; State Department of Research and Development." She selected the individuals, the government officials, and the staff of private institutions who are obligated to sustain the health and well-being of Native Hawaiians. Her agenda shifted from creating a center that was *owned* by her neighbors, and designed for the production of Hawaiian culture, to a center that would market Hawaiian arts and skills to the wider community of Hilo. The letter was first of all a plea for funding. "So inspite of what my writings say, I must concede to the reality of life and go out into the greater community for the kākoʻo [support] and kōkua [help] that is needed. I hesitated to do this, writing to all of you, because I planned it for Native Hawaiians." To win her case, she expanded the category of those who would be served. "However, I realize that in reality, Native Hawaiians are of all the colors of the rainbow too, and in this way, everybody is represented in this project."

The proposed location of the Center focuses the benefits of the plan on residents of Keaukaha-Panaʻewa. The HCC constituted a pointed reaction to a shopping mall, Prince Kūhiō Plaza, the Commission had been unable or unwilling to halt. Eleanor did not relinquish the idea that the Center be built on the land whose fate she had debated while commissioner: "in Hilo on Hawaiian Home Lands, in Waiākea Panaʻewa immediately in back of and adjacent to the Prince Kūhiō Plaza."[81] The HCC would be a compensation for the failure of agriculture to sustain the residents—"for Hawaiians to finally find a piece of Hawaiian Home Lands set aside for their economic well being," she wrote.[82]

Eleanor knew well the bitter fights that surrounded construction of the new shopping center on the edge of Pana`ewa. Members of the DHHL Commission spent months debating the appropriation of homestead acres for box stores, supermarkets, and access roads. During those months, Eleanor voted with the majority, but the resulting loss of land did not sit easily with her.[83] Once again, big business interests went hand in hand with state demands for revenue, more likely to be gained from real estate development and commercial enterprises than from the small houses scattered on farm lots. Architects, construction companies, state senators and representatives, as well as the majority of commissioners, convinced themselves and the public that a shopping mall would benefit the residents of Hilo County, the Big Island, and the state. Bulldozers slashed through the acres near and in Pana`ewa, and tenants made contracts: Borders, Wal-Mart, Safeway, Macy's, and McDonald's—the usual suspects. The invasion of Pana`ewa brought little profit to the residents. Moreover, the construction of a large mall drew business from downtown Hilo, from local shops, specialized stores, and movie theaters. No one walks in a strip mall and parking spaces, the only public gathering area, become precious commodities on a Saturday afternoon.

Hilo Hattie occupies one of the box stores in Prince Kūhiō Plaza. With its array of "genuine Hawaiiana," the corporation draws its profits largely from tourists who are shuttled the two or three miles to the Plaza from cruise ships in Hilo harbor or hotels on Banyan Drive.[84] A glaring example of the appropriation of Hawaiian arts and crafts, Hilo Hattie is not the only such enterprise. All over Hawai`i, shops sell "real" Hawaiian items, objects crowded together in glass cases or clustered with t-shirts on open shelves. In proposing the Hawaiian Cultural Center, Eleanor argued that Native Hawaiians should profit from the tourist demand for *Hawaiiana*. The concept of profit had multiple meanings in her proposal.

In August 1993, she sent a *Progress Report* on her plans to the Hawaiian Home Lands commissioners. The title of section 4 of the report is: "Hale-Kūha'o—Hawaiian Entreprenuership." Her plan had evolved into: "A shopping mall where every shop owner shall be Hawaiian and where labels on their wares shall include 'Made in Hawai`i'. A marketplace of self sufficiency, self-determined by the Spirit of *Aloha* and strengthened by the essence of 'Kū Kānaka.'"[85] Eleanor's report offers a particular version of a market, guided by generosity and by Hawaiian values. Yet it is a shopping mall, and she intended the profits to sustain residents of Pana`ewa and Keaukaha. She did not, however, equate profits with material wealth—or not only—but also with the gains to be won from practicing, extending, and transmitting cultural learning. Living on the land in the way the HHCA prescribed had not worked. With her plan for enterprise and marketing, Eleanor inserted the Native Hawaiian into the center of the American economic system—as the 1921 Act had not.

Eleanor included multiple strands in her efforts to gain support. In the *Progress Report*, she linked her proposal for a "Hawaiian marketplace" to the gains to the Native Hawaiian from a deeper share in the tourist business. And she emphasized the potential enhancement of Hawaiian culture in the "packaging" of arts and skills for tourists. Moreover, this aspect of her plan gave a strong role to the kūpuna—the elderlies who had the knowledge the younger generation lacked.

The *Report* opens with a clear message: "Kauhale Hawaiʻi. This shall be the heart of the Cultural Center. The Cultural heritage, traditions, customs, oral histories of our ancestors shall live and be passed on to our generation of poʻe Hawaiʻi and our progeny—for their future knowledge and enlightenment, thus enriching all who come to learn and share."[86] Those who would "learn" include local visitors and those who come from afar to see the romanticized Hawaiian Islands. Through the years I knew her, Eleanor often expressed her annoyance that the State Visitors Bureau did not do more to bring tourists to the Hilo area. In her view, culture learning would give Hilo a stake in the industry. She said: "People will learn about Hawaiʻi."

Hilo is a small town, whose central business district fell victim to a strip mall. Moreover, it is one of the rainiest cities in the United States, and few tourists travel across the Pacific to sit in a damp hotel. Most travelers to the Big Island, from the mainland or from Japan, use Hilo as a stopping-off point, on the way to Volcanoes National Park or to the other side of the island, where the sun shines on Kailua-Kona. In a letter whose recipients included the Hawaii Visitors Bureau, Eleanor complained: "Hawaii Island is being touted as a tourist attraction, our volcanoes, our Kona Coast, our people, our macadamia nuts, orchids, anthuriums, etc., but there is a great lack of cultural visual arts and attractions and or a place in Hilo to visit and learn about Hawaii and its native people and culture, history and traditions where they could gain a full, real experience of Hawaii." She added: "This project is so needed and very late in coming. The jobs generated and the taxes paid will help bring back a flame of life to our island economy."[87]

In linking her plans to tourism, Eleanor entered a complicated political arena. She proposed, in effect, to upset the existing hierarchy in that industry: Native Hawaiians work either in service sectors or as entertainers, rarely as resort owners, developers, or entrepreneurs.[88] The proposals she drafted required the business and political elite of Hawaiʻi to support the entry of Hawaiians into just those roles, ones they had been excluded from for decades. She reminded the reluctant Home Lands commissioners that she had received "legislative support" from two US senators. Daniel Akaka offered to make contact with the American Indian Affairs Committee and Dan Inouye promised an "inquiry." But like the state, the federal government remained uninterested.

Eleanor took a bold stand. From her perspective, Hui Ho`omau Keaukaha-Pana`ewa moved beyond homestead associations whose agendas focused on narrow, immediate issues. And she distinguished Hui Ho`omau from the traditional Hawaiian civic clubs, whose agendas were exhausted in events co-sponsored with the elite business community.[89] Her plans are determinedly pragmatic and long term, from a center in which Hawaiian owners practice and pass on Hawaiian culture to a center that is an alternative shopping mall, where culture is displayed and "arts and crafts" are marketed. Over time, her plans moved away from consumerism and toward a social service model. She transformed the center into a wide-ranging Hawaiian community complex. "My kōkua [help]," she wrote, "will be Hawaiian in its truth."

The introduction to the *Progress Report* explains: "There are several targeted areas of interest in The Complex. Each area of interest here is called a Component." Following the formal introduction, she lists the components, using Hawaiian phrases and adding an English gloss in parenthesis. With respect for the Hawaiian language and its complexities, she did not attempt a literal translation but rather used words that captured the "spirit" of her plans.

The first component is Kauhale Hawai`i, the cultural "heart" or "village" at the core of the program. The subsequent six components imbue specific welfare and remedial programs with Hawaiian values. Each component illuminates the ways in which state and federal governments neglect the Hawaiian people.

The second component in her list is "Mālama Nā Kūpuna (kūpuna housing)" in which care for kūpuna becomes the Americanized "housing." The third component, Mālama Na Mamo, translates "care for children/generations to come" into a "day care center." In the fourth component, Hale Ola Mau, Eleanor expresses concern for the health and well-being of her people in the border-crossing "medical clinic." Hale Mālama a Maluhia, glossed as "archival museum," represents a place for caring for artifacts, peacefully maintained. An "auditorium (for cultural performances)" comes before the last component: "Hale—Kūha`o—Hawaiian Entrepreneurship."[90] In her last component, Eleanor turns the nuanced meanings of kūha`o into a word that might appeal to the practical interests of those who supervise land distribution. With every component, she calls on the DHHL commissioners to account for their betrayal of a responsibility to the Native Hawaiian people.

The *Report* insists on the "community" that is served and created by the complex she describes. The components are clear, instrumental, and urgent; the spirit behind these practicalities is Hawaiian. The complex would be a shared space in which people came together to kōkua, to "nurture" the space, and to act as a collectivity. Moreover, alongside functional services like day care and a medical clinic, in this new iteration the center is a place for celebrations, reunions, and rituals.

The background for that version of the Hawaiian Cultural Center lies in Eleanor's memories of her childhood and the significance of the hall she talked about in a later interview. In 2001, she participated in an oral history project sponsored by the Hilo County Department of Parks and Recreation. She described the community center that sat on the road separating Keaukaha from the ocean.

"I first entered when it was down Kalaniana`ole Avenue. We used it for church, luau, meetings, weddings, and graduation and for commission [Hawaiian Homes Commission] meetings, which was often, because it was the only structure that the people in this community had so it was put to good use when it was in the front [of Keaukaha]." The Hall served multiple purposes. There was a library, and right next to it, a maternity clinic. "Hawaiian Homes had a pre-school in that same building before the maternity clinic was there. … [T]he only time you would take your baby out was when the center was closed. Other than that, the public health nurses would do all of the immunization for the children." People came, she remembered, not only for joyous celebrations but also for health care, for counseling, and for advice about DHHL rules. "The community was really supported by the people back then."[91]

On 1 April 1946, an enormous tidal wave washed the Hall away. A temporary structure replaced the old building for over fifty years. Finally, in 2001 the Parks and Recreation Department commemorated a newly built structure by eliciting the mo`olelo of kūpuna, who, like Eleanor, remembered its former capacities. The current website for Kawananakoa Hall reiterates the old mission. The Hall, the Internet text reads, is intended "to protect, to serve, and to support all who come to utilize her [the Hall] to its fullest potential."[92] But for Eleanor, important as a model, Kawananakoa Hall still did not go far enough in serving the people. The "components" in her cultural center plans provide the missing pieces: learning by doing, social services, enterprise, and, above all, self-sufficiency.

After her proposals for a cultural center failed, Eleanor did not give up her commitment to the future of Native Hawaiians. She extended her vision of a gathering of *the people* beyond the borders of Hilo County and the American state of Hawai`i. Her idea grew, from a center whose activities focused on local problems to a center from which Hawaiian values would permeate relations among *peoples*.

"Like a Lighthouse, a Flame"

On a July day in 2002, Auntie Eleanor and I drove to Volcanoes National Park, twenty or so miles from her house in Keaukaha. We were on our way to the prime tourist destination that overshadows Hilo and that attracts millions of visitors to Hawaiʻi every year. For Eleanor the land that lay at the foot of the volcanic mountains had many meanings, which she shared during the afternoon. As we drove up the road from Keaukaha, she talked about the areas we passed: the suburban housing developments on acres that once held sugar plantations, the expensive residences on former farm lands, and the flimsy commercial establishments set up for tourists.

Her stories brought us to the entrance of the National Park. A uniformed park ranger stepped out of his small hut and informed us of the cost of entry. Eleanor drew herself up and refused to pay. "I am kupuna," she told him, and "I do not have to pay to enter *our* land." After a pause (and perhaps wondering about the haole driver), the ranger asked whether she intended to "conduct religious services in the park." She assured him that she would teach me "ancient chants" and the stories of "sacred places." He let us go in, reminding us that under the terms of our entry we were not permitted to eat at the Volcano House Restaurant, which John had helped construct a half-century before. We had our picnic outside, with the saimin and rice we had picked up in Hilo.

Behind us loomed Mauna Loa, a 13,769-foot-high intermittently active volcano. So close as to be almost indistinguishable stands Kīlauea, a volcano whose frequent eruptions are a featured aspect of tourist trips into the National Park. Across the island, invisible to us, stood Mauna Kea, a non-active volcano and a sacred space in Hawaiian mythology. Religious shrines, rock shelters, and ancient petroglyphs dot the land beneath the summit. Today the 13,800-foot-high mountain houses a cluster of observatories, the world's largest site for optical, infrared, and submillimeter astronomy. The land the Astronomical Project occupies is protected by the US Historical Preservation Act under the guise of its significance to Hawaiian culture. The act does not forbid the construction of new equipment to test weather, wind, and climate change from an "ideal" location.

Most of the land between the National Park and the observatories is used by the United States military, as a weapons testing range and training ground for American soldiers. The Pōhakuloa Training Area (PTA) covers more than 109,000 acres and reaches about 6800 feet up Mauna Kea and 9000 feet up the sides of Mauna Loa where Eleanor and I ate our lunch. Three core American institutions—the progress of science, the power of the military, the preservation of national icons through a National Park service—thus rule over the volcanic landscape of the Big Island.

Eleanor was well aware of the presence of the US military in the center of the island. She knew the history of Volcanoes National Park, her brother's Civilian Conservation Corps camp in 1941, and its disputed use as a bombing range during World War II. She had participated in protest marches against the construction of new observatories on the top of Mauna Kea.[93] She told these stories against the background of the place we sat in that afternoon. While we shared our saimin, Eleanor reminded me that we were on space belonging to Pele, the "creator" of volcanoes. Although the mountains behind us were quiet that day, for most of the decade lava had been flowing down from Kīleaua. From time to time, red-hot lava covers the houses at the foot of the mountain, wiping away all traces of life and leaving only the black moonscape tourists photograph.

Eleanor explained that the destruction was never arbitrary or random. Pele is a stern and demanding force, a personage who regularly wanders through the small villages in her domain. She asks for welcome, for food, and for water, and refusal brings her wrath.[94] In 1990, Eleanor told me, the small fishing village of Kalapana fell victim to Pele's punishment. From April through December of that year, lava flowed relentlessly, burying the town and the Royal Garden Subdivision under ten meters of molten rock. The town was destroyed but for good reason; this was not simply a *natural* catastrophe. Eleanor elaborates: one day an old and haggard woman came around begging for sustenance. Some residents closed the door in her face, sending her away. Other residents gave generously, welcoming the "ugly one" into their households. Those households, Eleanor continued, were spared as lava ran in streams to the ocean.[95]

Tourists buy Pele t-shirts and mugs, wander over the hard lava, and peer into the smoky holes left in the wake. Occasionally, Pele stretches her power over tourists, punishing the reckless and the thoughtless; the media report on the deaths of ignorant or arrogant tourists. Early in our friendship, John gave me a videotape of volcanic eruptions. "Show it to your class," he advised, "so they know the story of Hawai`i." He told me about another village that was destroyed by lava. The people there grew pakalolo (marijuana), he said, showing disrespect for the `āina and for the youth in the community.

Not only the National Park itself, but also the residues of volcanic eruption constitute prime tourist sights. The black sand beach that covers the shore of a former fishing village, the sulfur that still smells along the pathways in the park, and the shiny lava rocks attract travelers who are circling the Big Island. Across the island, the United States welcomes curious tourists to explore the cluster of observatories, sign of continuing progress in the archipelago. Mauna Kea State Park abuts the Pōhakuloa Training Area, offering a safe spot from which to view the vast US military land area. A road leading through the middle of the island, from Hilo to Kailua-Kona, bisects the training area. Eleanor told me not to drive there; her stated reason was the possibility of gunfire, but I suspect her actual reason was objection to the ownership of sacred land by the American military. The road was recently rebuilt, ostensibly for travelers, quite possibly to help move the army vehicles stationed at PTA. In 2006 the Army bought 24,000 more acres, to house the armored Stryker vehicles. The vehicles were used to train soldiers for "modern warfare" in this rocky landscape, a euphemism for the preparation required for deploying troops to Iraq and Afghanistan.[96]

In some sense, this was a last straw for Eleanor, who had protested the nearby observatories built on sacred land. The spread of Stryker vehicles symbolized a long history of military takeover and the contemporary use of force by the United States in its domestic as well as its foreign policy. By then, Eleanor's protests mainly occurred in her mo`olelo, in letters to newspapers and officials, and in the "books" (notebooks) she kept for the younger generations. She continued, however, to be open to the political currents swirling around her. She listened when a visiting activist told her about the discovery of hundreds of petitions signed by kānaka maoli in opposition to American takeover of the Hawaiian nation.[97] Around that time, she identified herself as the *subject* of a foreign regime, her American citizenship illegitimately granted. I am, she said, a *citizen* of the Hawaiian Kingdom, and her mail came addressed to "E. Ahuna, Kingdom of Hawai`i."

But she also knew quite well the entanglement of her life, as of all Native Hawaiians, in the United States—its economic and social institutions, its health care and educational system, and its constitutional guarantees. Medicare and social security checks came in her mail, too, with the Keaukaha street address plainly written. When a presumptive king joined us for lunch, she listened to his claims and looked at his genealogy, recorded in notebooks. He stated his kinship with the Kamehameha line, and he asked Eleanor to persuade Big Island kūpuna to support his bid for the throne. Patient with his story, she yet rejected his plan to institute an independent government for the Hawaiian people. In her view, neither the return to a kingdom nor any other form of "state" was a realistic proposition. Or, in fact, a necessary one. "We already have sovereignty."

Sovereignty meant for her the endurance of culture—of the bases for action, for improvement, and for self-sustainability she had long been advocating. Sovereignty also meant, a new mo`olelo revealed, exercising the "spirit" of a people, their "way of being." The ideas came out in her vision of a Peace Center. Reminiscent of the Hawaiian Cultural Center, the Peace Center bypassed a direct relationship with the American Congress, the Hawai`i State Legislature, or the DHHL.

"One night after I got my stroke, I prayed and asked the Heavenly Father to tell me what that word [*aloha*] meant. And it came to me, what that word meant."[98] She explained: "that word is a god-given word: come-before-me-for-life-and-breath." The story went on. "And I asked for the word Hawai`i." *Ha*, she said, is life and *wai* is water. "Without water, there is no life. Together the words represent *Hawai`i*." The understanding led to another, which became the core of her plan. "In the names of nations lay their spirits; in their greetings lay the terms of their interactions." She concluded: "And that's what I want to write for the Internet. I want to write to the world council [possibly the United Nations] and find out what other nations say, their names and their greetings."

Her revelation about place is simultaneously an insight into a people. "Hawaiians are a peaceful people." In the early twenty-first century, her emphasis on peacefulness was not trivial: Hawaiians, she implied, are not part of a United States that is waging war in Iraq and in Afghanistan, despite their service in and employment by the military. The Peace Center represented a way of resisting the "militarism ... deeply embedded" in Pacific Island nations.[99] Furthermore, her proposal resisted the specific consequences of war in land appropriation; the prerogative of national security translated into "public use" permits the unabated stealing of Hawaiian acres. Like earlier wars, too, the twenty-first-century actions bring thousands of military personnel to the Big Island, supported by strongholds of ground and air weaponry. Considering that neither DHHL nor the state government prevent the ravaging of land, Eleanor created an alternative, a place for the ʻāina and for her people in a global arena and a location for the practice of aloha—generosity, compassion, and forgiveness.

The Peace Center represented her most forceful criticism of the United States. Through the vision of a Peace Center, Eleanor condemned the armed takeover of the Hawaiian nation and she censured the culture that represented the "spirit" of the United States. Her Hawaiian Cultural Center posed a milder critique, in the outline of programs to improve the conditions under which Native Hawaiians lived. That plan was a kind of step-by-step confrontation with the failures of state and federal programs. The Peace Center was less programmatic than visionary—a projection onto the world screen of a marginalized people.

Eleanor chose Panaʻewa as the location of a Cultural Center, and she placed the Peace Center on the farm lots as well. The Hawaiian Cultural Center returned to the original purpose of the 1921 Act, providing sustenance to the kānaka maoli and reserving a space away from the grasp of developers, businessmen, or a county government needing revenue. The Peace Center returned to the 1921 Act in another way, by "rehabilitating" the spirit of the Hawaiian people, restoring the place of Hawaiʻi in the world, and diffusing Hawaiian values beyond the boundaries of a homestead or of the fiftieth state in an American union. The premise for the center transformed the concept of "nation" from a nation-state to something closer to the lāhui of old. Inclusive, based on mālamaʻāina, laulima, and aloha, the "nation" represented in the Peace Center introduced a radical view of nationhood.

"The picture doesn't go away. It would be on the mountainside, with glass around so it will sparkle. At night, they'll see the light, like a lighthouse, a flame." In her vision of a Peace Center, Eleanor skirted the political talk about states and state sovereignty, instead asserting the self-confidence of Native Hawaiians to stay their own course—stand firm. She constituted a Hawaiian nation on the basis of the values that threaded through the eulogy she gave for her brother in June 1996. These were the values she and he associated with life in Keaukaha—not a return to the past, but rather a turn to "old ways" for guidance in a late-twentieth-century world. And these were the values Eleanor and John referred to all their lives—through the American public school they were compelled to attend, the English they were required to speak, and the social position they were expected to assume in an American territory and state. In 1930, John took a short walk to Keaukaha Elementary School, and three years later Eleanor followed him down the dirt trail. The walk both took marked the beginning of a lifelong journey between being 100 percent Hawaiian and a citizen of the United States.

Notes

1. According to Mary Kawena Pukui, E. W. Haertig, and Catherine A. Lee, *Nānā I Ke Kumu* (II), "The hānau mua was the accepted source of wisdom, the arbitrator of family disputes, the trouble-shooter in family problems, and the custodian of family history," 126.
2. Hawaiian Homes Commission Act of 1921: Hearings on H.R. 3500. Committee on Territories, 66th Cong., 3rd Session (1920), 70.
3. See Lawrence H. Fuchs, *Hawaii Pono,* chapter 6.
4. Davianna Pōmaika`i McGregor, "`Āina Ho`opulapula: Hawaiian Homesteading," 1.
5. While there is dispute about exact numbers, Native Hawaiian scholars agree on the demographic disaster that followed upon the arrival of settlers to the islands; see, for instance, Jennifer Noelani Goodyear-Ka`ōpua, "Rebuilding the Āuwai."
6. This was not the first such plan. "The record shows that Hawaiians had consistently advocated for homesteading by Hawaiians since the Land Act of 1895 set up five methods of homesteading upon the former government and Crown lands by the general public"; Jennifer Noelani Goodyear-Ka`ōpua, "Rebuilding the Āuwai," 7.
7. See J. Kēhaulani Kauanui, *Hawaiian Blood,* for a detailed discussion of the debates in the US Congress.
8. So persistent is the ideal of farming that the Homestead Act endured until 1976 on the mainland, and until 1986 in Alaska.
9. Such a break up, Secretary of the Interior Columbus Delano already argued in 1874, "will bring them to abandon roving habits, and teach them the benefits of industry and individual ownership." Cited in Francis Paul Prucha, *The Great Father,* 660. See Clarkson's *Recent Developments* for the significance of the twisted history of HHCA and the General Allotment Act in the *Rice v. Cayetano* decision of the US Supreme Court in 2000.
10. The Dawes Act was, in part, reversed by the 1934 Indian Reorganization Act, which restored "self-determination" to American Indian tribes. See Prucha, *The Great Father,* chapter 21.
11. Crown and Government lands comprised one of three divisions made in the 1848 Great Māhele. The other two parts were designated for ali`i (chiefs) and commoners (maka`āinana). "Probably no single event so drastically changed the social system

of Hawaii as the Great Mahele"; Fuchs, *Hawaii Pono,* 14. Territorial status erased the "crown" designation, replacing it with the somewhat euphemistic "public." See Jon Van Dyke, *Who Owns the Crown Lands of Hawai`i?,* chapter 4.

12. "The Hawaiian language does not even have a word for private property ownership of the land. The word kuleana, which was used to translate the law, refers to personal possessions such as clothing"; McGregor, "`Āina Ho`opulapula," 38.
13. According to Fuchs, "only 2 per cent of the lands set aside was suitable for cultivation;" Fuchs, *Hawaii Pono,* 174.
14. Memorandum by Eleanor Ahuna, Keaukaha Hawaiian Homeland Homestead, 30 September 1993 (in the author's possession).
15. Robert C. Schmitt, *Demographic Statistics,* 74, 120; John P. Rosa, "Race/Ethnicity," 55; see David E. Stannard, *Before the Horror.*
16. Noel J. Kent, *Hawaii,* 70. "With the exception of Davies, who was British, all these corporations were run by American missionary descendants (though American Factors Ltd. was German-controlled as H. Hackfield and Company until 1918)"; Kauanui, *Hawaiian Blood,* 69.
17. Ibid., 37.
18. Kauanui goes into detail concerning the differences between the General Allotment Act and the Hawaiian Homes Commission Act, in terms of the blood quantum as criterion and the ultimate goal of each policy. See Kauanui, *Hawaiian Blood,* chapter 2.
19. Memorandum by Eleanor Ahuna, Controversies on DHHL Policies and Administration Rules, Memorandum, 6 December 1990 (in the author's possession).
20. Prince Jonah Kūhiō Kalaniana`ole died on 7 January 1922, six months after the act passed. He did not witness its implementation in his homeland.
21. See Karen L. Ito, *Lady Friends,* for a discussion of the preservation of Hawaiian values in an urban population.
22. Rona Tamiko Halualani discusses this burden on applicants in *In the Name of Hawaiians,* chapter 3.
23. Memorandum by Eleanor Ahuna, Controversies.
24. Ibid.
25. In his discussion of "Native Hawaiian Land Rights," Neil M. Levy argues that the 999-year leases of small acreage at no cost represented "the portion of the act most suited to native Hawaiians," 863.
26. See Van Dyke, *Who Owns the Crown Lands,* 196–199.
27. See Ulla Hasager, "Localizing the American Dream."
28. As Fuchs put it: "The Hawaiians leased their own leased land to major pineapple companies, thus entirely defeating the original purpose of the rehabilitation program." Fuchs, *Hawaii Pono,* 72.
29. Thomas G. Thrum, *The Hawaiian Annual,* 118.
30. Simeona, John, *Life Story,* MS., 6 (in the author's possession).
31. Rhea Akoi, ed., *Ku`u Home I Keaukaha,* 41.
32. Ron Takaki, *Pau Hana,* chapter VI.
33. Akoi, *Ku`u Home,* 43.
34. Ibid., 70.
35. Ibid., 71.
36. Ibid., 72.
37. Ibid., 5. The choice of this gloss on the name reflects a self-conscious process of documenting mo`olelo that inspired the booklet in the first place. Other ways of translating the phrase include "the passing current," which can be interpreted as another mode of carrying past into present. Auntie Eleanor's granddaughter points out the relevance

of "time of writing" inasmuch as "many Hawaiians were writing their thoughts at that time."

38. That both parents were "100 percent Hawaiian" implies the blood quantum that would give John and Eleanor the "over 50 percent" required for getting a homestead lease. As I show, John's use of "100 percent" more often referred to his self-identification as Native Hawaiian than to his blood quantum.

39. In *Ku Kanaka*, George Kanahele describes the significance of place, concluding, "and no history could have been made or preserved without reference, directly or indirectly, to a place," 175–176.

40. John Simeona to the author, 21 November 1994.

41. Simeona, *Life Story*, 1.

42. Akoi, *Ku`u Home*, 70.

43. Thanks to an anonymous reader for pointing out the significance of shifts between Kimona and Simeona.

44. In Waimānalo, Helene told me she had changed the name of her daughter to counteract an infant illness the first name brought. "Names have *mana*," Karen Ito writes, "and an improper choice can bring the child bad luck, illness, misfortune, or a wandering spirit called `uhane hele, which can be interpreted as a loss of self"; Ito, *Lady Friends*, 110–111.

45. Ahuna, "Mama," 12–15.

46. Simeona, *Life Story*, 5.

47. Memorandum by Eleanor Ahuna, Controversies.

48. Simeona, *Life Story*, 1.

49. McGregor, *Na Kua`āina*, 24. McGregor explains the wedge-shaped form: "Ahupua`a boundaries coincided with the geographic features of a valley," 26.

50. In "Localizing the American Dream," Hasager describes the pono/harmony established in the homesteads of Molaka`i, in an appropriation of the meanings of land by homesteaders. See Hasager, "Localizing."

51. Simeona, *Life Story*, 6.

52. Ibid., 3.

53. Ibid., 7.

54. Ibid., 6.

55. Ibid., 8–9.

56. Ibid., 13.

57. Ibid., 7.

58. See J. Noelani Goodyear-Ka`ōpua, "Rebuilding the `Auwai"; Aikau, *A Chosen People*, 177.

59. See Ito, *Lady Friends*.

60. Fuchs notes that, "By 1920, more than half of the part Hawaiians and 36 per cent of the pure Hawaiians in the Islands lived in Honolulu," *Hawaii Pono*, 69.

61. Schmitt, *Demographic Statistics*, 117.

62. For a detailed account of the case and its consequences, see David E. Stannard, *Honor Killing*.

63. Rosa, "Local Story," 95.

64. Ibid., 104.

65. "It was the first time 'the people of Hawaii were brought up flatly and traumatically against the power of American racialism,'" writes Rosa, quoting John Reinecke; "Local Story," 104.

66. Ty P. Kāwika Tengan, "Re-membering Panalā`au," 35.

67. See Gary Y. Okihiro, *Cane Fires*, chapter 8.

68. According to Fuchs, "By 1934, more than 10 per cent of the Hawaiian or part-Hawaiian men between the ages of twenty and fifty-four were on relief, triple the proportion of Japanese and almost ten times that of Filipinos"; *Hawaii Pono,* 73.
69. In January 1920, a *Honolulu Star-Bulletin* article "describes overcrowded, filthy tenement slums"; cited in Rich Budnick, *Hawaii's Forgotten History,* 47.
70. http://www.Papakolea.org, accessed 3 July 2010 (currently under construction).
71. Edgy Lee's film documents women's roles in the struggles to retain land. Edgy Lee, *Papakolea: A Story of Hawaiian Land,* DVD, FilmWorks Pacific 1998.
72. See Ito, *Lady Friends.*
73. http://www.kawelina.net/hosts/papakolea., accessed 6 May 2013.
74. Ibid.
75. John Simeona to the author, 26 July 1989.
76. Ibid., 10 August 1989.
77. Minutes of the Hawaiian Homes Commission meetings 1980–88, Department of Hawaiian Home Lands, Series 239, Hawai`i State Archives.
78. See Samuel P. King and Randall Roth, *Broken Trust,* for a detailed history of the land policies of the Bishop Estate / Kamehameha Schools.
79. Her use of the word *local* is calculated: she refers to those with power granted by the state but presumably acting in the interests of Native Hawaiians. Her usage differs from the more common application of the word to "working class" or descendants of plantation workers. Sally Engle Merry, "Law and Identity," 125; see Rosa, "Local Story."
80. Eleanor Ahuna to the Honorable Trustees of the Kamehameha Schools and the Bernice Pauahi Bishop estate, 29 September 1992 (in the author's possession).
81. Eleanor Ahuna to all elected members of the Hawaii County Administration and Council, The Hawaii State legislators (and nine other institutions), 31 January 1993 (in the author's possession).
82. Ibid.
83. Minutes of the Hawaiian Homes Commission meetings 1980–88, Department of Hawaiian Home Lands, Series 239, Hawai`i State Archives.
84. In 2008, victim of the financial crisis, Hilo Hattie filed for bankruptcy.
85. Eleanor Ahuna to the Honorable members of the Hawaiian Home Commissioners, 25 August 1993 (in the author's possession).
86. Ibid.
87. Eleanor Ahuna to all elected members of the Hawaii County Administration, 31 January 1993.
88. Ramsay R. M. Taum claims, "Despite the wealth generated from the integration and use of Maoli culture in the promotion and marketing of the islands as a premier destination, very little of that wealth directly reaches host communities or their cultural practitioners"; Taum, "Tourism," 33.
89. A Hawaiian civic club existed in Keaukaha, named after David Kawānanakoa, brother of Prince Kūhiō. Their mother, Victoria Kūhiō Kinoiki Kekaulike, belonged to the royal lineage of Hilo District and was Royal Governor of the island. The founding of Keaukaha Homestead and the establishment of a civic club carried forward her attachment to the area. The civic club was conventional, according to Eleanor, a view born out by a newsletter: Prince David Kawananakoa Hawaiian Civic Club "participated in many Hawaiian community events such as the Merrie Monarch Festival, Kamehameha Day Celebrations at the Kohala *lei* draping event and Moku Ola (Coconut Island) and the 'Plantation Reunion Days' sponsored by the Hilo Downtown Improvement Associa-

tion," from *Nuhou I Ka Makani* (newspaper of Hawaiian Civic Clubs), October 1996, 6.

90. Eleanor Ahuna to the Honorable members of the Hawaiian Home Commissioners, 25 August 1993. I am grateful to Eleanor's granddaughter, Grace K. Mamoali`iokalani Bezilla, for offering her interpretations of the meanings attributed to Hawaiian phrases in the document.

91. Kawananakoa Hall Oral History Project. Under the sponsorship of the Department of Parks and Recreation, County of Hawaii, Gary Francisco, project coordinator, Hilo, Hawaii: October 2001.

92. http://keaukahavbc.org/Kawananakoa_Hall.html, accessed 6 May 2013.

93. These protests continue today: "Although the mountain volcano Mauna Kea last erupted around 4000 years ago, it is still hot today, the center of a burning controversy over whether its summit should be used for astronomical observatories or preserved as a cultural landscape sacred to the Hawaiian people"; http://www.namoka.com/catalog/spirit/maunakea_temple.html, accessed 25 April 2012. See also http://kahea.org, website of the Hawaiian-Environmental Alliance.

94. "Had not Pele herself, when refused food and drink by a selfish woman, destroyed the stingy one in a flow of lava?" Pukui, Haertig, and Lee, *Nānā I Ke Kumu* (II), 54.

95. "Pele is the magma, the heat, the vapor, the steam, and the cosmic creation which occur in volcanic eruptions. She is seen in the lava, images of her standing erect, dancing, and extending her arms with her hair flowing into the steam and clouds." From the *Pele Defense Fund*, quoted in McGregor, *Nā Kua`āina,* 188.

96. See Kyle Kajihiro, "The Militarizing of Hawai`i" and "Resisting Militarization in Hawai`i."

97. She may have heard about Noenoe Silva's uncovering of these documents, published in *Aloha Betrayed* in 2004.

98. The combination of a Christian God and Hawaiian tradition is not unusual. "A number of Hawaiians … continue to pray to `aumākua and sometimes to both `aumākua and God"; Pukui, Haertig, and Lee, *Nānā I Ke Kumu* (II), 138.

99. Ty P. Kāwika Tengan, "Re-membering Panalā`au," 29.

2

"Educating the Polynesian American"
Two Worlds of Learning

When I first saw John Simeona, on 17 May 1989, he was standing at the front of a large room pledging allegiance to the American flag. He led a group of women and men in the ritual, the people he would later call the *elderlys*. All stood together, hands on hearts, and all followed the pledge by singing "Aloha Oe," to represent the spirit of Hawai`i. John had learned the pledge over fifty years earlier, in the public schools of Hilo, where he recited the phrases every morning of every day. The elderlys, too, spoke the words easily, apparently as familiar to them as the patriotic song composed by Queen Lili`uokalani.

In 1989, John was president of the Waimānalo Senior Citizen Club, an organization established by the Hawai`i Department of Parks and Recreation. The statewide clubs serve several purposes: providing services to a growing population of seniors, offering recreational activities, and building community relations. John invited me to meetings and to events sponsored by the Waimānalo Seniors, often reminding me that I would learn "to be Hawaiian" from the seniors, whose events, he said, celebrated Hawaiian custom.[1]

The Waimānalo Seniors group embodied a benign policy of welfare and education begun by the missionaries in the 1820s. At the same time, the diversity of the group belied the connection with the past. Based on age and not on ethnic or racial identity, the seniors were diverse in their negotiations of American citizenship and in their embrace of Hawaiian causes. In 1994, when John urged the group to join the protests against land policies at the state legislature, most refused to accompany him. He called them "stubborn," equally so, he wrote, when he tried to teach them Robert's Rules of Order. He had better luck when he rehearsed the group for a Memorial Day ceremony or a celebration of King Kamehameha Day. In the 1980s and 1990s, reenactments increasingly played a part in the transmission of Hawaiian culture and history, supplementing a public school curriculum that still gave short shrift to those subjects.[2]

The elderlys energetically took the roles of historical figures, in front of an audience of children, grandchildren, and occasional visitors. Such performances constituted a lesson in Hawaiian history that the kūpuna passed down to a younger generation. For those who looked on, the dramatized renderings presented a story that the Western narratives provided by American public schooling distorted or denied altogether. In the senior clubs, a cultural renaissance and official recognition of kanaka maoli status fostered an effort to reinstate a story most members rarely—or never—heard in their childhoods. Club members created a moʻolelo that supplemented a curriculum still largely focused on American history and the "great men" of that tradition. John complained to me that his children and grandchildren learned the same stories he had, experienced similar stereotyping, and suffered from analogously strange standards of conduct. As in the 1930s, so in the last decades of the twentieth century, Americanized public schooling disciplined a population into the character befitting a citizen of the United States—and, not incidentally, distinguished that character from the alien.

And Everybody Had to Wear Shoes

John entered the first grade class at Keaukaha Elementary School one morning in September 1930. He was five years old, and the school was brand new. Keaukaha opened that September, an early sign of attention to the education of Native Hawaiian children growing up on the home lands of the territory. Despite its origin in a program designed for Native Hawaiians, the school looked much like elementary schools scattered throughout the islands—from the older, crowded Lincoln Elementary in a Hawaiian neighborhood of Honolulu to the small schools on outer islands. Regardless of the students served, teachers acquired the same pedagogical agenda from a centralized Territorial Department of Public Instruction (DPI).

John learned American history from teachers, some of whom were recruited from the mainland and all of whom were presumably fluent in English. The teachers he encountered were heavily imbued with American pedagogy, a mixture of progressive ideas of public education and traditional disciplinary methods of instruction. And they had to follow a curriculum that suppressed the pidgin dialect most children spoke at home—and Hawaiian was not even considered. In classes across the islands, teachers relied on a civic education in which children had to memorize passages from the US Constitution and Bill of Rights.

In *Life Story*, John writes that the school was only a "ten minute walk through a trail" from the house he shared with his parents and his sister Eleanor. Everything between the lines, however, indicates the vast distance that separated his hours at school from his life in the ʻohana.

At school, John encountered the full thrust of American colonial policy. He bore the brunt of a civilizing mission that had gradually relinquished its explicit Christianizing component. While adults might attend church, the ineffectiveness of Sunday sermons puzzled the missionaries, who, by mid-nineteenth century, determined that teaching native children promised a more predictable "taming" of the savage than preaching to adults. "If Christian institutions are to be perpetuated," wrote missionary Richard Armstrong in 1847, the work must be accomplished mainly where it has been so prosperously begun, *in the education of the young.*"[3] A century later, in the 1930s, public schools in Hawaiʻi educated the "young" along the lines of an assimilationist movement that spread from the mainland to the territory. By the time John went to Keaukaha Elementary, the only traces of Christianity in the curriculum lay in "moral discipline." As the superintendent for education in 1936 put it, public schooling should provide every student "a free education as well as prepare him to perform his duties as a citizen and to live usefully and wholesomely under the conditions of life in these islands," conditions that called for basic skills and not for higher education.[4] The weight lay on the three Rs of American education: reading, writing ('riting), and arithmetic ('rithmetic).

The missionaries had initiated a focus on the youngest residents of the islands, small children who might benefit from the ABC's of American life. The Lymans and the Coans arrived in Hilo in 1824, and immediately divided the tasks at hand. Mr. Lyman and Mr. Coan wrote out sermons for the adults they hoped to attract to church. Mrs. Lyman and Mrs. Coan recited the twenty-six letters of the English alphabet to the youngsters who gathered around them. And they discovered, with an astonishment recorded in letters home, that the Hawaiian children learned these unfamiliar sounds instantly. The "uncivilized" children, in fact, seemed to learn reading and writing far faster than their own children. (The older mission children went home to New England to be "properly" educated—a separation by age that would influence education in the islands well into the twentieth century.) Across the island from Hilo, in Kona, Lucia Ruggles Holman noted in her journal: "The natives, common people, with whom our house is constantly surrounded, have caught the sound of some of our letters, while we have been teaching [the king and queens]—so that wherever we go, we can hear ʻa, b, cʼ &d."[5]

The outcome exceeded expectations. The Hawaiians quickly became literate in English, and the missionaries became suspicious that the real meaning of the words escaped their pupils.[6] Nor was the facility the kānaka maoli achieved in reading any proof that they understood the lessons in the Bible the missionaries had painstakingly translated into written Hawaiian. Facile in both English and Hawaiian, the natives outdid their tutors, prompting discomfort among the missionaries and their descendants. The new tools might be put to other uses than those the Christian civilizers intended, and literacy offered a way for the Native Hawaiian to store his own body of knowledge. Newspapers in Hawaiian flourished in the mid-nineteenth century, and articles draw on the kaona even a literate missionary might miss. The mo'olelo Silva describes in *Aloha Betrayed* created a community of readers that excluded well-meaning teachers and advisors—and "native" stories posed a threat to the stories the missionaries were assiduously conveying.[7] Literacy also gave Native Hawaiians access to the documents the malihini brought to the islands. An example from John's family indicated the quick appreciation of writing: in the late nineteenth century, his uncle signed a contract for land on which to build a Church of Jesus Christ of Latter-day Saints.[8]

In one way or another, the very literacy upon which the mission families counted seemed poised to backfire in the precarious new order. Lucia Ruggles Holman predicted more than perhaps she knew when she complained that the common people took to the alphabet intended to serve the "kings and queens." Mr. Coan had a solution to potential shifts in the social structure of the islands. He applied lessons from home to complete the training of ordinary natives. "We teach them industry, economy, frugality, and generosity; but their progress in these virtues is slow. They are like children, needing wise parents or guardians," he wrote in his journals.[9] Coan and his successors established the blueprint for a pedagogical method, a curricular content, and a measure of success that well-meaning—and self-proclaimed—experts only adjusted over the decades. Well into the twentieth century, experts on educating the native considered the English language the fundamental core of a satisfactory curriculum. To this, administrators added a version of Coan's prescription for teaching proper comportment and the puritanical standard of behavior that distinguished *civilized* from *savage*.

English did come first. When John entered Keaukaha in 1930, nearly 100 percent of Native Hawaiians could read and write in English.[10] His first task was to learn those skills. "It was the hardest thing to learn to speak English," his cousin and contemporary Henrietta remembered. "I cried every day going home from school because I didn't know where to start or how to begin and my mom couldn't help me and it was compulsory that I speak English at home."[11] At home, however, pidgin dominated and neither John nor Henrietta addressed members of the 'ohana in the stilted language of a classroom. Yet their parents insisted on the importance of learning English. As Eleanor recalled, "my mama and stepfather said, 'you learn English. That's where your life is gonna be.'" In the mid-1990s, sitting in John's living room, I heard him say to a grandchild, "don't talk like a tita"—using the pidgin for *sister*. Sixty years after his own struggle to learn English, he scolded any member of his household who neglected the English taught in school. John knew then the implications of pidgin for shutting a person out of the jobs, the educational opportunities, and the resources of an American state.

English may have been the hardest for children whose primary use of the language was at a desk, in a row of other children, with a teacher correcting pronunciation. Other lessons were also hard. Coan's emphasis on comportment, behavior becoming a citizen, transformed into pedagogical dictates that had more to do with clean hands, proper clothing, and stiff demeanor than with the experiences familiar to a Hawaiian child. "And everybody had to wear shoes, the whole thing," Henrietta remembered. "I mean you had to dress nice, they check you out when you go to school, your hair had to be nice. If you had, if you had long hair, you had to have your hair braided, no such thing as letting your hair loose, always had to be braided."[12] John threw off his shoes, he told me, as soon as he walked out of the school building—often jumping into the ocean for a break. "At times I would stop at a pond area and take a dive for a little swim," he inserted in his account of school.[13]

A "little swim" provided temporary relief from the drills and inspections, regimentation and rules that filled the day. John spent hours reciting lessons in Standard English, and listening to a teacher who sat "coldly" behind a "block desk," as Auntie Eleanor recalled. He suffered, too, from the required shoes, long pants, and "tightly buttoned shirt" a boy had to wear. "We were taught very New England," recalled Eric Enos, twenty years younger than John. He continued, "So I would say it was very colonized."[14] In the 1980s, Enos participated in the creation of the ʻŌpelu Project, a restoration of ahupuaʻa forms of sustenance on the Waiʻanae Coast. The project is designed to counter the "colonized" education of his generation and generations before him.[15]

In the public schools, trained teachers continued to perpetuate a "colonized pedagogy." Other staff members, however, escaped the tight controls exerted by the DPI. John and Eleanor remembered the non-teaching personnel more fondly than their teachers, the school nurse, for example, or the dental technician. John distinguished the school dietician in a list of people he appended to his brief account of the elementary school. Fifteen years after he and Eleanor were pupils, two younger sisters followed them down the trail. "You know what I really liked about Keaukaha Elementary School was that we had a nurse, a dental nurse, she had an office there in our school," John's sister Winona remarked to me.[16] Auntie Eleanor's list included the principal and "Mrs. Kelso, who was a Hawaiian." Mrs. Kelso taught first grade and perhaps taught the homestead children with more understanding than other teachers showed. John also mentions Mrs. Kelso by name.

She was not the only Hawaiian teacher in the public school system of the territory in the 1930s.[17] But like other Native Hawaiians, then and now, she may well have struggled against the formal pedagogy prescribed by the Department of Public Instruction each time she entered the square brick building in the middle of the homestead. The DPI imposed severe rules for teachers as well as for pupils, and apprenticeship-style learning was not among the practices territorial administrators approved.

"Take More Part in Discussions"

By law, John had to go to school until he was sixteen years old. A century before, in 1840, haole advisors convinced King Kamehameha III to approve a new constitution; a statute soon followed, imposing compulsory school attendance on the children of the land. The early law compelled every child in the kingdom to remain in school until she or he was fourteen years old. Under the Minister of Education, Richard Armstrong, teachers conveyed mission values, training the children in "moral and industrial discipline."[18] They did not, however, teach in the language of the missionaries. Until the 1870s, educating native children in "common schools" meant teaching in Hawaiian and not in English. "The theory of substituting the English language for the Hawaiian, in order to educate our people," argued the president of the Board of Education and father of King Kamehameha V in 1864, "is as dangerous to the Hawaiian nationality, as it is useless in promoting the general education of the people."[19] And even when as president of the Board, Charles R. Bishop—banker, merchant, investor, and husband of a descendant of the royal family—argued for English instruction in the common schools, he had to admit that there were not enough able teachers available to implement such a reform.

As the century came to an end, education—like much else in the government of Hawai'i—came under the control of pro-annexationists, who used the fact of "total schooling" to argue for the incorporation of the kingdom into the United States. "The laws of Hawaii already provide that school attendance by all persons of school age shall be compulsory, and also that the English language shall be the universal language taught. The effect of these two enactments is the most beneficial and far-reaching in unifying the inhabitants which could be adopted."[20] The sentences appear in an 1898 report by a federal commission "in pursuance" of a resolution to annex the archipelago. The wording implicitly justifies the armed takeover of the kingdom in 1893 and the reign of haole under a regime euphemistically deemed the "Republic of Hawai'i." By then, the age of compulsory schooling had been raised to sixteen and English had been installed as "the medium and the basis for instruction in all public and private schools."[21] Considered a necessary tool for success in the modern world of nation-states by the Native Hawaiian elite, English became the crucial medium for unifying and disciplining a polyglot population.

The federal commission report continues: compulsory schooling "operates to break up the racial antagonisms otherwise certain to increase and to unite in the schoolroom the children of the Anglo-Saxons, the Hawaiians, the Latins, and the Mongolians in the rivalry for obtaining an education. No system could be adopted which would tend to Americanize the people more thoroughly than this."[22] Optimistic and agenda driven, the report puts a double burden on the public school system to Americanize a diverse population and to exemplify a racial harmony mainland states failed to sustain. English constituted the first step toward Americanization, and policymakers assumed a common tongue produced social integration. In 1900, the annexationists won their political victory. A Territorial Department of Public Instruction was charged with implementing the commission's report.

Throughout the ensuing decades, the DPI distributed one curriculum to all public schools in the territory.[23] Lesson plans expose the limits of language for Americanizing the young residents of the islands. "Use good English," a DPI brochure urged upon pupils. "Be ashamed of the so called 'pidgin English.' Take more part in discussions. Do not be afraid to make mistakes. It is better to make a mistake and profit by its correction than to refuse to see a mistake."[24] It was not enough to "parrot" the words of English; the booklet prescribed an active use of the language—in debate and in argument. An insistence on speaking out, asserting a position, and competing with fellow students: these were the lessons taught to John who, years later, gave me different advice. Be quiet, watch, and listen, and above all don't be nosey—*niele niele*.[25] Attend to the stories you hear, he added, and respect the knowledge a person's actions convey.

He introduced me to the learning in an ʻohana, and to the values he absorbed under the tutelage of uncles, grandparents, and parents. These values appeared in his *Life Story*, where John described in appreciative detail the Hawaiian-style education he received at home in Keaukaha. "At the age of six or seven, I learned all these experiences mentioned above, by going with my Uncles and Aunts, and also my Mom. I would watch them do the things they do to gather fish from the ocean or shallow water. Also get things from the dry or shallow waters of the reef."[26] On the next page, he underlines the significance of observing these tasks: "We would cook lots of ulu and taro. When it was finished cooking, everyone would help to de-skin this fruit [ulu] and make ready to pound into poi [taro], two to three times a week. Those old days were wonderful because I got to learn more of my Hawaiian culture."[27]

Twenty chapters later, John reflects on being a parent himself, and he dwells on the chores he set for his children. Like his parents, he woke the children at 4 AM to clean yard and cook rice. All the tasks had to be done before school began and all, he continues, carried Hawaiian values into "modern times." While the children grumbled (and still complained to me years later), he maintained a tie to the ways of old. "By taking their part in so far as age and skill permitted in the respective activities of the older men and women of their household and of the ʻohana," write E. S. Craighill Handy and Mary Kawena Pukui, scholars of Hawaiian tradition, "boys and girls acquired knowledge and skills by natural process, rather than by artificial means as in formal education."[28]

During the elementary school years, John and his siblings followed two paths to learning. And they suffered from two modes of punishment. Scolded at home for missing chores, John and his siblings were reprimanded at school for coming in tardy and tired. Impatient and susceptible to stereotypes of the Polynesian that accompanied the earliest efforts to "discipline" the native, teachers translated fatigue into laziness, indolence, and lack of ambition. If Mrs. Kelso, "who was Hawaiian," had insight into, and sympathy for, Hawaiian-style childrearing, she also had to toe the line presented by the DPI. The brochures she received stressed haole-style learning and, emphatically, character building. As Titus Coan pronounced a century earlier, literacy alone did not make a citizen and speaking English was not a sure route to assimilation.

In 1930, along with every teacher in the territorial public schools, Mrs. Kelso received a small booklet entitled *Character Education.* A portrait on the cover anticipated the lessons inside: Abraham Lincoln, bearded and solemn, represents the moral virtues Hawaiian children are to emulate. Nine concepts caption the portrait: Leadership, Cooperation, Loyalty, Accuracy, Initiative, Love, Health, Effort, and Labor. Not easy to execute, the conglomeration of desirable traits cast a shadow over classroom efforts, confounding the teacher who had to promote both love and leadership, ensure accuracy and initiative, and generally keep a restless group of children in order. John lost his patience, and after-hours swimming did not compensate for hours of instruction clothed in "foreign" virtues. He played hooky often.

He was not alone. Laws compelling attendance, plus the drumming in of basic reading, writing, and counting skills, built in resistance. In fact, the problem of absenteeism haunted the very first attempts to keep Hawaiian children in the confines of school for the major part of a day.[29] The problem also gave rise to a new class of civil servants, the truant officer, the first enforcers of law a child encountered. Uniformed and stern, these men chased down children who failed to appear in the classroom and brought them back. Too many such occasions and the officer turned to the parents to impose control. "And if you played hooky, the consul [truant officer] would go and get you and you would have one chance only," Henrietta told me. "The second time you did that they would put you into detention at home, because you're not being parented well."[30] Like earlier missionaries and later parent-training experts, truant officers placed the burden of disciplining a child for American public school education on parents. The faults lay in childrearing, according to this wisdom, and not in the failure of formal schooling. Blame for playing hooky rested not on the colonizers but on the colonized.

John moved from Keaukaha Elementary to a school at Waiākea Kai, where he finished fifth and sixth grades. On the road to Volcanoes National Park,

Waiākea Kai involved a much longer walk from the homestead, and separated John even further from the life of the ʻohana. After the two years, he enrolled in Hilo Intermediate and High School, traveling in another direction away from Keaukaha—five miles into town. In that setting, of secondary education, John met another version of the US imperial imprint on the residents of Hawaiʻi.

"Home of the Vikings"

Founded in 1905, Hilo High was the second public high school in Hawaiʻi, and the first under territorial status. Ten years earlier, in 1895, Sanford Dole, president of the Provisional Government of Hawaiʻi, argued for the establishment of secular high schools for the children of Hawaiʻi. Head of a government established by force, Dole attempted to soften the blow by introducing "democratic" principles throughout the former kingdom. The descendant of missionaries, Dole recognized the importance of "schooling" the natives of Hawaiʻi, and he continued that mission when he was appointed governor of a territory in 1900.[31]

Neither Dole nor the elite of Hawaiʻi anticipated the flood of enrollments that followed. In the eyes of the ruling oligarchy, high school education differed from the compulsory elementary school education advocates had touted in pleading for the annexation of Hawaiʻi. Territorial economic and political institutions rested on a strict division of opportunity, which the spread of secondary schooling appeared to undermine. With the promise of mobility, public high schools brought an aspect of Americanization the elite in the territory blocked, under an array of euphemistic rationales. The Big Five controlled the DPI, along with virtually everything else in the islands, and warned against allowing too many Native Hawaiians freely to partake of high school education. The group of men initiated a long lasting drive to restrict entry into the public schools Dole had promoted.

"Industrial leaders continued to be opposed to the extension of schooling into the secondary level," remarked Hubert Everly, a historian of education in Hawaiʻi. "Their alarm at the 315 per cent increase in secondary school enrollment between 1920 and 1930 was based on two factors. They felt that the cost of the new program fell largely upon them as the largest tax payers, and that high schools were disadvantageous to the economic welfare of the Territory, inasmuch as they encouraged youth to leave rural areas and to seek ʻwhite collar' employment in the cities."[32] Caught between an American ideology of universal education and the needs of a plantation economy, the ruling elite discovered a pragmatic solution in fees. In the 1930s, the DPI instituted a tuition fee for public high schools and charged for the requisite textbooks. John attended high school, but in retrospect he complained about an imposition of fees that kept him from continuing his education. "I lived with a poverty life so I could not have a good education."[33]

Other factors than money limited the rewards of education for John. Like anyone else who managed to enter a public high school, he met a rigorous scheme for placement. The policy of tracking—of dividing students by perceived capacity to learn—spread through mainland schools and across the Pacific into Hawai`i's school system. The basis on which capacity was judged also crossed the Pacific, and in the territory racial discrimination fell hard on the Native Hawaiian. Despite the extraordinarily high rate of literacy in the population, attributions of sloth and of incapacity persisted. The tracking system existed side by side with an emphasis on *public* schooling open to all. The DPI ran buses from outlying rural areas, to ensure access for "plantation kids."

At the same time, high schools were a primary mechanism for maintaining categorical distinctions among the children of the land. "The most prominent curriculum decisions were English-only instruction, separate schools primarily for whites and curricular tracking emphasizing vocational education for local youths and academic preparation for whites."[34] *Local* referred to the kānaka maoli and to the children of plantation workers—Filipino, Portuguese, Korean, and the Asians the teachers defined, with concern, as the most conscientious students. The locals were further divided, into those trained for agricultural labor and those—the Hawaiians and part-Hawaiians—who learned the manual skills (mechanics, construction) that supported a plantation economy.

Mixed messages, then, characterized the educational system in the territory. Against the democratization Dole intended to institute was juxtaposed the notion of natural capacity that excused the racism in territorial policies. The existence of levels of education permitted a resolution. In reports on education in the US possession, elementary schools came to represent integration, equality, and racial harmony. The high schools bore the brunt of divisions based on race, and adolescents were schooled less in the three Rs than in the techniques that placed them properly into the workplace—manual workers separated from potential "white collar" workers.

Writing up their observations, federal and territorial authorities praised the harmonious interactions among children of all backgrounds in the elementary schools across the archipelago. These schools were the visual justification of the American incorporation of Hawai`i. "All about the islands children of various races are seen trudging to school, ruddy with health, and neatly dressed in American-type clothes."[35] The quotation is from a 1932 report on elementary education sent to the US Department of the Interior, at the time John and Eleanor were "trudging" to school along with other children from the homestead. The classrooms they entered were relatively homogeneous, and they only encountered the diversity of races extolled in the report when they went to Hilo High.

Even for a Hawaiian child who grew up outside a homestead, elementary school was a fairly homogenous environment. During one of our afternoon conversations on the beach, Henrietta described going to school on the Big Island in the 1930s. She too walked a trail from home to the square brick building of an American public school. And she remembered her fellow pupils: "We had just several white children that went to our school in particular. The rest were Orientals and Filipinos and just a handful of Chinese children, handful, the rest were all Hawaiians, Hawaiian children." She added, "we all worked cane." These were working class kids, compelled to wear American clothes and the girls, as Auntie Etta complained fifty years later, were told to braid long hair into "knots." Her experience of racial diversity was compounded by class differences when she went to a public high school. But she did not say much about the restrictions she encountered then.

Depictions of territorial high schools in government reports and archival documents corroborate—and offer the official rationale for—the experiences John and Henrietta recalled. An emphasis on *racial harmony* gives way to a discussion of natural capacities that justifies not only tracking in the schools but also distinctions in the wider social context. Three years after the glowing report on elementary school integration, a 1935 report to the Department of the Interior defended the importance of training students to fit into the "prevailing economic scheme," based on large-scale plantations and supporting infrastructure.[36] A photograph in the Hawai'i State Archives illustrates the outcome of designated differences in Hilo High School: the picture shows a boy crouching down to turn the wooden wheel on a car. In blue jeans, kneeling, the figure has dark features; the caption points to the "success of vocational training."[37] His ethnicity is evident by implication: he is not white and he is not Asian. The boy could have been John. Along with other students from the homesteads, he took courses in auto mechanics, carpentry, and construction.[38]

Eleanor did not talk much about her experiences in elementary or high school. Her younger sister Priscilla conveyed the gist of training for a Hawaiian girl—not technical skills for a labor market but household skills for the domestic arena. Priscilla started school in the mid-1940s, just as Hawai'i was emerging from the war, from an industrial boom, and from the new versions of racial diversity brought by thousands of military men and women. She was blunt about the persistent racial stereotyping that restricted her education. "Being a Hawaiian, there was no other aspects [of education]—no idea of going to college," Priscilla recalled. "We didn't partake of Hilo Library because we stayed in the homestead area. The library wasn't meant for us."[39] More than curricular tracking is at issue, as Priscilla implies. The message she conveyed in her anecdote about the library refers to the subtle marks of discrimination—the librarian who frowns when a Native Hawaiian girl walks in, the teacher who does not hear the comment made in words closer to pidgin than to Standard English. Symbolic as it may be, the library represented the exclusion, and relegation, of Hawaiian students to the margins of mainstream American society. Priscilla claimed she "stayed" in the homestead.

Thinking back, she mentioned another sign of discrimination in the territorial schools. There was not a sign in the Americanized, and centralized, curriculum of Hawaiian history and culture. "In school, no one taught us about Hawai`i, Hawaiian culture," Priscilla remarked. "Only American history. No one actually told us about the kings and the queens." The instructions from the Department of Public Instruction did not vary: a school in Hilo taught the same lessons as a school in the heart of Honolulu or in an isolated area of Moloka`i. Under the American flag, in the 1940s and 1950s, students heard an account of discovering and democratizing the Pacific that bore little relation to the mo`olelo their parents and grandparents taught. A day that began with the pledge of allegiance to the United States of America continued with stories of Abraham Lincoln, equality for all, and marks of "good character."

Little changed after statehood, and the newly named Department of Education distributed a curriculum that did not differ substantially from the one Priscilla recalled. "We learned little about kanaka maoli traditions in high school," writes Dennis Kawaharda, a non-Hawaiian who came to the state as an adolescent. "An elective called 'Hawaiiana' was offered—simplified crafts and modern adaptations of arts. It was not for college-bound students, not as serious study of the traditional culture."[40] In response to gaps in his education, Kawaharda founded Kalamakū Press to preserve Hawaiian traditions. If well meant, Kawaharda's response reproduces the asymmetrical relations of teacher to pupil, and of outsider to "native." From the perspective of Native Hawaiian scholars, he assumes the kuleana that rightly belongs to kānaka maoli.[41] Ku`ualoha Ho`omanawanui articulated the criticism in a 2008 essay in *Asian Settler Colonialism,* where she accuses Kawaharda of "inserting himself, a settler, into the land and culture" not his own.[42] In response to Kawaharda's focus on his education, Ho`omanawanui points to a colonial regime that has historically denied indigenous people—their epistemology and their icons—significant roles in the schools of Hawai`i.[43]

When John entered the halls of Hilo High, he immediately encountered the image of a bold, helmeted Viking. The school mascot, the navigator-explorer-settler from a northern climate, greets every pupil, decorates football jerseys, and adorns the cover of the yearbook.[44] Rather than the stalwart Polynesian navigator that William DuPuy praised in his report on elementary schooling, high school students encounter a figure that represents the conquest by Europeans of unknown lands.[45] The instructions every teacher received from DPI supported the narrative, constructing a history that delineated the progress and modernization American settlers brought to the islands.

DuPuy's "bold mariner," "magnificent in physique," would be as inadequate a mascot as the Viking. The depiction, if well meaning, downgrades the traditional skills of the Hawaiian navigator. The rhetoric, as Ty P. Kāwika Tengan and Jesse Makani Markham show in their analysis of American football, falls into a long tradition in which images of island masculinity "authorize the scripts of American conquest and imperialism while also defending hegemonic notions of white masculinity."[46]

When John walked into Hilo High under the figure of the Viking, he confronted the script for his role as Native Hawaiian male in an American society. There was no mistaking where he belonged in a racist and gendered setting, his masculinity disciplined by the doctrines of work and of obedience. His sisters, too, experienced a gendered and racist education: *We stayed in the homestead,* Priscilla told me, never thinking about college. Adamant in her self-image as protester, Eleanor hardly talked about school at all. And John found relief in after-school diving and swimming. In the eyes of 1930s school administrators, happy to accept the stereotype of docility, Native Hawaiians posed no problem "to their Uncle Sam."[47]

The growing "Oriental" population did pose a threat. "What is being done to Americanize these various racial strains in Hawaii?" asked an observer in 1926. "The most vital and pressing problem in Hawaii to-day is that of the education of her polyglot population, especially the children who will soon assume political domination of the Islands. Will these future voters be Americans or will they still be Japanese?"[48] The public schools were filled with the children of Asian settlers, but the Nisei, the second-generation Japanese, troubled the authorities most of all. Observers remarked on the ambitious, hardworking "alien" pupils in American high schools, and set this against the attendance of these very same pupils at Japanese language schools. The fear spread that granting the benefits of public education to those who spoke Japanese and practiced Japanese customs promised disaster in the territory. The irrational fear acquired a concrete manifestation in a Honolulu high school: McKinley High, in the middle of the city, had so many Japanese students that newspapers (and members of the DPI) nicknamed it Tokyo High.[49]

The opposition of the Big Five to public high schools intensified, fueled by the exponential growth of the Japanese population—up from 61,000 in 1900 to 140,000 in 1930. Moreover, every Japanese born in the territory was an American citizen and recipient of the rights granted by the US Constitution. The ruling elite had reason to dread the possibility that well-educated Nisei would demand positions in the dominant economic and political institutions of the territory. Congressmen in Washington, DC, contributed to the growing alarm by spreading rumors about Japanese nationalism and its appeal to the Issei and Nisei residents of Hawai'i. Media accounts carried stories into the public domain: the Japanese, these stories asserted, were loyal to the emperor and supporters of the "Rising Sun" empire in the Pacific. From this point of view, lessons in patriotism in the territorial public schools held no candle against a presumptive *inherent* loyalty to Japan.

The numerous Japanese language schools came in for the deepest suspicion and, eventually, attack. Alarmists at every level declared that language schools actually indoctrinated students in pro-Japan sentiments. The fact that every teacher in a Japanese language school had to swear an oath of loyalty to the United States of America did not lessen accusations that these teachers were inculcating Japanese nationalism.[50] In the mid-1930s, according to an official report on territorial education, 45,000 children were learning the "alien" language and, by implication, *disloyalty.*[51] Less than five years later, Japanese principals, leaders of the community, and parents succumbed to the pressure from the federal and the territorial government; virtually all Japanese language schools shut their doors. The assumption American politicians made that people who spoke a foreign language could not be good citizens—or, worse, were loyal to another nation—won the day.

The heavy-handed clamp down on those speaking and learning Japanese was not necessary in the Native Hawaiian case, given that fewer and fewer kānaka maoli spoke the "mother tongue" in public. In households like John's and Eleanor's, parents who spoke Hawaiian urged the children to learn English. On homesteads, in rural sections of the islands, and in crowded urban neighborhoods, a generation of Native Hawaiians heard only smatterings of a language they were forbidden to use.

"Our Language is Who We Are"

English is where your future is going to be. Sarah and Thomas Pakele spoke Hawaiian at home, primarily, Priscilla told me, when they wanted to keep secrets from the children. John spoke English with me and, after some time, he apologized for not being able to teach me Hawaiian. He did not know enough, he said. Deeper into our friendship, he used the pidgin he had spoken in the schoolyards when a teacher was not around and punishment was not likely. Whether or not a teacher washed a child's mouth out with soap—the well-known treatment of American Indian children—every Hawaiian boy and girl recognized that severe punishment resulted from not speaking English.

John and Eleanor learned a form of English the DPI deemed adequate for the Polynesian American. Teachers in the public schools they attended passed a language test, but did not have to meet the high specifications for teachers in designated English Standard schools. Six years before John entered Keaukaha, the first English Standard school, Abraham Lincoln Elementary, was founded in Honolulu. Six years after setting up an elementary school, the

DPI established the first English Standard high school, named after President Theodore Roosevelt, architect of US expansion across the Pacific. Both Lincoln and Roosevelt are located in the district of Honolulu that includes the dominantly Hawaiian neighborhood of Papakōlea. In these still *public* schools, tests of elocution, spelling, and grammar set a high bar—for teachers as well as applicants. English Standard schools separated the "good" speakers from the less fluent. And a system based on differential linguistic ability reinforced ethnic inequalities in schooling.

Behind the banner of democratic education and equal opportunity for all students, the entry exams for the English Standards, while presumably based on merit, actually sorted students by racial background. This was not a new story, but had a legacy in the first schools established in the islands.

In 1841, missionary families in Hawai`i founded the Punahou School. A select group of children entered: English speakers, Protestant, and almost always from an elite haole family. Punahou is the first in a long line of private schools that sustain segregation through schooling. Hawai`i still has the largest proportion of students in private schools of any state, leaving in tact a persistent structure of inequality and discrimination.[52] Nor does the existence of a prestigious private school for children of Native Hawaiian ancestry neutralize the structural disadvantages in the school system as a whole.[53] Founded at the end of the nineteenth century, through a bequest left by Princess Bernice Pauahi Bishop, the Kamehameha Schools are devoted to the education of children of Hawaiian ancestry. Yet, like other private schools, the Kamehameha Schools impose standardized entrance tests, and these exclude a large majority of Native Hawaiian children.

If accepted into Kamehameha, a Hawaiian of John and Eleanor's generation encountered a curriculum that resembled the one distributed to all territorial public schools. Perpetuating the conviction that English and the principles of American citizenship promised success in a modern world, the schools did not support courses in Native Hawaiian history and culture. "The aim was to produce an assimilated and docile citizenry by individualizing students, [and] drawing them away from their cultural roots and social networks."[54] An elderly kupuna remembered her years at Kamehameha: "I went to a Hawaiian school because I wanted to be Hawaiian. Then not to be allowed to be Hawaiian! Of all things, for a Hawaiian school not to be Hawaiian!"[55]

Private and public schools shared an ideology that downplayed diversity in the interests of incorporation. The ideal dominated a school for children of Hawaiian ancestry as thoroughly as it regulated lessons in an English Standard school, filled with sons and daughters of the elite.[56] The public schools had the same aims and fewer resources with which to meet those goals. Teachers in the non-Standard schools often lacked the ability to remedy the linguistic disadvantages their pupils faced. John and Eleanor were likely to learn English from teachers who had not achieved the fluency required by an English Standard school.[57] Nor did they have much opportunity to socialize with children who spoke Standard English, thus losing another route to crossing linguistic barriers. Charlene Sato, a language expert, remarks: "Recall that almost all haole children attended the private schools and were therefore not available either as play partners or as language models in the classroom."[58] Surrounded by children and adolescents who spoke the same way they did, John and Eleanor were fluent in the pidgin that identified a local, bridged ethnic differences, and resisted linguistic hegemony.

Eleanor rarely spoke pidgin with me. She was careful to use English, but she frequently sprinkled her moʻolelo with Hawaiian words. Unlike John, she had retained the language her parents spoke, and she reactivated her ability in the 1970s, under the influence of the cultural renaissance. With some qualms, she undertook to teach others the rudiments of a nearly lost language.

She recalled how she got drawn into teaching. She was working in a small shop on the edge of Keaukaha when an elderly Hawaiian woman came in. According to Eleanor, the woman asked for her items "in perfect Hawaiian." Eleanor answered in the Hawaiian words she knew. A *kumu hula* (master hula teacher), Edith Kanakaʻole represented the vanguard of the cultural renaissance on the outer islands of the state. "You should not be doing this work," Eleanor continued her memory of Auntie Edith's conversation. "You should become a teacher of Hawaiian language." Respectful of her elder, though uncertain about her abilities, she took Auntie Edith's advice. "I quit my job to learn the language and to learn how to teach the language." Eleanor enrolled in a community program the Department of Education instituted in response to demands by Native Hawaiians for a revival of the language. Hawaiian was still banned from the schools, and teaching took place in neighborhood settings.

My first pupils were kūpuna, she told me, who could speak the language better than I could. She taught the group of seniors formal rules of grammar for speaking and for writing in Hawaiian. "I was good at grammar because I had learned English so well." She encouraged the kūpuna to record their memories, to describe the "ancient arts" they practiced, and to talk-story on paper. Eleanor did writings along with her pupils, a habit from which I benefited when she offered me the gift of her books. She had published several, in English and in Hawaiian. I have the ones she wrote in English. John had her Hawaiian books on his shelves in the Waimānalo house, although neither he nor his children could read them.

One of the books Auntie Eleanor gave me is called *Hawaiian Shores and Foods*. A contribution to a cultural education project sponsored by the University of Hawaiʻi at Hilo, the book is dedicated to "the memory of my Dad Thomas Kanehunamokuhunakaleikamoku Pakele." With line drawings accompanying (and occasionally interrupting) the words, the book tells the moʻolelo of her ancestors. "Hawaiian Shores ^^^^ And foods. Hawaii's shores ^^^^ rocky shores, boulders, cliffs, papa, moku, and sandy beaches are storehouses of seafoods. One need not possess any elaborate kinds of equipment to harvest enough food for his family. Fish, shellfish, and seaweed, all rich in the vitamin and mineral resources we need in our daily diet, lie in abundance at our beaches. ... In Hawaii, one should never go without food, especially a 'keiki 'o ka Aina', for 'ina a'ole molowa ke kanaka, ola ke kino.'" Eleanor wrote in English, but she used Hawaiian words and phrases in order to capture the spirit of her teachings. "One should never go without food: if the person is not lazy, the body will be healthy, will thrive, and will live." Her granddaughter offered me this interpretation of concepts that do not translate easily into English. When Eleanor wrote her book, a younger generation learned in English and not in the native tongue—'*ōlelo makuahine.*

Hawaiian Shores and Foods sits on my bookshelves, part of my culture learning. Next to it are four other books Eleanor wrote, textbooks on Hawaiian grammar. She wrote those in English, too, using the still-dominant language of the state to spread the language of her ancestors. Like the kūpuna who provided mo'olelo to the cultural projects a renaissance generated, Eleanor turned the skills she acquired in an American public school to the task of preserving core Hawaiian values.[59] The English language Sarah Pakele urged her children to use—"for the future"—served as a tool with which John and Eleanor transmitted the arts and skills their parents practiced. In her books, Eleanor took one more step, outlining the structure of Hawaiian in a mode familiar to those who attended public school: distinguishing the parts of speech and parsing a sentence.

Two decades later, still frustrated by the dominance of English, Eleanor returned to the importance of language for identity. "The language makes us what we are." And she elaborated: "Language comes from the kūpuna, the ancestors," she told me. "If you know the language, you can live like they want you to." Ever pragmatic, she also insisted on the importance of learning other arts for living like the ancestors. In 1976, she was appointed Hawaiian Cultural Specialist for Hilo County and in that capacity she taught more than grammar and writing. "I taught Hawaiian arts and crafts. I taught language, *lei*-making, *lauhala* weaving, and quilt making."

In November 1978, voters in Hawai'i approved four amendments to the state constitution. Each acknowledged the claims of an indigenous population and supported the preservation of cultural resources. The first amendment established the Office of Hawaiian Affairs, charged with distributing revenue from land held in trust for Native Hawaiians. The second required the state to promote the study of Hawaiian culture, history, and language in all public schools. The third amendment offered protection to subsistence, cultural, and religious rights of Native Hawaiians, and the fourth made Hawaiian and English the two official languages of the state.

Our language is who we are. Yet throughout the state of Hawai`i, opportunities to learn the language remained relegated to neighborhood associations and after-school programs. The 1896 School Act requiring that all instruction in Hawai`i's schools be in English remained on the books for a century, and all the children "of the land" learned their lessons in the tongue of those who had taken over the archipelago.[60] Teachers trained in English taught history based on "manifest destiny" and the benefits of assimilation into the United States. Alternative stories—of Polynesian customs, of diverse populations—received brief and superficial coverage, shorn of the meanings Hawaiian concepts convey. A scatter of words, like *aloha* and *mahalo,* in a classroom recitation resonated more with tourist brochures than with the mo`olelo told by an older generation. And for many Native Hawaiian youth, the primary language was Hawaiian Creole, the pidgin that prompted bitter controversy among educators, linguists, and policymakers.[61] The move to rehabilitate Hawaiian as a language of instruction left the fate of pidgin in limbo.

The Hawaiian cultural renaissance brought `ōlelo makuahine to the forefront. Parents, community leaders, and teachers organized to implement the constitutional amendment that promised to protect Hawaiian culture and language. A model existed across the Pacific in New Zealand. There Maori teachers and parents established language-immersion schools, called Maori Kohanga Reo, or language nests. In a step toward holding the state accountable to its constitution, parents and teachers developed a plan for comparable nests in Hawai`i.

The plan gained little official support. Despite a movement on the mainland to create language-immersion schools, the Hawai`i State Department of Education (DOE) refused to approve such schools. Decades earlier, administrators had concluded that English unified a population, and though Japanese schools presented a particular threat in the early half of the century, the assumption that a common tongue fostered social integration persisted.[62]

Obstacles thrown up by the DOE notwithstanding, success came in 1983, when the first Hawaiian language-immersion school opened. A preschool, `Aha Pūnana Leo (Nest of Voices) enrolled the youngest children, who transferred to American public schools or, if possible, to secular and religious private schools for the rest of their education. Still, the state of Hawai`i DOE refused to grant approval to the Pūnana Leo schools, which violated the law by teaching in Hawaiian. Despite the fourth amendment to the state constitution, English remained the official language of instruction until 1986. In that year, the state legislature finally annulled the 1896 law prescribing English-only in Hawai`i's schools.

One year later, in 1987, the DOE established a full Hawaiian language-immersion program, Ka Papahana Kaiapuni Hawai`i. In 1992, the DOE extended its approval of Hawaiian language teaching to secondary education, and in 1999, the first class of students entirely educated in the Hawaiian Language graduated from Ke Kula `O Nāwahīokalani`ōpu`u on the Big Island and from Ke Kula Kaiapuni `O Ānuenue in Honolulu. A decade later, in May 2011, approximately 2000 students attend the K–12 programs in twenty-one Hawaiian language immersion schools.[63]

Initially, the immersion schools faced a shortage of teachers and virtually no textbooks in Hawaiian. Drawing on the wisdom of kūpuna who had retained the language, teachers taught themselves along with the four and five year olds in their classrooms. They solved the textbook problem in a pragmatic way, writing down Hawaiian words and pasting them over the English words in schoolbooks. English disappeared, banished from the playing fields and recreational areas as well as from the classrooms. "The lessons continue at recess: using English is also banned then," reported the *New York Times* in 1994. Respectful and supportive in its intentions, the article simultaneously evokes the old stereotype of the gentle, childlike Hawaiian. "Hawaiian is a melodic language with soft edges," practiced by young children who "chat under the leafy boughs of a mango tree," wrote the reporter.[64] Ten years later, another *New York Times* article on Hawaiian immersion schools reiterated the familiar stereotype. "The Hawaiian rendering of the Lord's Prayer, with the soft, round vowels of the native language, tumble over the crowd like a wave coming to shore."[65] Behind the description lies an image of the native who learns the language—docile, natural, and not a threat to the US public school system or to the goals American schools imparted. The description is reminiscent of missionary perspectives, with its relief that the Hawaiian children remain in the frame of a Western canon, reciting the Lord's Prayer even if they speak a foreign language.

At the end of the twentieth century, alternatives to the conventional American public school appeared, and charter schools spread across the fifty states. The state of Hawai`i is not an exception, and these special-interest schools exist in rural and urban areas, as well as in the homesteads.[66] With a curriculum organized around a particular topic, and introducing innovative pedagogical techniques, charter schools incorporate not only Hawaiian history and culture, but also Hawaiian-style teaching/learning. "As Hawaiian-focused public charter schools, Nā Lei Na`auao schools are committed to provide a quality education rooted in traditional Hawaiian culture, values, and pedagogy."[67] Teaching traditional modes of subsistence and care for the environment, charter schools exemplify commitment to a new three Rs: relations, relevance, and rigor.[68] Carrying the goals of educational innovation further, J. Noelani

Goodyear-Ka`ōpua argues that changes in the schools must go hand in hand with reform of economic and ecological systems—allowing Hawaiians "again to feed ourselves and our `āina."[69]

Charter schools are public, free, and open to all residents of the state. In Keaukaha, Auntie Eleanor encouraged members of her `ohana to take advantage of the options for their children and her mo`opuna (grandchildren). Of this younger generation, several followed her advice. In May 2004, Eleanor invited me to the graduation of her great-grandson. He was graduating from a charter school in the homestead.

Ke Ana La`ahana Public Charter School was established in January 2001, its mission to foster educational experiences that "root the child and the parents to the specific land." The website continues: "It will be through the uniqueness of the environmental setting of Keaukaha that pedagogy will be rigorously enhanced."[70] Eleanor's great-grandson was one of thirteen graduating seniors. The ceremony took place in the gymnasium of the elementary school John and Eleanor had attended, and the bleachers quickly filled up with family and friends. An ancient welcoming chant brought the seniors in, and they performed a return chant. Then Auntie Eleanor rolled forward in her wheelchair to give the opening prayer in Hawaiian. She wept throughout, reaching for Kleenex along the way. Others wept, and the seniors laughingly passed around packets of tissues during the speeches and music that followed the prayer. Finally, all thirteen gathered together in front of us for the culminating moment, restlessly waiting for a turn. The principal called the names one by one, and a relative or friend came out of the bleachers to hand each graduate a diploma. More tears were shed, combined with laughter from the students and the audience.

The head of the DOE gave a speech, remarking on the success of the school and the promising future for the graduates. Her dark blue business suit contrasted with the colorful clothing—flowered dresses and aloha shirts—in the bleachers. A representative of the foundation named for Auntie Edith Kanaka`ole also made a speech: the Kanaka`ole Foundation sponsors Ke Ana La`ahana. Life had come full circle for Auntie Eleanor, whose language teaching Auntie Edith first inspired. Language and custom merged perfectly in the graduation ceremony, and, prominent on the front lawn, two canoes the students built fulfilled the mission of connecting learning to the `āina. But the school also accomplished another mission: six Ke Ana La`ahana graduates were going to college, seven to vocational schools. Auntie Eleanor's great-grandson applied to a culinary institute, planning to make Hawaiian food his specialty.

On the Big Island, public and private schools increasingly provide classes in Hawaiian language, history, and culture, as prescribed by the state constitution. In August 1996, the Kamehameha Schools opened a Hilo campus, and the curriculum includes academic courses in Hawaiian language and culture along with standard college-preparatory courses. According to its website, "Kamehameha Schools is a dynamic and nurturing learning community committed to educational excellence. We assist people of Hawaiian ancestry to achieve their highest potential as 'good and industrious men and women.'" The rhetoric is a hodge podge, mission language of industriousness sitting side by side with Hawaiian concepts of nurture and ancestry.[71] Two of Auntie Eleanor's grandchildren traveled up Volcano Highway to the Kea`au campus for their education—past Waiākea Kai, where John attended school. Both young women studied Hawaiian language at the University of Hawai`i at Hilo, and to my ears are fluent in the language. Long lists of Hawaiian words paper the walls of the house next door to Auntie Eleanor's in Keaukaha.

Children in the Keaukaha Homestead fare better than children in the Waimānalo Homestead, where John watched over the education of his grandchildren. Two elementary schools serve the town's children, one within the homestead and the other some distance away on Kalaniana`ole Highway. Neither school offers courses in Hawaiian language, and culture learning occurs under the prompting of an individual teacher or librarian.[72] The high school is a distance away from the homestead, in a relatively affluent suburb. Like their grandfather, the children in the Waimānalo household moved from a comparatively homogeneous elementary school to the heavily mixed classrooms of a public high school. And like their grandfather, the four girls opened textbooks that told of American presidents and American war victories, and read novels that described life in American mainstream towns. One evening in 1998, Ana showed me her eighth-grade textbook. A twenty-year-old American History text, it devoted a single paragraph to the "discovery" of the Hawaiian Islands by Captain James Cook. A whitewashed story of the spread of American democracy filled the next few paragraphs.

Ana learned about a Hawai`i discovered by a British sailor and civilized by missionaries from the New England states. Sixty years earlier, John did not even learn that much about Hawaiian history. Instead, the texts distributed by the DPI in the 1930s skirted history—and American imperialism—with references to unnamed nations and places or, in one case, to a country lacking much relevance for a Hawaiian high school student. A 1935 text informed pupils of "clean streets" in an unspecified "large city, in a small town, in the country and in Holland."[73] Revisions of the public school curriculum over the decades eliminated such blatant irrelevancies but maintained the emphasis on character training, with its dose of patriotism. For Ana, as for her grandfather, Lincoln's Gettysburg address, the Bill of Rights, and the story of American achievements replaced the mo`olelo of her ancestors. Like her grandfather, too, Ana learned from her teachers the importance of being assertive, expressing an opinion, and shunning the sharing that, in the individualized setting of an American school, is called cheating.

In the summer of 1991, I first met Helene, who became one of my closest friends. She was then the educational specialist for the Kū I Ka Mana mentoring program at the Waimānalo Elementary School. She had been a substitute teacher in the school, and she would become the facilitator for the Parent Community Network Center in the Waimānalo Homestead. In her view, the teachers in Waimānalo, trained in formal pedagogical methods, ignore the learning-style Hawaiian children bring from home. A generation younger than Eleanor and John, she denounced the atmosphere in classrooms in words similar to the ones they used: a teacher sat behind a "big block desk" and compelled the children to sit quietly in orderly rows, one behind the other. Few teachers, she told me, could relinquish the emphasis on "tedious" verbal instruction and "they would be punished by the system if they did." In one anecdote and another, Helene conveyed the erasure of Hawaiian culture from the classrooms, in content and in approach to the children. Most drastically, she said, teachers shut down the futures of these children. "The teachers don't care about the children. They think they'll just be garbage collectors anyway."

She spoke as a parent and as a teacher, and she was not far wrong. Reports on education for Hawaiian children continue to be dismal, and public school teachers reportedly fail to see beyond the stereotypes that were planted in the nineteenth century. "Native Hawaiian children were considered to be stupid, lazy, and troublemakers," Maenette Benham and Ronald Heck wrote in 1998, and the conclusion remains true for conventional public schools in the state.[74] The remarks of the two educational experts coincide perfectly with Helene's observations, and the string of adjectives rings true to the attributions John and his sisters remembered. The Hawaiian child who attended public school in the 1990s, like the child in the 1930s, stayed in the homestead—figuratively, if not in the literal sense Priscilla implied.[75] College "was not for us." "When he ask a question," John wrote about his grandson at the University, "they shut off his plea for information and where he can get help."[76] While girls represented one pole of the stereotype of the Polynesian, docile and pleasant, boys took on the other side, deemed unambitious, untrustworthy, and intractable.

At Hilo High in 1940, teachers accused John of being disobedient and causing trouble. "I was being accused of wrong doings without my accusers knowing what the problems were."[77] One March morning he walked out of the home of the Vikings, never to return. He was not alone in dropping out: "at least one third of all children of the Territory were out of school at 15, and one half at 16 years of age," stated the 1935 US Department of the Interior Bulletin on Public Education in Hawaii.[78] Decades later, John chided his children for succumbing to the temptation he had not resisted.[79] He punished his children for playing hooky.

"I Learned the Tasks for My Future"

John quit high school two months before his scheduled graduation. Two weeks later, on 20 March 1941, he joined the Civilian Conservation Corps. "I was sixteen," he wrote to me in 1995, "then I enlist in the CCC camp for further education on type of job that I can qualify for. I had move my age from sixteen to seventeen to get into this program." A month after he joined, the CCC lowered the enrollment age to sixteen with a proclamation in the monthly *TH* (Territory of Hawaii)-*CCC News*. "Under the banner of the great American flag that commands the spacious areas of the Hawaiian CCC Camps, these young chunks of clay will take shape—to their own advantage and to the advantage of America—in better citizenship and as better workers."[80]

While his decision to enroll might appear to be a leap from the frying pan into the fire, John's accounts of the CCC place that American organization into a realm far different from Hilo High. In John's stories, CCC methods for *shaping* boys resonated with the approach his uncles, grandparents, and parents adopted for teaching a child. Designed to put men to work during a depression, the CCC concentrated on activities and not on verbal instruction. Men worked to plant—or to cut down—trees, to run roads through wilderness, and generally to construct improvements on local land. John joined in Hilo, and he was assigned to a camp about twenty miles from town in an area designated as a national park. In his retrospective accounts, on paper and in conversation, the CCC camp plays a striking role. His moʻolelo of that period of his life weave together three themes: ma ka hana ka ʻike—knowledge/learning comes from work; kōkua, or help, in sustaining the land; and, the significance of Volcanoes National Park where he served his six-month contract.[81]

"I enrolled or signed up for this job and my place of employment was in the Volcano CCC Camp. This place, if you want to learn, you would accomplish your goal and when you leave this CCC Camp, you would find jobs anywhere in the world," he wrote in his *Life Story,* where the CCC takes up several thickly detailed pages.[82] His accounts mimic the language the CCC used, of jobs and employment. Yet there is another message in his references to the CCC. In utilizing the language of work, John asserts a capability that teachers, administrators, and employers caught in a colonial frame of reference denied to the Hawaiian "boy." His appreciation of the CCC distinguishes that American program from other territorial institutions. There were, John learned, variations in the institutions the United States inserted into the life of a Native Hawaiian male.[83]

He had enrolled at an employment agency, the Territorial Employment Service in downtown Hilo. And he joined, he wrote, in order to "learn more about different types of work." CCC brochures emphasized the significance of work, and the skills boys learned from doing tasks. "In other words they have learned by doing," stated the *TH-CCC News*.[84] The *Work History* John composed for me in 1994 begins: "This is my life working and learning at the same time."

John learned by handling a drill, a jackhammer, and a chain saw. He listed his acquired skills on the first page of *Work History*: "gas weld, truck driving, road repair." A few sentences later, he combined the skills into "construction work," continuing, "like drilling holes in the ground to put dynamite to losen the ground." These tasks extended the reach of the national park Woodrow Wilson had approved in 1916. John applied the same skills a few months later, when he joined the work crews assigned to extend the Bellows Airfield on Waimānalo Bay. He describes these *improvements* to the land in terms of the hard work he did and the lessons he learned. His stories avoid dwelling on the signs of American power that lay in the extension of a national park and the expansion of a US military station.

CCC documents assiduously downplay the connection with national security and a looming war. A New Deal program initiated in response to an economic crisis, the CCC emphasized the *training* offered to boys from declining farms, from impoverished urban areas, and from deserted villages throughout the United States. This training, newsletters assured the recruits (and their families), would "help the boys find jobs readily."[85] Articles focus on the future, and on the extension of opportunity for *all* enlistees, regardless of background. In a typical piece, the *TH-CCC News* touted an array of benefits for the boys of Hawai`i. "The work of protection and improvement of the forest lands of the Territory has been pushed ahead at five to ten times the best rate that had been possible before the Corps was established here, while the boys just coming out of school have had the opportunity to see more of the Islands and learn more of the value of the forest areas to the welfare of the community than would have been normally possible in a much longer period had they gone directly into usual plantation and commercial lines of work."[86]

At the same time, the CCC program trained the boys for the agricultural and construction work that would make up the future for most of them. Like John, a majority of the recruits in Hawai`i learned tasks that supported the dominant economic institutions of the territory: plantations, the military, and a nascent tourist industry. For ten to twelve hours a day, the boys hauled boulders, wielded axes, and dug ditches; exhausted at the end of the day, few of these boys took the "educational" courses camp administrators provided. And, furthermore, camp officials justified a division of labor that supported the racial hierarchy in the islands. The rationale was clear, and a strong echo of the doctrines issued by the Department of Public Instruction, the men in the Big Five, and local lawmakers. The division of labor, the *TH-CCC News* claimed, respected the *natural abilities* of recruits. "A CCC lad is lucky right at the start. He is fortunate to be in an organization that is designed and operated to direct his aims and aptitudes into the specialized channels which fit his abilities."[87]

The CCC prepared John for a future presumed to suit the abilities of a Native Hawaiian man. The skills he learned shaped him for manual labor and not for the white collar jobs that were reserved for haole residents of the territory. Nor did the program encourage his participation in courses through which he could acquire the high school degree he had rejected and allow him to take advantage of opportunities in higher education. The CCC administrators organized boys according to perceptions of ability, separating those with intellectual potential from those who were "fit" to handle a jackhammer or drive a truck. And while most of the boys in the CCC shared a background of reduced resources, the CCC accentuated divisions within this context that upheld the racist categorizations in mainstream American society. For John, however, teamwork and devotion to a concrete task distinguished the CCC from Hilo High and covered over the continuity of racism from one American institution to another.

In his stories of the CCC, John refers only obliquely to racial discrimination. He remarks on the fact that a haole was promoted ahead of him, when they had done the same work and showed the same capability. In another, longer anecdote he talks about working with the "Park rangers" and considers that a privilege. The rangers were haole *men* who had been trained on the mainland, yet, as John continues his account, the haole "needed" the expertise of a local *boy.* "I had the privilege of working with the Volcano Forest Rangers. This particular job was to rid the National Forest, Mauna Loa Mid-heights to the ocean at Helena Pali-Puna, of wild goats." And he continues, in one of the longest paragraphs in *Life Story*: "About six CCC Camp boys and two park Rangers would go up to the forest range area and we would camp there for the night." He details the particular skills he brought to the "job," and he concludes: "It was a remarkable experience."[88] This was John's first experience working side by side with haole and with men from all parts of the islands. He colors the period brightly in *Life Story* and again in *Work History.*

Two months after he enrolled, the *TH-CCC News* published the demographic profile of his camp: 35 pure Hawaiians, 19 part Hawaiians, 37 Portuguese, 20 Japanese, and 24 "others" (it is not clear how many "others" were haole).[89] His racial classification appeared on the certificate of discharge he pasted in a photograph album. The caption under the text reads: "His color was 'Hawaiian.'" The CCC turned its continual tabulation of racial composition—based, as John's certificate implies, on physical features and not on self-identification—to positive effect. Descriptions of the Hawai`i camps repeat the praise of "racial harmony" that runs through virtually every document a US agency prepared on the territorial possession.

Throughout the 1930s, observers from the mainland continued to visit the islands, ostensibly to check on conditions. In September 1940, the federal supervisor of CCC education and training appeared; he summarized his opinion in the *TH-CCC News.* "In considering the racial composition of the camps a good policy would try to preserve the friendliness and companionship already existing between the races therein, and would establish the basis that blood is red in spite of the color of the skin under which it flows."[90] And while the supervisor resisted appropriating the Hawaiian word *pono,* he resolutely presented a picture of harmony and well-being in the social interactions among different "races."

On the ground, the camp officials worked with equal resolve to insure the harmony among boys that visitors reported back to Washington. Consequently, while the distribution of tasks segregated men according to natural ability, wages were the same for every task. Equal pay made the divisions appear to be fair, just, and democratic. With the exception of the 6 percent who were appointed leaders, the base pay was $30.00 per month. "Eight dollars per month is allowed for personal and canteen purchases," the April 1941 newsletter reported.[91] The boy had either to save the $22.00 remaining after "purchases" or to send it to his family. John claims to have followed the rules: "Out of this [$30.00] $22.00 would go home to the family, leaving me with $8.00 for toilet articles, snacks, stamps and envelopes, laundry and other PX items."[92]

He probably also wore the regulation clothing. Beyond control through strictly regulated wages, the camps imposed sumptuary uniformity. Shirts and long pants meshed the boys into an apparently homogenous crowd. "The sight of men on duty in Camps wearing shirts of many colors and clothes of many kinds indicate [sic] lax discipline all around," reported the *TH-CCC News,* a lapse that was quickly corrected: "The sight of brawny CCC crew in blue denim pants stripped to the waist and sweating is a satisfying sight because the clothing is the right kind to wear when working."[93] Perhaps, too, John gained the 7 or 8 pounds the CCC proudly touted as another accomplishment.[94] Brawny, hefty, and dressed in blue, the only thing left to distinguish one camper from another was the color of his skin—and the training accorded on that basis.

The policies and the practices of the Territory of Hawaii CCC suited the interests of the Big Five, as the businessmen made clear to CCC administrators. In 1938, Robert Fechner, the director of the CCC, took a trip to the islands. Like every other observer, he reported back on his positive findings; his report referred to the enthusiastic support the men he met gave to CCC training. "I was told that our method of feeding enrollees, our provision for organizing recreation and our effort to help enrollees carry on their education had been of distinct interest to the plantation managers and had resulted in these features of plantation life being substantially improved."[95] He further noted that these representatives of Hawai`i's elite credited CCC practices with promoting "beneficial" changes in plantation life. The gist of Fechner's report indicates that the benefits lay in the CCC's validation of racial hierarchies upon which the plantations had long rested.

Hawaiians and part-Hawaiians withdrew from plantation field labor in the nineteenth century, and the CCC did not buck this trend. Instead, the administrators trained Native Hawaiians to run the heavy equipment and drive the trucks that support a plantation economy. They saved agricultural training for members of those groups whose grandparents and parents had (by and large) worked cane—the Portuguese, Japanese, and unidentified "others" in the Big Island camp. John learned skills for the growing construction industry in the islands, working the jackhammers and drills that placed him on building sites in the future. Native Hawaiians left the CCC able to perform the tasks that contributed to the blanketing of the islands with roads, shopping centers, and military bases in the second half of the twentieth century.

John learned the skills in an organization filled with contradictions and double messages, which newsletters and public relations material glossed over. The CCC was officially a conservation program. In reality, the program adhered to the ambiguous goals of the 1916 federal statute that established a National Park Service. Conservation of the Volcano area was intended to promote a part of the Big Island in a way that left the park "unimpaired for the enjoyment of future generations."[96] To accomplish the goal, John and his co-workers engaged in tasks directed toward transforming the ʻāina into a place where visitors would be welcomed. Together the "boys" cleared the mountainsides of rough underbrush, wiped out "pesty snails," and planted erosion-control trees along the roadsides.

Tourists constituted the explicit embodiment of "future generations." The potential for attracting visitors had justified the appropriation of presumably unused and unoccupied land in 1916, and prompted the environmental improvements assigned to John and fellow enrollees in 1941. Federal government definition of *public use* of the land for military purposes remained obscured by the continued emphasis on tourism.[97]

John ran wires into the Volcano House restaurant, designed for the (rightly) anticipated thousands of visitors—and from which his sister Eleanor was excluded fifty years later. He also ran electric wires into the Kīlauea Military Camp, a rest and recreation facility the military never surrendered to the National Park Service (a barely noticeable sign informs visitors of its existence). John's accounts skirt both the commercial and the military goals of "caring for" the land. This avoidance was easy enough: the CCC kept both goals under wraps, in publicity focusing on skills, on "saving rare native species," and on teamwork. Training in Volcanoes National Park stayed far away from the regimented drills and trumpet calls of a military camp.

John did not, however, lose sight of the towering volcanoes that gave the park its name—and its appeal. A century earlier, the missionary Titus Coan succumbed to the spell of the intermittently erupting Kīlauea, distracted from his spiritual duties but not from his religious language. "Two mighty antagonistic forces were in conflict," he wrote in 1840. "The sea boiled and raged as with infernal fury, while the burning flood continued to pour into the troubled waves by night and by day for three weeks."[98] Kīleaua did not erupt in 1941, but John encountered the power of the volcano in another version.

He took a job as a night watchman in the camp. In the dark, the glowing light of the volcano added a dimension to the landscape as John did his rounds. "While checking the buildings, I would come upon people crying, singing, arguing, playing music and barking like dogs," he begins a paragraph in *Life Story*. "Also some would be having fits with white foam all over their mouth and face. Some would be pounding the floor with their fists and crawling all over the place." Noise and music came from the sleeping barracks, and then from the toilets. There was banging in the cafeteria and the shuffling of feet from invisible presences. His nighttime tour of duty over, he writes, he returned to the cafeteria where, "I would make my own coffee and fry my Ham and eggs."[99]

Caught in the diurnal tasks of a US federal program, John preserved his Native Hawaiian identity under the shadow of the adjacent Mauna Loa and Kīlauea Mountains. He does not mention Pele in his story, but the mysterious noises and shuffling evoke the presence of an unseen force. Spooky and beautiful, weird and chilling, the sounds of the night contrasted with the exchanges of the day, and the presence of Pele kept the CCC boy attached to the stories told in his ʻohana. "My experience in CCC camp was a tremendous success and I really appreciated it very much."

Success went beyond tasks, teamwork, and training. In Volcano, caught between the extensive construction of a site for strangers and the mountain space Pele ruled, John moved from perceiving a stark conflict between two cultures into the negotiation of distinct ways of life that characterized his adult years. He participated in the making of an extremely successful tourist destination that, under Army and Navy pressure, accommodated military exercises during the war. In the end, Volcanoes National Park came through World War II relatively unscathed; only a few stray unexploded bombs and cracks in the roads exposed the weapons testing nearby neighbors overheard. The concrete John poured and the telephone lines he ran intruded more severely into Pele's land. Yet, as John's nighttime encounter revealed, the takeover of Hawaiian ʻāina was not absolute.

For John the half year in the CCC shaped his "manhood" in ways not anticipated by administrators, who bragged of making *boys* into *men*. The skills he learned, and the ways in which he learned them, resonated with his childhood experiences in the homestead while preparing him for work in an Americanizing society. The positive experiences he reported in letters and in conversations occurred as the unintended consequence of a program designed to insert men into the existing political and economic institutions of a rapidly changing nation. The consequence for John was a broadening of the ways in which he could negotiate his kanaka maoli identity—his Hawaiian manhood—in the context of a colonial economic and political system: being Hawaiian, he would say, against the values imposed by the Untied States.[100]

He served out the full six months of his contract. On 18 September 1941, one year to the day before the CCC was "liquidated" (in the words of the *Honolulu Star-Bulletin*), John was honorably discharged. He took his eight dollars and boarded a ship to Honolulu. He had never before been off the Big Island of Hawaii. He arrived in Honolulu in early October 1941. Two months after he arrived, Japanese bombs fell on Pearl Harbor.

Notes

1. While John did occasionally refer to my "being" Hawaiian, his meaning is closer to the notion that I could learn to *act* in appropriate ways. See Karen L. Ito, *Lady Friends*, "Introduction," for a discussion of similar lessons during fieldwork.
2. Such reenactments originated before the late twentieth-century cultural renaissance; Amy Ku'uleialoha Stillman, "Nā Lei O Hawai'i," 103. Ty P. Kāwika Tengan discusses the tensions between reenactments and enacting cultural practices in *Native Men Remade*.
3. Quoted in Lee D. Baker, "Missionary Positions," 40.
4. Quoted in James R. Hunt, *Education in the States*, 300.
5. Lucia R. Holman, *Journal*, 30 [1820].
6. See Ralph S. Kuykendall and Herbert E. Gregory, *A History of Hawaii*, 131–134, and Patricia Grimshaw, *Paths of Duty*, 160–161.
7. See Noenoe Silva, *Aloha Betrayed*.
8. "My uncle Ioane Simeona was one of the founders of Kamakau Mau Loa Church"; John Simeona, *Life Story*, MS., 14 (in the author's possession).
9. Titus Coan, *Life in Hawaii*, 254–255.
10. "In 1930, the percentage of literate school age [ten] and older people was: Hawaiian 96 percent and Part-Hawaiian 99.3 percent"; Maenette K. P. Benham and Ronald H. Heck, *Culture and Educational Policy*, 170.
11. Interview with Henrietta, 26 June 1989.
12. Ibid.
13. Simeona, *Life Story*, 8.
14. Interview with Eric Enos, 15 June 1990.
15. The goals of the project are "To promote and encourage the physical, mental, spiritual, social, cultural and economic health and well-being of people and their communities through fostering an appreciation and understanding of the traditional Hawaiian cultural concepts of Aloha 'Āina (Love the Land) and Lokahi (Cooperation), and reestablishing the relationship between people and the 'Āina (Land) and the Kai (Sea)"; *'Ōpelu Project, Inc.* manuscript (in the author's possession).
16. "The health program is furthered, too, through a division of dental hygiene in the department of public instruction"; Katherine M. Cook, *Public Education*, 36.

17. In figures he provides for 1920, Fuchs notes that 40 percent of teachers were haole, 25 percent Hawaiian or part-Hawaiian; Lawrence H. Fuchs, *Hawaii Pono*, 283.
18. Baker, "Missionary Positions," 40. King Kamehameha III had appointed the missionary Richard Armstrong as Minister of Education in 1846. See Jennifer Noelani Goodyear-Ka`ōpua, "Rebuilding the `Auwai," for a discussion of the role of the Hawaiian monarchs in shaping the educational system.
19. Quoted in Ralph Simpson Kuykendall, *The Hawaiian Kingdom: 1854–1874*, 112.
20. Hawaiian Commission, *The Report*, 10.
21. 1896 Laws of the Republic of Hawaii, Act 57, section 30.
22. Ibid.
23. After statehood, the Department of Public Instruction became the Board of Education. Hawai`i still retains the only centralized school system in the United States.
24. Territory of Hawaii, Department of Public Instruction, *Curriculum Brochure*, 33.
25. In *Lady Friends*, Ito reports a similar lesson, adding the further, even more severe condemnation of someone who is *maha`oi* or *really inquisitive*, 10–11.
26. Simeona, *Life Story*, 4.
27. Ibid., 5.
28. E. S. Craighill Handy and Mary Kawena Pukui, *The Polynesian Family System*, 177.
29. In *Colonizing Hawai`i*, her thorough account of US colonization of Hawai`i through law, Sally Engle Merry includes a discussion of compulsory education laws and their failures. "School attendance also remained sporadic and difficult to police," 83.
30. Interview with Henrietta, 26 June 1989.
31. Secondary education was not new, having been an early missionary initiative. "In 1831, a high school to train boys of exceptional promise was founded on Maui under missionary sponsorship"; Fuchs, *Hawaii Pono*, 263. Non-denominational secondary schooling was relatively new, coming at the end of the nineteenth century as an element in Governor Dole's construction of the Republic of Hawaii. See John S. Whitehead, *Completing the Union*.
32. Hubert Everly, *Education in Hawaii*, 49.
33. John Simeona to the author, 8 June 1995. A 1933 territorial law required public high school students to pay $10 tuition to help fund teacher salaries; see Rich Budnick, *Hawaii's Forgotten History*, 70.
34. Benham and Heck, *Culture and Educational Policy*, 155.
35. William A. DuPuy, *Hawaii and its Race Problems*, 121.
36. Katherine M. Cook, *Public Education*, 38–39.
37. In Ralph K. Stueber, "An Informal History of Schooling," 30.
38. Like the American Indian who attended Carlisle and the African-American who went to the Hampton Institute, the Native Hawaiian learned the manual trades deemed suitable to his natural capacities; see Baker, "Missionary Positions."
39. Interview with Priscilla McGuire, 23 May 1990.
40. Dennis Kawaharada, *Local Geography*, 45.
41. See Sam L. No`eau Warner, "'Kuleana': The Right, Responsibility, and Authority of Indigenous Peoples to Speak and Make Decisions for Themselves in Language and Cultural Revitalization."
42. Ku`ualoha Ho'omanawanui, "'This Land is Your Land, This Land was My Land,'" 142.
43. See Manulani Aluli Meyer, "Our Own Liberation."
44. A figure of the Viking was still on the cover of the Hilo High Yearbook when Auntie Eleanor showed me a copy in the late 1990s.
45. The Hawaiian, DuPuy wrote, is a "stalwart race … straight haired, magnificent in physique, as bold mariners as ever sailed the main," *Hawaii and its Race Problems*, 100.

46. Ty P. Kāwika Tengan and Jesse Makani Markham, "Performing Polynesian Masculinities in American Football," 2414.
47. DuPuy, *Hawaii and its Race Problems*, 124.
48. E. Guy Talbott, "Making Americans in Hawaii," 281.
49. "By 1920, Oriental children … constituted 60 per cent of the enrollment" in public schools; Bernhard L. Hormann, *Integration*, 6. DuPuy reported to the Department of the Interior that "Japanese and Chinese students spare no whit of drudging application to master whatever is taught there," *Hawaii and its Race Problems*, 117. "High schools on the outer islands were over 50 percent nisei and sansei"; Fuchs, *Hawaii Pono*, 291. Franklin Odo, *No Sword to Bury*, 37.
50. "Beginning in 1921 the [Japanese language] schools were licensed by the territorial Department of Public Instruction. Teachers had to demonstrate a grasp of the English language, American history, and the ideals of democracy, and they had to pledge themselves to teach their students loyalty to the United States"; Gavan Daws, *Shoal of Time*, 309.
51. Katherine M. Cook, *Public Education*, 51.
52. At the start of the twenty-first century, the *New York Times* reported, "nearly one in five children in Hawaii attends private schools, the highest percentage of any state," 12 October 2001, A12.
53. "Thus, the socioeconomically subordinate groups, including Native Hawaiians, Filipino Americans, Latinos, Samoans, and other Pacific Islanders, comprise a majority of public school students"; Jonathan Y. Okamura, *Ethnicity and Inequality*, 65.
54. Goodyear-Kaʻōpua quoted in Tengan, *Native Men Remade*, 46.
55. In M. J. Harden, *Voices of Wisdom*, 99.
56. English Standard schools were finally eliminated in 1948.
57. "There was, no doubt, considerable variability in the 'standardness' of their English as well, since many of the teachers were Hawaiians and part-Hawaiians who were themselves non-native speakers of English"—and, by implication, not well trained; Charlene Sato, "Linguistic Inequality," 263.
58. Ibid.
59. For one example of kūpuna stories, see *Voices of Wisdom*, edited by M. J. Harden. Much of the credit for preserving the words of a silenced generation can be given to the Ethnic Studies Oral History Project at the University of Hawaiʻi, Mānoa.
60. The law was signed by Sanford Dole, Governor of the Republic of Hawaiʻi . The goal of educational policy was, and remained, the assimilation of diverse ethnic groups, an Americanization that lasted well into the period of the Hawaiian cultural renaissance; Benham and Heck, *Culture and Educational Policy*, 155.
61. "For many native Hawaiians and descendants of plantation laborers, speaking Hawaiʻi Creole English has been a mark of their ethnicity and history"; Eileen H. Tamura, "Power, Status, and Hawaiʻi Creole English," 453.
62. J. Kēhaulani Kauanui analyzes the difference between views of the Japanese as alien and of the Native Hawaiian as subject in *Hawaiian Blood*. See also Merry, *Colonizing Hawaiʻi*, 16–17.
63. http://www.ahapunanaleo.org/eng/ohana/ohana_immersion.html, accessed 12 February 2010.
64. *New York Times*, 17 August 1994, B7.
65. *New York Times*, 22 February 2003, A18.
66. See Manulani Aluli Meyer, "Our Own Liberation: Reflections on Hawaiian Epistemology," which shows how Hawaiian ways of knowing have spread across the islands

"since the Hawai'i legislature passed Senate Bill 62 in 1999, which allows for twenty-five charter schools in Hawai'i," 146.

67. Katherine A. Tibbetts, Kū Kahakalau, and Zanette Johnson, "Education with Aloha," 149.

68. Ibid.

69. Goodyear-Ka`ōpua, "Rebuilding the `Auwai," 46.

70. http://www.edithkanakaole foundation.org/ke_ana/, accessed 19 June 2010.

71. http://www.ksbe.edu, accessed 19 June 2010.

72. In the early 1990s, Helene described a project instituted by the librarian. The third and fourth graders collected oral histories from the residents of Waimānalo, gathering a story that went beyond the boundaries of the homestead, the beach lots, and the village. Copies of the tapes were to be deposited in the Waimānalo Elementary School library.

73. Territory of Hawaii, Department of Public Instruction, *Character Education,* 56.

74. Benham and Heck, *Culture and Educational Policy,* 169.

75. In 2005, only 12.6 percent of Native Hawaiians twenty-five years or older obtained a Bachelor's degree, while the average in the state was 26.2 percent; S. K. Kana`iaupuni, N. Malone, and K. Ishiboshi, *Ka Huaka`i,* 125.

76. John Simeona to the author, 27 January 1995.

77. Simeona, *Life Story,* 11.

78. Katherine M. Cook, *Public Education,* 33. At the same time, another report suggests that in 1930, 92.6 percent of sixteen and seventeen-year-old Hawaiians and Part-Hawaiians were in school; Benham and Heck, *Culture and Educational Policy,* 171.

79. The school dropout rates for Native Hawaiian children continue to be among the highest in the state; Okamura, *Ethnicity and Inequality in Hawai`i,* 69.

80. *TH-CCC News,* April 1941, 2. The Territory of Hawaii Civilian Conservation Corps newspaper was published monthly by the US Department of the Interior, National Park Service, Honolulu.

81. Six months was the standard CCC contract across the United States.

82. Simeona, *Life Story,* 21.

83. See Tengan, *Native Men,* 139–140.

84. *TH-CCC News,* April 1941, 1.

85. *TH-CCC News,* September 1940, 4.

86. *TH-CCC News,* April 1941, 4.

87. *TH-CCC News,* February 1941, 2.

88. Simeona, *Life Story,* 23.

89. *TH-CCC News,* June 1941, 8.

90. *TH-CCC News,* September 1940, 2.

91. *TH-CCC News,* April 1941, 10. Even assuming the "leaders" tended to be haole, the CCC did not replicate the strict racial hierarchies imposed by Hawai`i's plantation owners. Thanks to an anonymous reader for emphasizing the difference.

92. Simeona, *Life Story,* 23.

93. *TH-CCC News,* July–August 1941, 2.

94. "A report received from the work supervisor of the camp located at Schofield Barracks, Territory of Hawaii, stated that gains in weight averaging six or seven pounds ... were recorded within the first three weeks after the men enrolled in the camp." *Memorandum for the Press,* 12 September 1934. Civilian Conservation Corps, Territory of Hawaii. Records, CCC Headquarters, Territory of Hawaii, University of Hawai`i, Mānoa.

95. Alison T. Otis, William D. Honey, and Thomas C. Hogg, *The Forest Service,* 68.
96. National Park Service Organic Act, 1916, US Congress Title 16, section 1.
97. See Francis Jackson, "Bombs in a National Park."
98. Titus Coan, *Life in Hawaii,* 72.
99. Simeona, *Life Story,* 22.
100. Tengan's *Native Men Remade* provides a penetrating account of the way constructions of gender maintain the "colonial subject" in an American state.

3

Work, War, and Loyalty
The Impact of World War II

As the *man* the CCC built from the *boy* who enrolled, John was ready to leave Keaukaha. In school, along with other children of the homestead, he had experienced the efforts to socialize him into an American citizen, through a heavily ideological American public school curriculum. In the CCC, he discovered another version of Americanization. The emphasis on learning-by-doing, accomplishing concrete tasks, and cooperating rather than competing suited the traditions he had grown up with under the tutelage of kūpuna. The CCC promise of "making men" included building bodies, and John came out of camp with increased physical strength and stamina. He also came out with a new experience of working side by side with men of different backgrounds, capacities, colors, and temperaments.

John started the decade of the 1940s with a strong sense of himself as a worker. He was ready to put his skills to the test of a larger environment than the one of his childhood. In a document entitled *Work History,* he told a wartime story, beginning with a trip from Hilo to Honolulu and ending half way around the world in the occupied city of Berlin. Work provided John with a place in an American territory, carried him through months of martial law and front-line combat, and then "opened the future" for him in the post-war economy. Work also exposed the hypocrisy in US policies. Government propaganda preached democracy, equality, and justice for all. On the job, John discovered something different: denunciation, discrimination, and outright racism.

Two weeks after his official discharge on 18 September 1941, John boarded a boat for Honolulu. "We rode steerage on the Hualalai, an interisland freight and passenger ship," he wrote in *Life Story.*[1] Over a decade later, he described the trip to me in a letter. "I got out of this CCC Camp School and came to Honolulu, with only $8 dollars in my pocket, $4 for my ship fare and left me four dollars balance."[2] He had a place waiting for him in Honolulu, with "my moms sister," he explained, sketching his absorption into the urban branch of his ʻohana. He distanced himself from Keaukaha, from his mother and his sister Eleanor, and from the stepfather he did not respect. Two sisters were born while he was gone; he met them five years later, in the spring of 1946.

This was John's first trip off the Big Island of Hawaii. It was to be the start of a long journey that brought him through a war-torn Europe before he returned home in the wake of a devastating tsunami. In writings, tape recordings, and conversations, John tells a story of war that reveals the complexities of Americanization in the second half of the twentieth century.

"I Was a Young Punk"

In the *Life Story* he wrote for his ʻohana, John describes his arrival in the Port of Honolulu, far bigger than the Hilo docks from which he dove for pennies. Honolulu was nothing like Hilo. "When I stepped down on the dock I was amazed to see so much things going on. The town was huge. There were lots of street lights.... There were lots of beautiful people, lots of automobiles and trolley cars. It was like something that I never knew could exist." He writes of his amazement, in the words of the country boy coming to a big city. "I kept Ohing and Ahing because I couldn't get over it."[3] In *Work History*, he confesses to the pleasure that preceded a job search. "Now I'm walking the street to see the sights. Very beautiful and big."

Honolulu *was* big, and in 1941 a crowded city. Over the previous decade, the American military had added personnel to the armed forces already in the territory, further swelling a population that expanded exponentially in the early part of the twentieth century. From a slow-moving colonial town of 40,000 in 1900, the year of annexation, Honolulu became a bustling American city with 180,000 residents in 1940.[4] What the census figures do not capture is the density, the push and pull from the growing influx of soldiers and civilian workers as well as outer islanders who came for work. The city's people were constantly on the move.

Six months before John's arrival, the US Navy deployed 42,000 American sailors to the city to engage in war games and rehearse defense strategies.[5] Thousands more followed, and a flood of brown, blue, and white uniforms spread across the archipelago. No longer restricted to barracks and bases, servicemen were seen on every street, filling the shops, bars, and "night spots" of Oʻahu. In early December 1941, the popular magazine *Paradise of the Pacific* could still write about the recreation the islands offered: "As each week unrolls one sees thousands of enlisted men swarming to the beaches, especially to Waikiki.... Saturdays and Sundays find the parks filled with visitors from the fleet, unslinging cameras and snapping exotic shots to be sent back to the folks at home."[6] By the end of the war, millions of men and women had passed through the territory, some staying just weeks and others deciding to settle permanently in the strange yet familiar place. When John arrived in Honolulu in the fall of 1941, military attire was the outstanding sartorial mode in the city.

Honolulu had nearly eight times the population of Hilo, which, although the second largest city in the territory, remained a sleepy backwater. Only 24,000 inhabitants lived in the urban center on the Big Island. John had left behind a place whose geography and demography he knew well—a landscape that was familiar and seemingly stable. He had left behind a place where ethnic and racial differences were reinforced by the plantation economy, the school system, and the policies of a territorial government. Honolulu, by contrast, witnessed a constant stream of newcomers, who entered a setting in which interactions between members of different ethnic groups followed increasingly precarious norms. The propaganda depicting racial harmony was harder to uphold in the chaos of new faces and the clash of stereotypes imported from the mainland. Tensions lay not very far beneath the surface, erupting in labor strikes, struggles over housing, quarrels on street corners, and even murder.[7] If still deemed a "paradise of the pacific," the cliché referred more to physical landscape than to the integration of races. For a Native Hawaiian from an outer island, the rapid urban changes lent Honolulu's "beauty" a disturbing undertone.

John set out to find a means of support, to contribute to his aunt's household, and to establish himself in the new environment. With the confidence he had acquired in the CCC—and the skills he had learned—John strode the streets of Honolulu. It did not take long to find work: city and county were undergoing massive construction, and John's training qualified him well. Preparation for war brought "the sudden, overwhelming demand for labor for repair and construction," wrote a commentator about the work setting in those years.[8]

John elaborates, presenting a tale of coincidence and good luck. "I met a man on the road and asks him if any one place have opening for any type of job. I went to this location he had mention, and this place—low and behold they hired me as a laborer paying 50 cents an hour. I could not refuse it so I took it."[9] He refers to the company as Honolulu Constructors, and he presumably means Hawaiian Constructors.[10] This was a joint venture of three mainland companies put together by the Army Corps of Engineers to fortify the US Pacific outpost. The military commander in Hawai`i and the Corps used Hawaiian Constructors to build railway tracks, aircraft warning stations, storage holds for ammunition, and fortifications all over the islands. Formally, John was employed as a worker for a private company. Actually, even before the attack on Pearl Harbor he was under the command of the Corps of Engineers, which had taken over payroll services, time keeping, and procurement from the merged firms.[11]

His memories blur corporate titles and bureaucratic competencies, and emphasize the work he did. John was sent, first, to Waimānalo Bay to help transform an auxiliary landing field and gunner range into a full-fledged military airfield, Bellows Field.[12] "My first job was as a Jackhammer. The jackhammer weighed 90 pounds or better. We would drill holes in the hills for the dynamite, so that the hills could be leveled for the airfield."[13] Eight miles from Kaneohe Naval Air Station, Bellows Field became a feature on the beachfront that was once the playground of Hawaiian royalty and haole sugar plantation owners.

John joined a crew that was engaged in flattening the sand dunes for a full-fledged runway system. Like CCC assignments, construction at Bellows was physical, purposeful, and *hard*. And like his accounts of Volcano, his references to the time at Bellows stress the teamwork, cooperation, and coordination of the men. The clatter of jackhammers intruded into the nearby beach lots; the noise of dynamite blasts echoed against the Koʻolau Range, audible to residents of Hawaiian Home Lands and of Waimānalo Village. The people of Waimānalo grew used to the sounds of explosions, and obeyed the signs that forbid swimming, diving, and fishing in parts of the wide aquamarine bay.

Bellows formed part of a network of defense sites on Oʻahu that had already expanded in the 1930s. Responsible for shoring up these sites for imminent war, Hawaiian Constructors gathered a large labor force by offering a pay rate above the island's minimum wage: 50 cents to the normal 25 cents per hour.[14] "My wages was fifty cents an hour doing all this sort of jobs," John writes, embedding the sentence in a long account of the specific tasks he did for that rate—in addition to breaking up old cement, he set off dynamite blasts, dug tunnels, and helped pump sea water onto a coral runway "so the [steam] Rollers could roll on it to harden the surface."[15] Hundreds of local men worked side by side on these urgent tasks, and the company brought more men from the mainland as emergency measures intensified.[16]

Under sweeping treaty agreements, and covered by the claim of national security, the United States located military sites in areas defined as crucial, without concern for the history of those places. Bellows occupied the shore of what had once been an ancient Hawaiian settlement, on fertile land between the Koʻolau Mountains and the bay. Replaced by a sugar plantation owned by one of the sugar barons Eleanor castigated, much of Waimānalo lay under cultivation, cane replacing the "grass huts" that once dotted the valley floor.[17] In 1917, complying with a presidential executive order, the plantation owner leased acreage to the federal government, and "men and tents" moved in. The military installation replaced an open beach from which plantation owners, members of the royal family, and residents had launched ships and small fishing boats. Cane still grew, some miles from the shore, and residues of the old settlements remained in places the dynamite or the bulldozer missed. In his

Work History, John comments: "I did remove graves to a different location so they could make their airport runway for larger planes."

Seventeen years old, John did not pay attention to the past.[18] "I was a young punk ful with vinegar trying my best to do my job."[19] He was at the peak of his strength and eager to move ahead, and he concentrated on the skills he acquired on the job. "I became a pipe fitter, grease monkey, oiling all heavy equip., plus change oil also, began to move this equip around the area while the operator goes out to eat lunch. ... I was a driller, power man, watch man for Hon. Construction."[20] In both *Life Story* and *Work History,* John dwells on the job he did at Bellows, on the particulars of his day-to-day activities, almost as if there were no war in the background. In neither document does he refer to the Army Corps; instead he uses the other name under which the unit was known: the United States Engineering Department or, in an unintentionally ambiguous acronym, USED. John's emphasis on applied skills, and on the range of activities in which he engaged, suits the official history of the Engineering Corps. That history distinguishes between civilian and war efforts—a distinction without a difference that came with the first arrival of the Corps in the Pacific in 1898.[21] Faithful to its history, the Corps maintained that home front security and not warfare was at the heart of work in Hawai`i.

John did not wear a uniform and he did not answer directly to military personnel. He worked in "dungarees," occasionally side by side with a worker in uniform.[22] There, engaged in a shared and difficult task, the Native Hawaiian assumed the identity of worker, indistinguishable from other hot and tired men.

In the CCC, distinctions based on race had intruded into the teamwork. The haole men who arrived at the Volcano camp took the positions of administrator, ranger, and expert, separated from the ordinary boys in rank if not in clothing or pay scale. At Bellows and on other construction sites, John met haole laborers, who worked at the same manual tasks he did. "My partner all this time was a mainland haole man a little older than me, but we managed to do our job right," he writes in *Life Story.* Strained and sweaty, the two men developed a partnership, the outcome of which John describes: "Then one day, our Field Superintendant was elevated up to General Field Superintendant of Oahu. This left his position open. My mainland haole friend took the test and made field superintendant. The first thing he said to me was to get a higher paying job." With the help of the mainland haole, John got work on a crane, a prize job. "He put me with an old man operating a crane, that was going back to the mainland. I stayed on this crane as an oiler and in three days time I had his crane and was the youngest crane operator in the company."[23] On the crane, he received a good salary and the prestige attached to the position. "My boss really took care of me," he notes in *Work History.* That chapter was soon over.

A City Under Martial Law

On the morning of 7 December 1941, John had just completed a grueling seven-hour night. "I was working third shift on December 6, 1941, knocking hills down. Then our shift ended at 6:30 a.m. and we all went home. By 7:30 a.m. I had gotten home and all of a sudden everything started happening. The Pearl Harbor area was full of smoke. Overhead planes were zooming all over the area and also above our house. We did not know that the Japanese had attacked Pearl Harbor. Then the radio announced that Pearl Harbor was being attacked and for everyone to take cover. I already knew that help was needed in all areas."[24] John volunteered right away. He left Aunt Mary's house on Magellan Street, perhaps with a glance at the nearby Puowaina (Punchbowl) Crater as he walked toward the ocean; the crater would later be claimed by the United States for the National Memorial Cemetery of the Pacific.[25] At oceanside, he offered his help through Hawaiian Constructors, performing emergency tasks delegated by the US Army Corps of Engineers.

The Corps set up controls on all harbors, and sent John to Kewalo Basin, a small harbor between Waikīkī and Honolulu Harbor. "Although less congested than Honolulu, the basin was the only small boat harbor on leeward Oʻahu and thus thought to be a logical site for a potential Japanese invasion"—logical given the fear of subversives that had been brewing in the territory for over a decade.[26] John describes his job in *Life Story*: helping to "remove all radios and communication equipment" from the fishing boats—the Japanese sampans— at work that Sunday morning.[27] Caught up in the crisis, the commotion, and the confusion on that day, John threw himself into defense work: "sinking all the fish boats so they cannot do any damage to Kewalo Basin Area."[28]

Along with other volunteers, he moved from one designated danger spot to another. "Then I was sent back to Waimanalo Bellows Field," site of his first job in Honolulu, "but the situation was well in hand. Then I was shifted to Hickam Field in the night, helping remove the dead to an emergency mortuary, then going back to repair all the damaged runway areas."[29] Approximately 2400 Americans were killed, including 57 civilians; fires spread through the city, and smoke infused the lives of residents.[30] The Corps assigned men like John to defense sites, where planes had been badly damaged, runways torn up, and hangars destroyed. John worked for nearly a month—"smelly like a fish"—without a change of clothes, a bath, or, according to his story, any rest. Then he went home to the house on Magellan Street. Like every other neighborhood in Honolulu, the cluster of houses near Punchbowl experienced the swift imposition of martial law.

Late in the morning of 7 December, US Army General Walter Short forced Governor Joseph Poindexter to hand over all executive powers to the military. By the end of the day, marital law was imposed across the American territory. The military controlled all administrative activities, including the courts and civic institutions, and essentially ruled Hawai`i like an occupied territory. Martial law lasted in Hawai`i until 24 October 1944, well beyond the projection made by General Short. And he did not remain in office long. Sanctioned for the failed defense of Pearl Harbor, he lost his post in nine days and was replaced by General Delos Emmons. Plans for home front security were solidly in place: military personnel supervised the lives of residents, fingerprinting every resident, citizen and alien alike, and walking the streets to enforce the 6 PM curfew. Civil defense volunteers patrolled the streets, alarming people about the next attack. Children learned to run for cover in schoolyards, and everyone bought a gas mask.

Like every resident in the territory, too, John lined up to register and receive an identity card. He acquired his gas mask, and perhaps brought masks home for Auntie Mary and others in the `ohana; "special sponge rubber inserts were used to pad the faces of the masks to fit children and 'bunny masks' were devised for babies."[31] The emergency following upon the Pearl Harbor attack crept into personal interactions on the streets and in the shops of Honolulu, onto the buses, and into households. Food was scarce: ships carrying troops from the mainland did not stock large supplies of food. People had to make do.

"Only meat, poi and rice were always in storage," John writes, not mentioning that poi and rice were essential in the Hawaiian diet. "There was always people lining along side the sidewalks at the market or stores for the things mentioned above." Stores were instructed to sell only the "normal" amount of food, and residents of outer islands complained that O`ahu got a "better deal."[32] John remarks on one strategy individuals adopted to deal with shortages: "Lots of black marketing was going on." He also remarks that those who profited in the black market, broke the curfew, or disobeyed military authority ran the risk of being prosecuted. "If you were to break the law, other than a serious crime, the judge would make you buy War Bonds."[33] These were military judges, and a person accused of a serious crime had little latitude: Short had suspended habeas corpus, a deprivation of a civil right that lasted until the end of the war. Next to the threat of imprisonment, spending money on a war bond was a mild penalty.

For many residents, particularly those groups the United States defined as alien, dangerous, or subversive, life changed profoundly. For others, like John, the imposition of martial law veered between discomfort, inconvenience, and annoyance. "You must carry a gas mask," he remembered, "and also be age 21 to buy liquor." A self-described young punk, he had to be home by 6 PM, sitting behind pulled shades and keeping company with kin. His walks in the city were also transformed: deep trenches ran through neighborhood gardens and through schoolyards, shack-like emergency shelters spread across parks and recreation areas, and the beaches were officially closed. And while John does not mention the problem, his recreational diving became virtually impossible. The Army immediately strung barbed wire along the island beaches, less against submarine attacks than to prevent "collaborators" from contacting enemy ships. Wires stretched across the sand at Waikīkī, but, one resident remembered, "they left us a puka [hole] to go thru to swim."[34] The puka may have been as much for restless servicemen as for civilians.

Meanwhile, John left for work every day, gas mask in hand. Once the emergency work ended, the Army Corps went to work on projects that could no longer be defined as civil. Roosevelt had declared war, and the Corps set their sights on shoring up the military outpost in the middle of the Pacific. "The Army took over parks, schools, plantation fields, and vacant lots for barracks, supply depots, and offices. They dredged channels, drained swamps, reclaimed land, and cut tunnels into mountains."[35] For these jobs, the Corps added hundreds of men to the thousands already at work in Hawai'i. Gwenfread Allen noted: "1,500 civilian mechanics were transferred from Patterson Field, Dayton, Ohio."[36] Officers took rooms in a popular Honolulu hotel. "Hawaii's biggest [wartime] employer was the army's United States Engineering Department, which spent more than $400 million on the war effort and located its offices in the Young Hotel roof garden, a favorite local night spot."[37] In addition to occupying rooms at a downtown hotel, the Corps distributed men and machines all over O'ahu, creating a substantial and unmistakable footprint. Signs reading "USED" referred to a present and active territorial institution.

Life on Magellan Street proceeded as best it could under wartime conditions. "In 1942, Uncle Bimbo married Sarah Nahoikaika and I was his best man," begins a paragraph full of domestic details. The household was getting crowded, John continues, and he moves out. "In my house or home I had a kitchen complete with gas stove and icebox, one bedroom and big parlour. Boy was I set." He liked where he was living. "Down the street, about five minutes walk, was the CD (Civilian Defense) cafeteria, that was open all night for people who were doing odd jobs."[38]

Proving They Were *American Japanese*

In 1941, the US Army Chief of Staff deemed the island of O'ahu "the strongest fortress in the world."[39] Yet fear of internal subversion intensified, and the federal government, the US military, and local authorities warned of "enemy aliens" within the territory.

The perception of danger began well before Pearl Harbor, exacerbated by Japanese expansion into the Pacific and the nation's imperial stretch toward

American holdings in the vast ocean. According to a military history website, "The Hawaiian [War] Department had been concerned for years about the threat of sabotage by the large population of Japanese nationals in the event of a war with Japan."[40] In 1936, President Roosevelt declared, "every Japanese citizen or non-citizen on the Island of Oahu who meets these Japanese ships or has any connection with their officers or men should be secretly but definitely identified and his or her name placed on a special list of those who would be the first to be placed in a concentration camp in the event of trouble."[41]

By 1940, every Japanese resident of Hawai`i, citizen and non-citizen alike, came under surveillance as a potential collaborator. Women and men who worked side by side with Japanese and welcomed them into their houses became fearful. "We had had stories as far back as 1940 and all through 1941 that the Japs on the Is. were all set to kill or poison every haole on the Islands." And the woman goes on to report her terror when her "Jap cook" decided to buy ant poison.[42] The diary entry appears in *The First Strange Place,* one of many similar anecdotes historians Beth Bailey and David Farber collected. Media reports encouraged such responses, and territorial authorities confirmed the danger when they ordered all Japanese language schools to close—hotbeds of subversion, they claimed. Japanese cultural institutions and newspapers came under scrutiny, and the remaining Japanese newspapers changed their names: *Hawaii Hochi* became *Hawaii Herald* and *Nippu Jiji* became the *Hawaii Times.*[43] Nisei, who were citizens, told Issei parents to shed their kimonos, stop eating Japanese food, discard ancestral shrines, and, above all, not to speak Japanese.[44]

On 19 January 1942, the Reserve Officers Training Corps (ROTC) at the University of Hawai`i dismissed all Nisei members. Young and energetic citizens, these men challenged the racist decision made by ROTC officers and demanded a role in national defense. In dire need of laborers, the Army Corps bent its restrictions and accepted the nearly 160 volunteers. Each man had to swear an oath of loyalty to the United States of America. "All my friends," John remembered about the Nisei who joined the Corps, "had to prove that they were American Japanese or who ever their race was."[45]

In fact, he did not work side by side with the Nisei. They formed a separate unit within the Corps, under the name Varsity Victory Volunteers, or VVV.[46] And they took on a new ethnic identification, *Americans of Japanese Ancestry,* or AJAs. The territorial newspapers continued to use the term *Japs.* The local authorities continued to round up their relatives, teachers, and, in some cases, parents as potential threats to the security of the Pacific Island "fortress."

On 19 February 1942, Franklin Roosevelt approved Executive Order 9066. Considered the order that permitted the internment of people of Japanese ancestry in the United States, in the Territory of Hawai`i the order only reconfirmed the power the military already had over enemy aliens. Under martial law, there were "no legal barriers to prevent the Army from handling the large

Japanese minority in the islands as it wished."[47] The military police arrested 391 Japanese, aliens and citizens, a day after the attack on Pearl Harbor. On 9 December, the police picked up ninety-three Germans and thirteen Italians, considered potential traitors to the United States.[48] Although many of the early prisoners were released, the outcome of military policy toward aliens was not blanket exoneration.

A half-century later, John wrote to me about the injustice in an American policy that cut people off from a place they had cared for and considered home. In his memory, "lots of Japanese people being displace and out from their homes, give up their business and put in relocation areas in the mainland."[49] Looking back from 1995, John saw little to justify the "rounding up" of Japanese in the 1940s and much to resonate with Native Hawaiian experience. The sympathy he expressed, fifty years after the end of the war, occurred in a context in which new mo'olelo emphasized the devastating impact of colonization in the displacement, dispossession, and decimation of kānaka maoli.

In Hawai'i, however, local officials limited the impact of Executive Order 9066. The Japanese comprised nearly one-third of the population of Hawai'i, 160,000 of the total 600,000; Japanese were the largest single ethnic group in the territory. Police Chief John Burns and military governor Delos Emmons took matters into their own hands, refusing to banish thousands of residents to internment camps. Full-scale incarceration was impossible for practical reasons. Burns and Emmons recognized that the highly educated and enterprising Japanese were crucial to the territory's survival during the war. Furthermore, branding a whole ethnic group *collaborators* (in current terminology, *enemy combatants*) was doomed to fail, regardless of whether residents perceived their Japanese neighbors as enemy aliens likely to betray the United States at any moment. While "lots" of Japanese were displaced, the sweep was never so thorough as on the mainland.

The territorial military authorities chose to pursue a selective internment strategy, aiming primarily at leaders of the Japanese community—teachers, Buddhist and Shinto priests, and successful businessmen. In all, between 1200 and 1400 local Japanese were interned, along with about 1000 family members. On the mainland, 120,000 Japanese were sent to (euphemistically named) relocation camps; two-thirds of them were American citizens.[50] A few Japanese from Hawai'i sailed across the Pacific, in troop ships fitted out for the incarceration. After living in camps scattered along the west coast, many returned home to a post-war Hawai'i where people (at last) acknowledged the comment made by the head of the Honolulu Chamber of Commerce at the start of internment: "The citizens of Japanese blood would fight as loyally for America as any other citizen."[51]

Burns and Emmons obstructed but did not entirely halt incarceration in camps on the islands. Most of the Japanese who were arrested were sent to

Sand Island, a former quarantine station a few miles from Pearl Harbor. Separated from O`ahu by a small channel, Sand Island had been used to hold ships—and individuals—suspected of carrying contagious diseases. In 1941, little had to be done to outfit the place for prisoners, and the Army Corps contributed men to do the necessary dredging and buttressing. During his "long hauls of dirt and gravel," John could see the segregated tents, men on one side, women and children on the other. Over the next two years, conditions in Sand Island improved, and the Army constructed housing for families. Still, as John remembered, people were locked behind high fences, unable to leave the location, and treated like potential combatants. "The families were like prisoners of war, in living quarters with high fences around them."[52]

In March 1943, the Army closed Sand Island and sent remaining prisoners to Honouliuli, a camp not far away on the coast of O`ahu. The Army had no choice: Sand Island violated the Geneva Conventions and the federal government respected international laws of war. Although aliens and suspects remained incarcerated, Roosevelt shifted his policy on Japanese citizens in a nation at war. At around the same time as Sand Island closed, he lifted the ban on Japanese enlistment. The decision was pragmatic, based on the need for more fighting forces. It was also a response to propaganda from Japan that accused the United States of denying civil rights to citizens and establishing "concentration camps" for a racial group. In revising the military policy, Roosevelt stressed the rights of an American citizen: "No loyal citizen should be denied the democratic right to exercise the responsibilities of citizenship, regardless of his ancestry."

The lifting of the ban led to one of the most storied aspects of the war in Hawai`i. No sooner had the call gone out than 10,000 Nisei came forward to enlist, far more than the expected 1500. The men volunteered for the US Army, the only unit they were permitted to join; the Navy, Marines, and Air Force closed their ranks to Japanese-American citizens. By June 1943, the newly formed 442nd Regimental Combat Team was ready for battle and hundreds of Americans of Japanese Ancestry sailed across the Atlantic to Europe.

Driving a Bus: "We *Local* Boys"

John quit his job with the Army Corps in the summer of 1943. "We wasn't laid off. We quit, we local boys, and went with an outfit, HRT"—Honolulu Rapid Transit—he tells his `ohana.[53] He provides an explanation in *Life Story:* "I quit USED because the superintendant wanted to hang on to the mainland workers because we local boys were outshowing them on the job. We local boys all quit and went out to seek different types of jobs."[54] No matter how much the Corps officers argued that the haole had an expertise the local boys lacked, the decision to ignore hard work in promotions rubbed John the wrong way: a sign of discrimination that contrasted with his recollection of the CCC. Then haole shared his jobs and men were promoted on the basis of capability, he recalled, and not of race. The USED maintained a hierarchy in which experts were white, workers brown, and the program did not provide training for men whose backgrounds denied them access to engineering courses.

This time John hardly had to wait for luck and a chance meeting. Honolulu Rapid Transit, responsible for moving thousands of people a day, needed drivers. Under martial law, plantation workers were forbidden to leave agricultural labor, and the bus company necessarily recruited from available urban workers, like John. He had a driver's license, benefit of the CCC, and he took a job with the company. And he took a pay cut. "I was making 35 cents an hr compare with USED $1.75." In compensation, he gained a good deal of freedom, and some pleasure. Even before the war, HRT had phased out its "old-fashioned jitney buses" and replaced them with smooth-running electric trolleys.[55] John had an easy ride and eventually a desirable route through Waikīkī and into downtown Honolulu.

The ride was easy only up to a point. During the war, HRT buses were enormously crowded, packed with a daily average of 350,000 passengers. At its peak, the monthly load rose from 1.2 million to an astonishing 11.5 million.[56] The crowd was mixed, from housewives traveling to Chinatown for the rare fresh produce to drunken sailors rushing back before curfew, and everything in between. In between were mainland military personnel and civilian war workers who carried with them entrenched stereotypes—different depending on background, but often clashing against one another on a ride. Moreover, as John told me, echoing other commentary on the period, the malihini did not understand the way "race" played out in the territory. Newcomers disturbed the existing structures, and not always with puzzled looks.

"The motion of the buses down Honolulu's crowded streets threw people into each other, and an innocent step to regain one's balance could easily erupt into a fight."[57] John witnessed these fights, and his stories reveal the impact such outbursts made on his perceptions of American race relations. "At this time, the mainland haoles and whatever, hated all slant eyed people that they saw on the streets. Be they Japanese, Chinese or any other slant eyed person, they were constantly being harassed. I did not like this sort of thing and all or at least the majority of the bus drivers were forced to take up martial arts such as Judo, Karate, boxing and all other sorts of self defense, to defend ourselves from getting hurt while driving the buses."[58] He did not excuse the behavior, as some did, by the fact that the "mainland haole" anticipated hand-to-hand combat with enemy Japanese in tiny islands across the Pacific.

John intervened, and he defended the "Orientals" who were especially subject to aggression. His memories dovetail with later remarks by fellow drivers. In an interview conducted in 1993, a Japanese-American told his story of driving an HRT bus during the war. "And when these service guys, marines, soldiers, when they get little high, you know, oh, they see you're an Oriental. They throw all kind of wisecrack." Cracks erupted into a "lot of fighting, too. But those days we were protected by roving protectionists. Had big Samoan guys, Hawaiians. Tough guys." Fred Kaneshiro continues: "I've seen how they've beat up some soldiers and marines because they were giving the young, small Orientals bad time." The Japanese drivers did not hold back either: "The other incident was a little smaller Japanese guy driving the trolleybus from Waikīkī—coming up Waikīkī—loaded with servicemen. He couldn't take it." And he simply crashed the bus: "He drove the bus into [HRT, Honolulu Rapid Transit, headquarters on] Alapaʻi [Street], right in the [bus] barn."[59]

HRT drivers joined together against the violent behavior of "young guys" who knew nothing about the rules of interaction in Hawaiʻi. John calls the aggressors "mainland uneducated hillbillies and country jacks," but the men who threw blows could have been any guy stationed in Hawaiʻi before going into battle.

Neither John nor Fred Kaneshiro refers to another source of outbursts and fistfights. Beginning in 1942, African-Americans in numbers out of all proportion to the black population of Hawaiʻi passed through or were stationed in the territory. During the war, nearly 30,000 black servicemen were ordered to the islands, which had then a population of approximately 200 to 300 black residents. For some of these servicemen, Hawaiʻi represented a "paradise" of race relations, an experience of acceptance and tolerance contrasting with what they knew at home. For others, confronting white soldiers in the tense pre-battlefront setting reactivated all the biases they had known before. "Many black soldiers believed the biggest troublemakers in Hawaii were southerners straight from the mainland," Bailey and Farber write in *The First Strange Place*. "Unsurprisingly perhaps, many of the racial fights broke out in the buses bringing men back from Hotel Street to Pearl Harbor before curfew—buses in which Jim Crow-style, back-of-the-bus seating arrangements were disallowed by military order." Local drivers, reported one of their informants, showed "empathy" for the blacks. After a fight started, according to the interviewee, "a local bus driver would hold the bus doors closed as long as the blacks were winning."[60]

"We local boys," John says, describing the bus drivers. In his use, the term *local* refers to the solidarity the drivers established with one another, expressed in the protection offered to victims of racial attacks.[61] Drivers or passengers, the "Japs" on the bus were distinct from the "enemy" vilified by the media and personified in wartime propaganda. And even if not every driver learned judo or closed the doors during a fight between a white and black serviceman, the blatant racism malihini brought to the islands was alien to "local boys," in John's rendering. Between the lines of his anecdotes, the contrast is clear. In Hawai`i, racial differences, and even slang terms, did not prompt physical fights. During the war, mainlanders brought a new kind of racism to the territory, in the quick and unprovoked attacks based solely on the color of a person's skin. John singles out "hillbillies and country jacks" to represent the group most responsible for the fights, and thereby differentiates mainland whites from the haole at home. The racism attached to color on the mainland became more evident to John when he was conscripted, and the category of *local* more significant as an opposition to divisions instituted by the US government. [62]

HRT drivers had routes and troubles in common. They also occupied the same position vis-à-vis company managers, most of whom had close ties to the Big Five oligarchy. A strike in the first months of 1941 indicated how powerful the drivers could be by interrupting the transportation upon which thousands of servicemen and civilians depended. Four hundred drivers left the buses sitting in garages, and little moved for a month.[63] John did not participate in the work stoppage, but he came into a company in the aftermath of a successful working class action. "We local boys" were workers, and in his talk-stories the category distinguishes a group by class and not by race.[64] John's expressed solidarity with those who "work hard" created a new "we" group, in the context of highly fraught—and visibly precarious—us/them distinctions.

Local integrates diverse ethnic distinctions through a class lens. The term stood in juxtaposition to the slang terms that were part of territorial discourse, and not always innocently. For John, local overcame the *kanaka* he was called by a boss, the *native* in documents he signed, and the *Hawaiian* that placed him on a grid of racial, not cultural, categories applied by the federal government.

"Everyone Called Me a Nigger Because I Was Dark"

On 9 March 1943, John paid a visit to the US Selective Service Board in Honolulu. He had just turned eighteen and by law he had to register for the military. Six months later, he was drafted.[65] He was one of over 40,000 men from the islands who served in the war, voluntarily or, like him, compelled to join. The Selective Service Board kept track of the racial backgrounds of draftees, while military history provides a further breakdown by ethnic background. Not all John's fellow Native Hawaiians were inductees: "When the Hawaiian National Guard was mobilized in 1940, 28 officers and 732 enlisted men were listed as being of Hawaiian or part-Hawaiian ancestry." The Selective Service inducted a thousand or so more.[66] By the end of the war, 3,854 Hawaiian and Part-Hawaiian men fought for the United States, 11.9 percent of the total from the territory. AJAs made up 50 percent of the territory's fighting force.[67] Volunteers joined draftees like John for training at Schofield Barracks, on 18,000

acres in the middle of Oʻahu. The Japanese would be separated from other local servicemen when they reached the West Coast of the United States.

At the end of his training period, John sailed 2500 miles across the Pacific
Ocean to San Francisco, further from Hawaiʻi than he had ever been. On An-
gel Island, just past the Golden Gate Bridge, he received his first real Army
task: "to guard Japanese prisoners who were caught in the Midway and Wake
Island conflict."[68] These were *enemy* fighters, distinct from the local Japanese
servicemen with whom John sailed to San Francisco. Members of Japan's fighting forces, the POWs had little in common with the Americans of Japanese
Ancestry who had enlisted in huge numbers. Nevertheless, the Army acted
quickly to move the men of the 442nd to training areas far from California,
away not only from military prisons but also from the internment camps that
dotted the West Coast. Most of the trainees went south to Camp Selby, deep in
the heart of Mississippi, where racism had another face. John would not meet
Japanese-American soldiers again until after the war.

He was sent to Camp Hood in southwestern Texas. Camp Hood (now Fort
Hood) lies outside the small town of Killeen, 60 miles north of Austin and
nearly 4000 miles from Honolulu. The base extends 26 miles east to west and
24 miles north to south, and during the war hosted troops from all regions of
the United States. In 1943, when John arrived, the camp was one year old and
there were approximately 40,000 men in training—95,000 at the peak.[69] The
camp constituted a village that was twice as big as Hilo, which had a population of 24,000 in 1940.

Like every other Native Hawaiian, John received his Army placement as
a "Caucasian," and he moved to Camp Hood in a *white* unit. In the process,
the military replicated the story of colonization in Hawaiʻi, assimilating the
Native Hawaiian and minimizing the implications of the otherwise significant racial classifications imposed by the US government. For over a century,
kānaka maoli had been ruled and regimented by a dominating nation, and the
outbreak of World War II showed the pragmatic side of imperial policy. Native
Hawaiians served side by side with white soldiers in platoons and companies
that also included Native Americans.

The story of Native American service in the US Army exposes the difference in US policies toward the indigenous peoples within its boundaries.[70]
Both peoples had been pushed aside, decimated, and ultimately taken over by
an expanding American nation. But the outcome differed, as did the characterization of the victims of "manifest destiny." In the eyes of governing authorities, the American Indian remained a threat, dangerous, and resistant to the
civilizing mission well into the twentieth century. The Native Hawaiian, on the
other hand, received the not-less-demeaning characterization of docile and
obedient. When the First World War broke out, members of Congress debated
long and hard about letting the "savage" American Indian fight next to civi-

lized white soldiers. Meanwhile, Native Hawaiians were encouraged to enlist, and did so.[71] Only the Army was at issue—the Navy, Marines, and Air Force remained exclusively white until the Second World War. In the end, Congress was persuaded of the value the American Indian could bring to a nation at war. Placed in white units, the American Indians were given tasks that fit their perceived abilities, serving primarily as scouts and code-breakers.[72] They were rewarded with American citizenship in 1924.

When Franklin Roosevelt declared war in 1941, the problem of American Indian military status had been resolved by the earlier decision. Questions about Native Hawaiian patriotism and loyalty had been moot for decades. Enlistees and draftees from both groups of indigenous people were assigned to white units. "Colored" units were reserved for African-Americans who, accepted into service, were not accepted into Caucasian units. During training, John did not encounter a black soldier in any of the drills and practices. However, he may have marched next to a Navajo, a Mexican-American, an Italian American, or a Chinese-American. War with Japan distinguished the Japanese from the Chinese citizen; in one case, the home nation was enemy and in the other ally of the United States.[73] The blanket racial category of *Asian* that had determined immigration and naturalization policies for over a century broke against the nationalist assumptions of wartime. Japanese-Americans from the Territory of Hawai`i served in units separated from the heterogeneous group John joined.

He described the men: "we were of all nationalities." A retrospective comment, his statement ignores the segregation of Japanese—neighbors and fellow workers—and of African-Americans, whose arrival in Honolulu had exposed a new racism. At Camp Hood, John met another version of American racist attitudes and behaviors.

Some miles distant from his barracks, in a far corner of the camp, stood barracks that housed "Negro" troops. These were elite recruits, enrolled in the Tank Destroyer Officer Candidate School. Their families lived with them on the base, and during the day the children went away, to attend a segregated school in a distant town.[74] While the Army recognized the benefit of training African-American men to command African-American foot soldiers, the military did nothing to break down segregation inside or outside its training camps. The only branch of the US military with a racially mixed population, the Army took direction from a War Department that claimed to uphold the social and cultural distinctions of the country at large. "The War Department administers the laws affecting the military establishment; it cannot act outside the law, nor contrary to the will of the majority of the citizens of the Nation."[75]

If segregation represented the will of the citizens, that could not have been clearer than it was in southwestern Texas. In the small towns surrounding Camp Hood, neighbors expressed the *will* Army literature cites. Trips into town were risky for certain members of so-called white units.

"I was the only Hawaiian in my outfit," John writes, and he adds: "everyone called me a nigger because I was dark."[76] He says no more about the epithet in his writings. The story he tape-recorded for his ʻohana offers another version. "The white men were so furious when they see a black man on the road. They thought that we were black men but we fought for our rights. But we always end up in jail. But they come and get us out." The first *we* refers to the collection of dark-skinned men in his unit, indistinguishable from one another in a Texas town—a Mexican-American, a Puerto Rican, or an American Indian. *They* are, first, the furious white men; *they* are, too, the military officers who come and bail the boys out. The racial attitudes and nasty confrontations were, John told me years later with still strong emotion, "things I hate."

In the mainland, in Texas, incidents of racism were not limited to fights between tired servicemen, drunken sailors, or overheated civilians. The extent of anti-black sentiment became perfectly clear to John, and implicated him in ways that differed from his bus-driving days. On the tape, he refers to the "collecting" of all dark-skinned men together. He had seen a similar confusion of Japanese and Chinese at home, but the phenomenon in the American south had a different cast to it. Neighboring townspeople who attacked and imprisoned apparently "black" men did not have the excuse a young soldier, about to be shipped to the Pacific, had when he reacted hostilely to an Asian-appearing person. As John's fellow bus driver said, "But these were all young *Haole* kids that don't realize a lot of things. They just have one thing in mind. You're fighting a 'Jap.'"[77] One slang word was not the same as another, and *nigger* carried a message that had nothing to do with an enemy nation. Racism in the mainland south was simply, and blatantly, based on the color of a man's skin—and John had not experienced that version of the "will of the majority of the citizens" before.

Whether or not his experience of racism in the towns around Camp Hood reminded him of the changed racial situation in Honolulu, John decided not to go "home" for his rest and relaxation. He attributes the decision to fear that he would be sent to the Pacific to fight men who looked like fellow workers and neighbors. "Well, I didn't come home to see my family," he wrote to me fifty years later. "I have gone to Chicago for my 2 weeks RR, because I knew that if I went home, I would sure as hell be sent to Japan."[78]

Our Life Was Not Worth a Nickel

Chicago was an interlude. Two weeks later John joined his unit at Camp Kilmer, New Jersey, before sailing across the Atlantic. The unit left the United States on 14 October 1944, in a large convoy John remembered as containing "60 ships." The departure—leaving the lights of Brooklyn behind—initiates a moʻolelo in which memories are influenced by media accounts and, sometimes, by the mythologies of war. "The sea was full of German U-boats," he continues his story, but the convoy "out run them all" to come safely into port in England two weeks later. There the men on the ships, including a Native Hawaiian from a tropical island, confronted one of the coldest winters of the war, with freezing snow and subzero temperatures.[79]

John writes his experiences in *Life Story* and *Work History,* tapes episodes for his children and grandchildren, and reflects on war in his letters to me. He never wrote a separate war book, though he ends one of his letters, "this is my Army story to you." John fought with the 78th Infantry Division, one of four divisions in the 310 Regiment. Nicknamed *Lightning* and assuming the motto *Audaciter* (boldly), the regiment produced a wealth of material in histories that now fill the Internet. John's stories provide a counterpoint to these official, triumphant accounts. "Yes, Honey, it was awful, man cry, we all tried to comfort each other."[80]

His moʻolelo diverge from conventional American war stories in some respects, though not in others. He does not dwell on outstanding acts of bravery, courage, or risk-taking.[81] Rather, when John writes of men in battle, on the edge of death, he focuses on teamwork, cohesion, and the ways in which men "of all nationalities" protected one other. Not unlike narratives of multi-ethnic platoons in World War II films and novels, for John these attributes echo the values he attached to "ways of old," to Keaukaha, and to the harmony, or *pono,* of his best work experiences. As for other kanaka maoli men, serving in the Army provided an outlet for acting Hawaiian in a fully Americanized setting. Ty Tengan notes in *Native Men Remade* that service in the military was "one of the few ways" "ʻŌiwi men could achieve a masculinity based on notions of family, leadership, providing, strength, and mana."[82]

In his talk-stories when we sat on the beach together, John added to these expressions of "masculinity" another dimension of male solidarity in the face of war. Men who were frightened, he told me, took to teasing, squabbling, and drinking. Alcohol, he went on, calmed fears and eased the prospect of hand-to-hand combat with German soldiers. A month after arriving in England, trench warfare became a reality for the 78th Infantry Division. The men in John's unit fortified themselves for the trip across the channel to the battlefields of Northern Europe.

On a dreary Thanksgiving Day, 22 November 1944, the *Lightning* Regiment landed near Le Havre. Terror and tedium set in, as the men marched through snow and ice, from village to village in France, Belgium, and Luxembourg. "It was cold," John remembers in his *Work History.* "We had to make ourselves warm by wearing double socks and our snow shoes. Heavy overcoat. Also stay back to back in the fox hole." Freezing temperatures did not distract him from the conditions of the towns through which they passed, and he comments on the "devastating poverty" apparent in bare fields and abandoned houses. In *Work History*, he dwells on the personal impact of this march toward the border with Germany: "Life is worth 2 seconds on the front line or anywhere you are fighting either hand to hand combat or shooting your enemy. Mercy is not shown, because we were taught only to kill our enemy or they kill you."

On 8 March 1945, the 78th Infantry crossed the Rhine River at Remagen, engaging in a battle that took the Americans into German territory at last. The official history notes proudly that the 78th was "one of the first infantry division troops to span the Rhine." The history continues, in typical military rhetoric: "the German defense line along the Roer River had been smashed, and now the last remaining obstacle—the Rhine—had been crossed. The stage was set for the final, crushing blow of the offensive. Nazi Germany—its back to the wall, its vitals exposed—was ripe for the kill."[83] The next day was John's twentieth birthday and, with a contrasting perspective, he says: "I was lucky to be alive." The battle was not only glorious but also deadly: "Now more of my buddies got killed and wounded."

In his account of Remagen, John connects one of the most glorified actions in regiment history to the behavior of men engaged in battle. One letter tells a story of betrayal, disunity, and neglect of duty. The officers, he writes, "were not committed to us," and he concludes: "Honey, our life was not worth a nickle, we were expendable."[84] *Cannon fodder* is the more popular phrase, but the point is similar. Foot soldiers were often on their own in trenches and in no-man's land. Rather ambiguously, John adds: "We lost most of our top officers." Whether the officers were killed or behind the lines in command tents, John's emphasis falls on the ways in which he and his buddies worked together, gathering for the action they needed to perform. The men, he writes, "just picked ourselves up to lead the rest of our men to continue fighting."[85] He had survived the battle over a last-ditch German stronghold. He commemorated the teamwork among fellow soldiers. He does not talk of the *heroic annihilation of an enemy nation*, the phrase used in the official regimental histories.[86]

On the other side of the Rhine, in German territory, the 78th continued its march. But this was still war, and villages harbored enemies, who found hiding places in the deserted streets. John describes one village: "While they were firing at us, my buddy and I hurled hand grenades into this area and to my amazement there were about 65 German women in this building with guns and other weapons. They came out yelling with white sheets to surrender. I was scared and startled."[87] This would be one of the last danger points for John. In early April, the 78th entered the industrial town of Wuppertal. There, John writes, "the war ended for us." On 12 April, President Roosevelt died—"a big blow to us"—and on 17 April, the unit won a well-deserved rest before continuing to train for possible deployment to the Pacific. On 7 May, Germany signed surrender papers and the war in Europe was over.

Occupying Berlin 1945–46

Six months after the surrender John entered Berlin. On 17 November, the "first foot troops" and the "last elements" of the 78th Infantry Division replaced the 82nd Airborne Division in the divided city.[88] The American military occupied one quarter of Berlin, and the three allied powers held the other sections.

"Now I'm in Berlin and this city had been demolished by the Russians and the [US] Air Force," John writes about the capital of Germany.[89] The division took up quarters near the huge Nazi-style Tempelhof Airport, the biggest in Europe at the time. John lived a few blocks away from the airport in a neighborhood he called Marine Dorf in a near-phonetic rendering of the Berlin neighborhood Mariendorf. His unit served as a constabulary force, expected to maintain discipline in the troops, check for fraternization with the enemy, and keep a close—if winking—eye on black-market activities. In his descriptions, John's tasks combine policing, commanding, and disciplining men and women. "I did cover a very big area."[90]

He was assigned to enforce rules in a city that was in ruins and short of resources. The citizens greeted the surrender with relief, and residents of Mariendorf especially appreciated living in the American zone, where the soldiers appeared to be generous and openhearted. The men of the 78th met virtually no hostility or suspicion, and they threw themselves into life in a big city, compensation for months of trekking through ice, snow, and sniper fire. The *Lightning* newspaper marked their arrival in Berlin with a promising headline: "Man-About-Town Finds Berlin Rich in Hot Spots."[91] In his official role, John had to impose order on men eager to take advantage of such "spots." He had to transmit officers' orders to a group of men ready for "rest and recreation" before being sent back home.

"My job was to pick up everyday, one officer from different outfits and make a tour through the American sector," he writes in *Life Story*. "We checked for the behavior of the military, made sure they were clean and well groomed and carried themselves with respect for the military."[92] He adds a few details in *Work History*: "I checked on everyone," making sure men were in uniform, "hair cut, shoes polish." Women as well as men came under his purview: "they must be like the male service men and have the same punishment. No salute to the officer is an offense. No if or buts."[93] He demanded outward conformity and obedience, particularly when accompanied by a superior on his rounds, but he also took advantage of the opportunities a city offered. Still a "young punk," John assumed policing responsibilities without shunning pleasure, and he extended his adventures from city to countryside, swimming in lakes he recalled as "dirty and dark brown."

He imposed discipline, but he was not stricter about obeying formal laws than were his "buddies." In the tape-recorded moʻolelo for his ʻohana, John remembers: "We made big bucks down there [Berlin], where we were selling cigarettes, Pall Malls, the longest cigarette out in America. They were selling for $500 a pack and the rest, the other cigarettes, were selling for $300 a pack. And we would get this all from the PX, but I used to collect all the cigarettes … and I used these cigarettes to exchange for cameras and watches and whatever." He probably means marks and not dollars when he talks of *500* and *300*.[94] He made a profit, but the amounts were small—and fell under the radar of officers, who were tolerant of mild misbehavior by troops. "An army officer … wrote years afterwards that 'nobody who sold a few cartons was considered a criminal. It was the big wheeler-dealers who dealt in cars, diamonds and tens of thousands of dollars that the CID [Criminal Investigation Division] was after.'"[95]

Fraternizing with the enemy posed a more complicated problem. On the front lines, any contact with Germans had been absolutely forbidden. John refers to the law and the punishment: "If you got caught you would be fined $65.00"—a large amount at the time, but not as severe as a dishonorable discharge. "You couldn't even talk to anyone, even to an infant. That's how bad it was at that time." Still there was disobedience: "Soldiers would go in the forest or into the wheat field to hide from the Military Police to keep from getting caught."[96] As the war wound to an end, commanders recognized the futility of a non-fraternization policy and the absurdity in its implementation. In the spring of 1945, General Dwight D. Eisenhower, Supreme Commander of the Allied Forces, lifted the ban on American soldiers "talking to" German children and in October he abolished the rule forbidding "fraternization" with German civilians.

In Berlin, John and his fellow *Lightning* soldiers were free to pursue relationships with German citizens. John befriended a nurse, at a hospital near Tempelhof Airport. "I seen her everyday because I pulled guard in the hospital, so I would see her everyday," he tells the listeners to his tape. But, he adds without giving any further reason, I could not bring her home, "because she's a German." In this story for his children, grandchildren, and great-grandchildren, he stresses the elements of friendship and of concern, not of romance. He was "generous," he tells his listeners, and took care of her in a time of scarcity and shortage. "I used to go hunting up there everyday and bring all the deer and wild pigs to them and they clean it up, cook 'em and bring it to us." And he repeats the emphasis on *providing* that appears in his written account of "feeding" men in his platoon: "I used to hunt for deer and wild pigs and bring it home to the company and we would have lots of Barbecue meat."[97]

John exercised discretion for listeners in the younger generation. His retrospective account downplays the whole complex matter of sexual relationships in an occupying American Army. Although the official ban was gone, the association of sex and lack of discipline was not. Prudence and Puritanism framed the rules for men who were allowed to befriend civilians but not to disgrace the conduct expected of a soldier. The danger sex posed to the display of discipline and combat readiness erupted in a congressional hearing in 1946, when a returning commander mounted an exhaustive case against the US occupying forces.

Colonel Francis P. Miller offered a dismal picture of "the depredations of the American troops in Germany," through widespread trafficking in Army goods, black marketing, immoral conduct, and general disorder rampant in the American occupation forces.[98] He accused Lieutenant General Lucius Clay, the deputy military governor in Berlin, of tolerating "rotten apples" in his administration, and blamed the chain of command for laxness. At the end of his testimony, Miller did not hesitate to make the "Negro" troops—altogether 18 percent of the occupation force in 1946—scapegoat for all that struck him as wrong in the occupation of a defeated nation.[99] "The conduct of the white troops at times is reprehensible enough. ... But for generations to come, the German people will remember what undisciplined, uncontrolled negro troops have done to them." The white officers are afraid, Miller asserted, "to crack down on a Negro outfit."[100] Colonel Miller setting the tone, the senate hearing degenerated into a discussion of dubious statistical data, which showed higher venereal disease and crime rates "among the colored troops." The discussion included assessment of programs to reduce the number of black soldiers in the occupation army.[101]

The hearing exposed the still-existing racism not only in the senate but also in American society as a whole that made full integration of the military impossible. The testimony, and its reception by Congress, underlined the rift between the principles and the prejudices acted on by a mostly white professional officer corps and the honor code maintained by combat soldiers—who were "of all nationalities," John put it, omitting the fact of black segregation. His memory of the months in Berlin matched those he had of trench warfare: cooperation, reciprocal responsibility, and loyalty among men. John's wartime anecdotes ignore the racism promulgated in word and in deed by American politicians, officers, and, even, fellow soldiers. In his "war story," he relegated racism to non-combat arenas, not to behaviors under fire or actions undertaken by a victorious army in a defeated country.

Moreover, he recalled the months in service as a time when rewards were meted out on the basis of merit and hard work. John achieved a position of authority in the occupying force: "I was always sharp," he says, in a rare moment of explicit pride, "that's why I was picked up for this job" of disciplining "foot soldiers." In his tape, he adds another dimension: "I had good people in the service where I was. They respected me and liked me to help them."

The Army experience occasioned a turn in John's relations with American institutions. His reflections on his time in the military reveal an evolving perspective on the nation that governed life in the territory—soon to become the fiftieth state of the union. He appreciated the respect granted to a kanaka maoli and, in retrospect, he was grateful for the cultural experience he acquired during the one stay in Europe he would ever have.[102] "So that's what I did," he writes in *Work History*, "see how other people did, live, and what they think about us. Yes, I enjoyed all this places, that's why I can talk story of this experience which took place in my occupation in the Army in Germany."

At the same time, the war years exposed the gaps between principles and practices in United States governance. While John trained in a multienthic unit, the Japanese-American citizens with whom he sailed across the Pacific were placed in a separate regiment. Under the banner of a "fight for freedom and democracy," the military enforced a determination of loyalty based on national origin or, essentially, "racialized identity."[103] In southwestern Texas, John witnessed a form of American racism first hand, when he was arrested as a "nigger." These varied experiences in different places reframed his interpretation of the categories of identification he knew in Hawai`i. The term *local* took on renewed significance, distinguishing the finely managed social interactions "at home" from those outside the territory. In John's "war story," *local* sometimes refers to all long-time residents of the islands, not just to the men who labored with him on bus routes, in a training camp, and on the battlefront. Ultimately, however, the term expressed the solidarity of men who experienced war first hand. "Our local boys were all over the world fighting for freedom, also defending our country and the allied countries also."[104]

Home to Keaukaha

In the spring of 1946, John was beginning to get homesick. One evening in April, he went to the movies in a Berlin theater. The newsreel came on, and a dramatic segment showed enormous waves washing over the shores of the Big Island. "Instantly, I went to the Red Cross to try and get information, if any, of my family, if they got hurt or what kind of damage the tidal wave did to my family's living area." But there was no news. "Meantime, my chance to come home was getting closer. I contacted my Military leaders about how long before I could leave Berlin. They did good work and put me ahead of some old timers."[105] A month before the official deactivation of his regiment in May, he began the journey home. He sailed from Bremerhaven to New York, to the familiar Camp Kilmer in New Jersey, the first step in a cross-country trip back to Hawai`i. He celebrated with men in his unit. "Us guys found a Japanese restaurant and we had a ball," he writes, a choice that signaled a return *home*. "We had fresh Aku, we had sashimi, shrimp tempura, Lobster claws, chicken Hekka, shoyu chicken and more."[106]

The men traveled together from the East Coast to the West Coast, and into San Francisco. There John looked for Uncle Billie, his first step in a return not only to Hawai'i but also to the 'ohana. He failed to find his kin, and he boarded the boat with other decommissioned soldiers for the trip across the Pacific. "But then the sun came up and we were getting goose pimples for we could sight Oahu and were getting closer to Diamond Head, then we were in the harbor lanes."[107] John was home. He went first to the 'ohana he had left behind in Honolulu, where his sister Eleanor now lived. She wasn't there, and her memory of his return stresses its unexpected quality: "I was walking to work when I saw a man at a phone booth. From the back, he looked like my brother. I went up. He had come home from war." In the end, the family made a party for him, and, like returning soldiers all over the territory, John sat and talked-story far into the night.

"After seeing all my family in Honolulu I went home to Keaukaha, Hilo, Hawaii, to see my Mom and Family." Not only did he see his mom and step dad, but also two sisters born during the war. "I never knew I had a brother," Priscilla would remember in the 1990s, "until after the war." And he witnessed first hand the devastation caused by the worst tsunami to date in Hawaiian history.

Strong winds and high waves destroyed the docks he and Eleanor had jumped from as children. Hilo Harbor collapsed: "Giant blocks of stone, some weighing more than 8 tons, were strewn on the bayfront beach like grains of sand."[108] A few miles away, the oceanfront shore of Keaukaha lay under waste, trees down and the road demolished. The families who camped on the shore, anticipating summer weather, swiftly packed up tents, rushing to dry ground. "Mom them had run from the beach where they were fishing about 500 yards through bushes," John writes in his *Life Story*. Hollering "tidal wave," his parents warned their neighbors to safety. Not all could return: the catastrophe damaged or destroyed a number of the wood-framed bungalows of the homestead. No one in the 'ohana was hurt, but Eleanor later told me that the graves of their ancestors had washed away in the storm.

John stayed to help repair damages, but the natural disaster challenged him in severe ways. "I was always getting hurt," he writes, "falling all over the rocks or diving into the water and scraping my forehead and face." Reentry proved difficult, even softened by the familiar customs his mother still practiced.

Chapter XI of his *Life Story* tells a story of returning to the past in order to erase the years of distance from family, from Keaukaha, and from a way of life.[109] In a half-page-long chapter, John dwells on the continuities he perceives in the 'ohana. "When I came back from the Armed Service I thought of our old days of living, the kind of food we had, what Mom did when she had little money. As a youngster with my sister Eleanor, we had lived a poor life, but as long as there was Hawaiian salt and poi, like ulu, taro or palauwa, we were happy."[110] But the nostalgia fails to hold him, and in a few months John returned to Honolulu "to start a new, whole life again."[111]

"Service for Our Country"

John had not volunteered for the Armed Service. He was drafted toward the end of the war, and witnessed the surrender first of Germany and then of Japan as a private in the Army. On the days marking the anniversaries of those events, he participated in ceremonies and, in letters, reflected on the lessons from war. He extended his interpretations of American wars when Vietnam Veterans marched in a Veterans Day parade, or Japanese veterans attended a presidential speech on Pearl Harbor Day, or, finally, when there were young veterans from the 1990s war in the Gulf. He wrote letters to me on those anniversaries. "This day is very important to all service personnels who have gone into the service for our country and never returned to tell their storys about their life, like I am writing to you about."[112]

Celebrated on the mainland, these holidays commemorating American military victories had a special resonance in Hawai`i. Memorial Day is the most Americanized of the holidays, with its parades of children, school bands, and local clubs alongside uniformed veterans. John described "elderlys" from the Second World War and a few from the First going by in one parade, some on crutches and some in wheel chairs. Veterans from the Korean War were outnumbered by a contingent from the Vietnam War, a war in which the enlistment of Native Hawaiians increased exponentially.[113] As far as I know, John never marched. He did attend public commemorative ceremonies and from time to time he honored the dead on his own. The National Memorial Cemetery of the Pacific, often called Punchbowl for the crater it occupies in the mountains behind Honolulu, is a green and calming memorial. "I visit our national cemetery every year to see the graves where all service personnel is buried and of all culture," he wrote to me one Memorial Day, relishing the ethnic diversity he had appreciated during his service in an American Army unit.[114]

The letters show a more complicated response to V-J Day than to the other holidays. In retrospect, for John V-J Day became the point at which his path as a Native Hawaiian diverged from the one a Nisei veteran could take. Thousands of his neighbors had demonstrated loyalty by renaming themselves Americans of Japanese Ancestry, volunteering for the Army Engineering Corps and enlisting in mass when Roosevelt permitted these citizens to serve. Dramatic public recognition of the loyalty of a once-suspect ethnic group occurred immediately after Japan signed surrender papers. John stood by—along with virtually every citizen of the territory—when men of the 442nd received more medals than any comparable regiment in the American Army. The attention accorded these surviving servicemen pushed into the background the achievements of other troops, perhaps especially the Native Hawaiian, with his rejection of individual heroics.[115]

John considered the attention reasonable, a fair compensation for the prejudice and hostility the Japanese of Hawai'i had suffered before and during the war. Individuals whose families had dissolved, whose parents died in internment camps, and who themselves lost positions deserved recompense. "Now those who is Home again, worked hard to bring [back] their ways of living, and their children got educated and become high officials in the state government."[116] Yet he expressed ambivalence about the rewards that few kānaka maoli were given the opportunity to enjoy.

John's remark about the successful Nisei comes in the context of regret that he could not further his own education. In particular, he mentions his inability to take advantage of the GI Bill—the Servicemen's Readjustment Act Roosevelt signed in 1944 to stave off another depression. Like numerous local "boys," John did not qualify; he did not have a high school degree and, as he also told me, he did not have money for an education. The returning Japanese veterans met the criteria: many had left the University of Hawai'i to enlist, and others graduated from high school before enlisting. This generation of AJAs, John noted, successfully challenged the established haole elite. In the fifties and sixties, individuals of Japanese ancestry began to dominate state institutions and to win elections to local offices and to the United States Congress.

V-J Day was also a celebration of American triumph, and John's reflections on that day spread to a contemplation of the war for "freedom and democracy."

He wrote about the special role Hawaiians, residents of the islands, played in the fight to protect rights. The *locals* he described who risked their lives included the Nisei, men he had defended from attacks on crowded buses. When in early September 1995 President Bill Clinton came to the islands to honor the veterans of the fiftieth state, John participated in the events. He gave me his version of presidential rhetoric. "Today is a very special day of my life, because the celebration of our VJ day. I was happy to see lots of them [veterans], of all different ethnic culture and what we gave to our country and our people what they have today, a Democratic way of life in America."[117] Influenced by the collective spirit of a Second World War anniversary, John expands the category of *local* into the "we" who benefit from democracy.

He distinguished those who fought and understood what "war is really about" from residents who had no experience of battle and from mainlanders who did not know home front danger. In a letter written just before V-J Day in 1995, he condemned the "crowds" who protested against Truman's decision to drop bombs on Hiroshima and Nagasaki. "When the war ended in Europe, we trained hard for we were going to invade Japan mother land. America drop the A bomb which defeated the Japanese. They [protestors] hollered it was wrong.

President Truman did the right thing—the people of America United States did not feel the terrible blow we had at Pearl Harbor, I know how awful it was. We in Hawaii is the one who felt hurt."[118]

In the end, however, the war did not turn John into an uncritical American patriot. When he uses *we* in the "war story," he refers either to Hawaiians—the residents of the territory—or to the men (and women) who fought, never *we the people of the United States*. His experience in the Army left him with a more pragmatic than an ideological appreciation of US military service. The differential rewards—the signal success of the Nisei veterans—put a dent into the undifferentiated version of loyalty taught in public schools and reinforced by the punitive measures taken against "aliens" suspected of disloyalty, despite the oaths they swore. In his 1994 *Work History* and *Family History,* John regards the Army in somewhat the same terms he described the CCC: with an emphasis on the teamwork and cooperation that to an extent eroded the boundaries of class and of ethnicity—of "different nationality or culture, as you say."[119] He learned tasks in both institutions, he writes, that prepared him for a future in an American territory. Yet that future was a mixed business, as he implied when he mentioned the two Japanese-American senators or the Nisei who dominated the school system and, eventually, bought houses in the expensive suburbs of Honolulu.

John appreciated the opportunities the military offered to "young punks" like himself, and he encouraged the boys in the `ohana to choose careers in the military. After 1948, when President Truman signed the executive order for desegregation in the Armed Forces, a Native Hawaiian had an even better chance of being accepted into the formerly elite and exclusive Navy, Air Force, and Marine Corps. Once in, a Native Hawaiian could be trained, educated, and promoted on the basis of merit. From that point of view the military surpasses tourism, the other dominant industry in Hawai`i. The tourist industry does not open its doors widely or provide much opportunity for mobility through the ranks. Native Hawaiians are hired either in the service sector or, for a few, as entertainers. Rarely does a kanaka maoli achieve what might be equivalent to "command," the position of manager or corporate executive.

As head of an `ohana, John advised his sons to take advantage of the military and to shun the discriminatory tourist business. Neither a service job nor the role of entertainer accorded a Native Hawaiian recognition comparable to what he had won in the military. Appreciative of an institution where merit counted, John refrained from participating in protest marches against military installations, or the movement of armored vehicles onto the land belonging to Pele, or the docking of aircraft carriers in the harbors of O`ahu.[120] These were the activities his sister Eleanor would take on.

John made four tapes for his family in 1994 and in them he talks about the sons who entered the military, expressing pride in their decisions. One son,

John says, was making "good money, but then when the Navy call him, he drop his work and go in the Navy." Four sons and four sons-in-law entered the service, he tells the ʻohana in his recordings of "what to think about." While he intersperses his memories of battle in these lessons, his emphasis is not on bravery—or on fear—but on the advantages he gained: the respect of men, the status of US veteran, and the papers that testified to his "honorable" conduct. For his sons and sons-in-law, and then for his moʻopuna, the military offered similarly substantial rewards. Security, status, and training in skills were resources John was too pragmatic to ignore when he addressed future generations.

In his accounts of the US military presence in Hawaiʻi, John demonstrated a realistic assessment of the continued discrimination against kānaka maoli. The US military still offers a primary means of sustenance to marginalized and dispossessed residents of an American state that lacks a robust manufacturing sector and leaves most Native Hawaiians in low-paying jobs. In contrast with African-Americans, where the enlistment rate has sharply declined over the last decade, falling below the percentage in the population, the number of enlistees from Hawaiʻi and other Pacific Islands has increased and is well above the percentage of eighteen to twenty-four year olds in the population.[121] "The connection between work and militarization is an important one," asserts the anthropologist Ty Tengan, "for it is not only ideology but also employment that serves as a draw for Hawaiians who may not otherwise have opportunities for advancement or mobility."[122]

John, too, refers to continued participation in the military by members of his ʻohana in terms of employment. But he also dwells on another aspect of service: the shared stories members of the ʻohana tell that enhance unity, communicate aloha, and transmit Hawaiian cultural values. "So we can relate our experiences with each other and our children and grandchildren."[123]

Service in the American Army provided John a stepping stone to the next phase in his life. With a residence in Navy housing and a job at the Pearl Harbor Naval Shipyard, he married, began a family, and negotiated his claimed "100 percent Hawaiian" identity in the context of changes in US–Hawaiʻi relations in the last decades of the twentieth century.

Notes

1. John Simeona, *Life Story*, MS., 23 (in the author's possession).
2. John Simeona to the author, 11 October 1995.
3. Simeona, *Life Story*, 24.
4. Robert C. Schmitt, *Demographic Statistics*, 116, 118. Ten years later, Honolulu's population jumped to 250,000.
5. Rich Budnick, *Hawaii's Forgotten History*, 82.
6. *Paradise of the Pacific* 55, no. 12 (1941), 104.

7. "Sharp tensions in fact existed between and even within the multiplicity of ethnic groups that behued [colored] the island landscape." Allison J. Gough, "Messing Up Another Country's Customs," at FN 9.
8. James H. Shoemaker, *Hawaii Emerges,* 188–189.
9. Simeona, *Work History,* MS., 2 (in the author's possession).
10. A private company called Honolulu Construction and Draying existed on the islands, but in 1941 John was more likely to be working for the conglomerate.
11. Karl C. Dod, *Corps of Engineers,* 25, 41.
12. "In prewar days, 1,500 acres of sand dunes and cane fields at Waimanalo had been converted into an auxiliary landing field and gunnery range manned by personnel from Wheeler and Hickam Fields"; Gwenfread Allen, *Hawaii's War Years,* 227.
13. Simeona, *Life Story,* 24.
14. In October 1941, Governor Poindexter signed a law to establish 25 cents an hour as minimum wage on Oʻahu. Budnick, *Hawaii's Forgotten History,* 87.
15. Simeona, *Life Story,* 24.
16. In 1942, Hawaiian Constructors had a workforce of 7400; Allen, *Hawaii's War Years,* 234.
17. Quotation from *The Nalo News* 2, no. 10 (1978), 3.
18. Fifty years later, after the passage of the Native American Graves Protection and Repatriation Act (NAGPRA) of 1990 (finalized in 1995), the removal of graves and other scared sites became a subject of intense controversy in Hawaiʻi. Greg Johnson, *Sacred Claims,* chapter 2. See Edward Halealoha Ayau and Ty P. Kāwika Tengan, "Ka Huakaʻi O Nā ʻŌiwi: The Journey Home," 171–189. The repatriation process, they claim, is an appropriate way to "navigate through the harsh, often tragic realities of colonization," 186. Such concerns were not on John's mind when he began work at Waimānalo in 1941.
19. John Simeona to the author, 11 October 1995.
20. Simeona, *Work History,* 2.
21. The Corps entered the Pacific with a dual purpose during the war of 1898, America's first open embrace of imperialism—to build a modern infrastructure in the acquired territories for the military bases as well as to win "the hearts and the minds" of the civilians. See, for instance, for the Philippines, David Brody, *Visualizing American Empire,* 76–80; Dod, *Corps of Engineers,* 3; Paul A. Kramer, *The Blood of Government,* chapter 5.
22. "Side by side with uniformed personnel in Hawaii toiled war workers," writes Allen in a chapter titled "Warriors in Dungarees." *Hawaii's War Years,* 233.
23. Simeona, *Life Story,* 25.
24. Ibid.
25. "In ancient times, the extinct volcanic Punchbowl Crater was known as Puowaina which means 'Consecrated Hill' or 'Hill of Sacrifice.'" See http://www.hawaiiweb.com/punchbowl.html, accessed 10 June 2012.
26. Donald Fitzgerald, "Pearl Harbor," 189.
27. Simeona, *Life Story,* 25.
28. Simeona, *Work History,* 3.
29. Simeona, *Life Story,* 25.
30. The figures come from Budnick's *Hawaii's Forgotten History,* 89. In the confusion, deaths were caused by American fire as well as by Japanese fighter bombers. Allen, *Hawaii's War Years,* 7–8.
31. Allen, *Hawaii's War Years,* 116.
32. Ibid., 160–161.

33. Simeona, *Life Story,* 26.
34. DeSoto Brown, *Hawaii Goes to War,* 55.
35. Wilbur D. Jones and Carroll Jones, *Hawaii Goes to War,* 83.
36. Allen, *Hawaii's War Years,* 234.
37. Jones and Jones, *Hawaii Goes to War,* 90.
38. Simeona, *Life Story,* 26.
39. http://www.usarpac.army.mil/history2/dec7th.asp, accessed 20 February 2011.
40. Ibid.
41. Quoted in Gary Y. Okihiro, *Cane Fires,* 173. Roosevelt may have been responding to Army Colonel George Patton's suggestion that "126 Japanese" be arrested in Hawai'i as potential subversives; Budnick, *Hawaii's Forgotten History,* 75. Those arrests were not made.
42. Quoted in Beth Bailey and David Farber, *The First Strange Place,* 4.
43. Helen G. Chapin, *Shaping History,* 181.
44. Lawrence H. Fuchs, *Hawaii Pono,* 304.
45. John Simeona to the author, 30 August 1995.
46. See Franklin Odo, *No Sword to Bury,* chapter 6.
47. Stetson Conn, Rose C. Engelman, and Byron Fairchild, *Guarding the United States and its Outposts,* 207.
48. Okihiro, *Cane Fires,* 210.
49. John Simeona to the author, 30 August 1995.
50. http://www.hawaiiinternment.org/history-of-internment, accessed 22 February 2011.
51. Quoted in Bailey and Farber, *The First Strange Place,* 5.
52. John Simeona to the author, 30 August 1995.
53. John Simeona in a tape recording, June 1994.
54. Simeona, *Life Story,* 26.
55. Cliff Slater column, "Second Opinion," in the *Honolulu Advertiser,* 20 May 2002.
56. Allen, *Hawaii's War Years,* 345.
57. Bailey and Farber, *The First Strange Place,* 44.
58. Simeona, *Life Story,* 27.
59. In an interview with Fred M. Kaneshiro, published by Center for Oral History, *An Era of Change,* vol. I, 1082, 1084.
60. Bailey and Farber, *The First Strange Place,* 161–162.
61. According to Jonathan Y. Okamura, *local* became popular among non-white workers in early twentieth-century Hawai'i as a form of opposition to haole elite; Okamura in John P. Rosa, "Local Stories," 99.
62. The term *local* has accumulated multiple referents—denotative as well as connotative—and these change depending on the speaker and on the era. While Rosa argues that widespread use of the term came in the 1930s as a result of the Massie case, Sally Engle Merry emphasizes its establishment of working class solidarity in the islands in the early twentieth century. Rosa, "Local Stories," 94; Merry, "Law and Identity in an American Colony," 125.
63. Budnick, *Hawaii's Forgotten History,* 85.
64. Sally Merry writes that, "the language of 'local' emphasized long-term residence and working class status"; Merry, "Law and Identity," 125.
65. Just after Pearl Harbor, Congress amended the draft law, lengthening the term of service from one year to the duration plus six months and extending registration to all males between eighteen and sixty-five, with those between twenty and forty-five eligible for the draft. See *Mobilization: The U.S. Army in World War II. The 50th Anniversary,* 17. The document was prepared in the US Army Center of Military History by Frank

N. Schubert at http://www.history.army.mil/documents/mobpam.htm, accessed 9 February 2011.

66. http://www.history.army.mil/html/topics/apam/hawaiians.html, accessed 9 February 2011.
67. According to Gwenfread Allen, "The only racial breakdown of Hawaii's men in the service is of the 32,197 inducted by Selective Service Boards. Of these, 49.9 per cent were Japanese by ancestry; 14.8 per cent, Caucasian; 10.5 per cent, Chinese; 11.9, Hawaiian and part-Hawaiian; 8.7, Filipino; and 2.1, Korean." Allen, *Hawaii's War Years,* 264.
68. John Simeona to the author, 29 May 1995.
69. http://pao.hood.army.mil/history.aspx, accessed 9 February 2011.
70. See J. Kēhaulani Kauanui, *Hawaiian Blood,* chapter 1.
71. In 2011, Senator Daniel Akaka commemorated the service of both Native Americans and Native Hawaiians: "The service of Native Hawaiians in the United States Armed Forces, my own service included, predates Hawaii's statehood. A number of Native Hawaiians fought in the Civil War when Hawaii was still an independent nation. They also fought in the First World War." http://www.indian.senate.gov/news/pressreleases/2011-11-10.cfm, accessed 19 July 2012.
72. Alison Bernstein, *American Indians and World War II,* 46–56. Thousands of American Indians fought in the Second World War, and many took a heroic role that was later dramatized in Hollywood films like *Flags of Our Fathers.*
73. "The war thus constituted a major turning point for Chinese-Americans"; Rhonda Evans, *A History of the Service,* 32.
74. http://pao.hood.army.mil/history/1940/African-American percent20soldiers.htm, accessed 1 March 2011.
75. Quoted in Bailey and Farber, *The First Strange Place,* 1.
76. Simeona, *Life Story,* 30. His experience was not unique. "Former servicemen who were stationed for a time on the U.S. mainland remember comments and attitudes on their darker skins. Some of the men who were mistaken for Negroes and discriminated against in the South remember feelings of humiliation; others felt pride in pointing out they were 'different—Hawaiians for Hawai`i.'" Mary Kawena Pukui, E.W. Haertig, and Catherine Lee, *Nānā I Ke Kumu* (II), 306.
77. Center for Oral History, *Era of Change,* 1083.
78. John Simeona to the author, 29 May 1995.
79. "There, hail, sleet, snow, and cold harassed them [soldiers] until May 1945." Peter Schrijvers, *The Crash of Ruin,* 19.
80. Ibid.
81. "In a group of Hawaiians and part-Hawaiians asked to list what they considered 'Hawaiian qualities,' not one mentioned courage." Pukui, Haertig, and Lee, *Nānā I Ke Kumu* (II), 306.
82. Tengan, *Native Men Remade,* 49.
83. http://www.lonesentry.com/gi_stories_booklets/78thinfantry/index.html, accessed 2 March 2011.
84. John Simeona to the author, 29 May 1995.
85. Simeona, *Life Story,* 30.
86. http://www.lonesentry.com/gi_stories_booklets/78thinfantry/index.html, accessed 2 March 2011.
87. Simeona, *Life Story,* 31.
88. *Lightning* (the newsletter of the 78th), 17 November 1945, 1.
89. Simeona, *Life Story,* 32.
90. Simeona, *Life Story,* 33.

91. *Lightning,* 17 November 1945, 1.
92. Simeona, *Life Story,* 33.
93. Simeona, *Work History,* 10.
94. "A carton of any American brand, which cost the U.S. soldiers 50 cents in the PX, was worth 150 marks, $15 at the US rate of exchange, and in Berlin could bring several hundred dollars in marks. Matches were the small change." Earl F. Ziemke, *The U.S. Army,* 350.
95. The officer David Chavchavadze, in a memoir about his time in the OSS and the CIA, *Crowns and Trenchcoats,* New York: AIP, 1990, 142, cited in Kevin C. Ruffner, "The Black Market," FN 22.
96. Simeona, *Life Story,* 31.
97. Ibid.
98. *Investigation of the National Defense Program:* Hearings Before a Special Committee Investigating the National Defense Program, Part. 42, 80th Cong. 1st sess., 14 August 1946, 25834. See for the black market in Berlin and Miller's accusations, Kevin C. Ruffner, "The Black Market," and for the occupation of Berlin in general, Paul Steege, *Black Market, Cold War.*
99. Ibid. Miller at 25846. In his confidential report to the Select Senate Committee, the Chief Council George Meader summarized his investigations in Germany after the hearing: "A major difficulty with troops in Germany has been the proportionately large number of Negro troops used … in the Army's occupational duties" (26163).
100. Ibid., 25833.
101. As in all occupation armies, discipline was of course a matter of concern in Germany in 1945–46. Scattered data about "troop depredations" for a nine-week period, referring to a surge in crimes and venereal diseases in general and blaming African-American soldiers in particular, prove nothing else than the racism of those who used these figures. (Ibid. 26148 for Miller's rate of incidents.)
102. Unlike some of his fellow soldiers, John never went back to Europe. He did, however, visit Chicago again after the war.
103. Merry, "Law and Identity," 125.
104. Simeona, *Life Story,* 29.
105. Ibid., 33.
106. Ibid.
107. Ibid., 34.
108. W. C. Dudley and M. Lee, *Tsunami!,* 21.
109. "The tendency of the veteran to idealize all that he had left behind was in Hawaii, as elsewhere, a source of considerable difficulty in the period of postwar readjustment." Andrew Lind, *Some Problems,* 60.
110. Simeona, *Life Story,* 36.
111. Ibid., 37.
112. John Simeona to the author, 11 November 1994.
113. Kathy Ferguson and Phyllis Turnbull, "The Military," 47–52.
114. John Simeona to the author, 29 May 1995.
115. "Despite the significant contributions of Kanaka in the US military, their participation has been overshadowed by the accomplishments of the 100th Battalion 442nd Regimental Combat Team"; Tengan, *Native Men Remade,* 48.
116. John Simeona to the author, 30 August 1995.
117. John Simeona to the author, 3 September 1995.
118. John Simeona to the author, 30 July 1995.
119. John Simeona to the author, 29 May 1995.

120. For a strong comment on the dependence of Hawai`i on the American military, see Ferguson and Turnbull, "The Military."
121. http://prhome.defense.gov/MPP/ACCESSION percent20POLICY/PopRep2009, accessed 3 April 2011.
122. Tengan, *Native Men Remade,* 49.
123. John Simeona to the author, 3 September 1995.

4

Making a Way, Building a Family
Preserving ʻOhana in an American State

In the spring of 1946, John came back to a homeland in the process of righting itself and returning to stability after four years of severe disruption. The territory was reeling from clashing impacts: the return of thousands of residents who had been displaced by war and the departure of servicemen and civilian workers who populated a home front. Blackouts, curfews, and fingerprinting of residents had ended, and so had the construction of a wartime defense system that employed kānaka maoli alongside haole. The move toward stability linked Hawaiʻi more closely to the United States, its economy, its foreign policy, and, finally, the Cold War.

Returning veterans came "home" to a place whose landscape the war altered, toppling the memories each man had carried into a foxhole. John encountered a modernized American city in Honolulu and a homestead transformed by a natural catastrophe and an economic crisis. Neither place was the same as when he left, although the reasons for the transformation differed. In a decade of recovery and eventual prosperity, John began a journey toward settling down, with detours and false turns. He met his future wife, moved from job to job, married, raised a family, and gradually assumed the role of kupuna, head of an ʻohana.

His sister Eleanor also moved into adulthood in a post-war world marked by increasing Americanization. She went home from Honolulu to Keaukaha in the winter of 1946, and she stayed in the homestead for the rest of her life. That year, the United States signaled its plans for the territory by moving hearings on statehood from Washington, DC, to the islands. Although it would be another thirteen years before Hawaiʻi became a state, the distance to the mainland already diminished thanks to the replacement of troop by passenger ships, and of boats by airplanes. Workers crossed back and forth between the docks of California and the ports of Honolulu and Hilo. Union activists followed, persuading hundreds to join the ranks. Real estate developers flew in, predicting—and spearheading—a vast growth in tourism. Politicians arrived from the nation's capital, using statehood hearings to investigate the *loyalty* of businessmen, professionals, and union members.

In 1959, the US Senate finally approved statehood for the Pacific Island archipelago, Alaska having broken the barrier of non-contiguity and of a "non-American" population.[1] The change in status was less a radical shift than an inevitable end to hearing after hearing, sixty-three since 1919.[2] Presidential approval of the Statehood Admissions Act passed John and Eleanor by in the stories they told. For them statehood was a non-event, significant mainly for further tightening the federal threads around their daily lives. The American flag had flown over ʻIolani Palace for decades, guarding the bureaucratic offices of a US territory.

While congressional representatives visited Hawaiʻi to debate its future, John and Eleanor established the parameters of their future in an ʻohana intertwining *family* and *work*. Kinship and sustenance constitute the core themes in their lives after the war. The same poles support the structures through which the United States disciplines a native population. Settled, incorporated, granted statehood—Hawaiʻi's official status matters most in the impact on daily lives and domestic concerns. This chapter tells of the individual actions that make "intimacy" a key factor in eroding the hegemonic power of an imperial nation.[3] In building a family and sustaining an ʻohana, John and Eleanor acted politically, entering the domain of US–Hawaiʻi relations on the pathway of particular, personal decisions.

Commotions and Crews: Work in Post-War Hawaiʻi

After the flurry of welcome home parties in Honolulu, John flew to Hilo on "an Air National Guards plane."[4] In Keaukaha, John's mother and stepfather struggled to raise the two sisters he just met, "teenagers, but doing OK" he said, exaggerating their ages. Bitter quarrels with his stepfather and "mysterious" accidents at work on tsunami repair sent him back to Honolulu in the fall of 1946. His stay in Hilo had been brief and he returned to Honolulu to start "a new, whole life again."[5]

The population of Honolulu expanded from 180,000 in 1940 to approximately 217,000 on V-J Day, in August 1945.[6] After victory on the European and the Pacific fronts, the United States pulled defense-related industries out of Hawaiʻi, sharply shrinking the work opportunities for residents. By 1949, unemployment had risen to 17,500, compared with the 316 unemployment checks issued four years earlier.[7] In November of that year, Governor Ingram Stainback declared an unemployment emergency in the territory.[8] John escaped the worst of the post-war recession: after walking the streets in the fall of 1946, much as he had in the fall of 1941, he got a job driving a bus for Honolulu Rapid Transit. I was lucky, he told me, because "I had high seniority." His status as a US Army veteran did not hurt his employment prospects either. John was assigned one of the better bus routes, from Kapahulu, east of Waikīkī, through the developing tourist area, up to Liliha Street on the Western side of Honolulu. "It's beautiful driving," a fellow driver remembered the route, "You go down Kalākaua Avenue, see Royal Hawaiian [Hotel]. Beautiful shrubs in front Kalākaua Avenue."[9]

For John, the route had another importance: "I met my future wife." Rosario Kayomo Chu rode the bus to work every morning. She was one of thousands of workers at the Libby Pineapple Company, canning fruit to export from the territory. Still a bulwark for the territorial economy, pineapple plantations held on through the war. "By 1940, the 'king of fruits' accounted for plantings in 78,000 acres of land, and 35,000 Islanders were employed to grow, harvest, and seal the pineapple in tins."[10] Libby held hundreds of acres on Maui and on Moloka`i—part of the latter land leased from homesteaders in the "experiment" the Hawaiian Homes Commission instituted in 1921.[11] Soon after John met her, Rosario went to Moloka`i, "with all her Libby gang," to work in the fields, a refreshing break from a closed-in canning factory at the edge of Honolulu.[12] A few years later, Libby Pineapple lost its foothold in the American market and faced a steep decline in profits. Labor costs, high taxes, and cheaper pineapples from further-flung markets reduced the spread of Hawai`i's once-famed fruit. Libby gave up plantation land and fired workers. By then, Rosario had quit her job.

She had been a "hard worker," according to John, and a manager of other "ladies." His descriptions repeat the words he used about his mother Sarah Kealohapau`ole—tiny, energetic, and enterprising. Rosario, too, worked to support a family, an extended `ohana that included the two children she "took home" from their negligent father. The wages she earned contributed to survival in a setting where rationing and shortages limited the means of subsistence for an urban dweller. A mainstay of the family in just the way John described his mother, Rosario was dependent on an industry the United States promoted in its territory until the mid-1950s.

Pineapple also provided a living for residents of the outer islands during the war. Pushed out of regular work, not always welcomed in defense industries, men and women traveled to Honolulu to earn the wages an American economy provided. Eleanor joined the cannery workforce, traveling to Honolulu during the summers of 1945 and 1946 to help sustain the family in Keaukaha. She returned in the fall, to finish high school. In June 1946, she graduated from Hilo High School in a ceremony muted by the disaster of the April tsunami. At the end of that summer, Eleanor stayed in Honolulu, and she enrolled in courses at the University of Hawai`i.

In the fall of 1946, John and Eleanor shared a house with Auntie Flora, another relative on their mother's side. Eleanor rode the bus to the University in Mānoa, while John drove his route through Waikīkī, downtown Honolulu, and past the old internment camp at Sand Island. After four months, in mid-winter 1946 Eleanor went back to Keaukaha. She was pregnant with her first child, a daughter she gave to her mother to raise. "I came home and I stayed home," she told me in 1997, the start of a mo'olelo about her involvement in the homestead. Her education had been interrupted. Years later she urged her children and grandchildren to complete the college education she had had to forego, like many girls of her generation and generations after.[13]

Meanwhile, John quit his job at HRT. "There was too much commotion with the public and also with the company bosses."[14] Besides saying he was "frustrated" at the bus company, he does not elaborate in his various stories of work. But he could not have missed the signs of discontent among his fellow drivers. There had been a notable job action in the summer of 1946, when the drivers refused to take fares from passengers. Free rides for thousands of O'ahu residents substantially depleted bus company profits. Not a full-fledged strike, the action resulted in a victory for the drivers: better working conditions and the establishment of a new union, the Transit Workers Union of Hawai'i.

The "trick" John and other drivers practiced during the war—covering fare boxes—changed from a way of keeping extra coins dropped by careless malihini to resistance by an organized group. No longer a harmless trick, covering the fare boxes undermined the smooth running of a crucial institution in the territory. In the stories of work John did tell, he conveyed the importance of "harmonious" relations, the kind of work setting he attributed to a unit at war and before that to life on a Hawaiian homestead. He disliked the conflicts that split a "team" into opposing factions. And he was equally critical of the bosses who provoked splits among men through discrimination and unfair practices.[15] When tension between worker and boss intruded on getting the job done, John left.

He quit HRT, and he said good-bye to the "old timers" he knew from 1941. It did not take him long to find another job. Despite the downturn in the economy, construction moved on apace, and John found a job with the large and successful Dillingham Company. He had a certificate from the CCC and his discharge papers from the US Army to add to his qualifications—his ability to do "hard work" on a job site. Dillingham placed him, along with his fellow Hawaiians and part-Hawaiians, in semi-skilled positions, like heavy machine operator. This category included excavating and road grading, work John had done on runways at Bellows Airfield on Waimānalo Bay.

Dillingham was a sixty-year-old corporation, owned and managed by descendants of missionaries. The company was closely affiliated with the Big Five oligarchy, which effectively determined the politics and the economy of the territory for years.[16] A crying need for construction after the war increased the company's influence, and hundreds of men just out of the military joined its ranks. "Practically every road and building needs repair or complete reconstruction; the traffic and parking situation will need a wizard's wand," claimed a 1945 editorial in the popular *Paradise of the Pacific.*[17] Walter Dillingham was not a wizard, but he was an opportunistic and successful businessman. He placed his men on jobs all around the city and county of Honolulu. John worked at the University of Hawai`i quarry, on the roads that increasingly covered Honolulu with asphalt, and in residential and non-residential neighborhoods—"Manoa Chinese Graveyard's street curbing and the Woodlawn road curbings." He did not stay at Dillingham long. "I was assigned eleven laborers, all Filipinos, to work for me building sidewalks and parking lots. I knew what to do but the men under me were not trustworthy."[18]

In *Life Story,* he does not elaborate beyond that one sentence. The account in *Work History* is even shorter: "I worked many different companies." John's brief comment about the Filipinos recalls the bias that accompanied the manipulation of ethnic-based work groups on plantations.[19]

Or he may simply have been uncomfortable with men who resisted the orders he gave as foreman. In any case, his designation of an ethnic group as untrustworthy contrasts with contemporaneous accounts of near-perfect racial harmony in the territory.

A decade after John's experience at Dillingham, the sociologist Andrew Lind published a report on labor in post-war Hawai`i. He describes the breakdown of "ethnic divisions" and praises the demonstrable "racial equality and cultural tolerance" throughout the territory. "Actually the post-war decade (1947–57) has been distinguished chiefly by a further closing of the gap between the profession of racial equality and the actual practice," he concludes.[20] Thirty years later, in the mid-1980s, labor historian Edward Beechert reiterated Lind's conclusion. "On the job, unity was the prevailing order."[21]

The unity and equality scholars portrayed did not coincide with the experiences of workers like John in the post-war economy. Nor did every ethnic group enjoy the same possibilities of upward mobility.[22] For the Native Hawaiian and the Filipino worker, Lind's assertion of an end to discrimination rang false. His conclusions resonate more closely with the rhetoric of statehood hearings than with the actual conditions non-white workers in 1950s Hawai`i faced.

Veterans, however, had an advantage. The Big Five and its affiliates were hiring men returning from war. John moved from Dillingham to Theo. H. Davies, the smallest of the Big Five conglomerates. Involved primarily in wholesale and retail merchandising, Davies hired John as a "helper." John explains: "I assisted the driver, delivering merchandise and goods." This job did not last for long; he left because his boss "goofed off and got thrown into jail for misusing company funds."[23] *Commotion,* in his word, and competition and sometimes corruption marked the times, as residents took advantage of rapid economic and political transformations in the territory. When John left Davies, he moved almost immediately to yet another corporate entity in the Big Five oligarchy, Castle and Cooke Inc., with its many subdivisions, from pineapple plantations to transportation. He was again hired as a deliveryman. Big Five foremen and bosses applied the judgments of capability and of merit familiar from his days in the public schools of Hilo County. John's prospects were narrowing, the work was frustrating, and his tasks differed considerably from the "command" he had in Berlin. John quit Castle and Cooke after a few months and he joined the ranks of the nearly 20,000 unemployed persons in the territory. Still at Libby Pineapple, Rosario gave him money for lunch and for the bus.

Meanwhile his sisters and his mother flew back and forth between Hilo and Honolulu, visiting family and maintaining kin ties. They reported on the slow progress in repairing Hilo, the damaged houses in Keaukaha, and the ruined roadways between the homestead and downtown shops. John listened, and acting on a sense of duty, and perhaps the restlessness of being out of work, he decided to fly to the Big Island. He bought a ticket on a Trans-Pacific airplane, no longer needing to take the slow boat ride across 220 miles.[24] In Hilo, John contacted a familiar US institution. The United States Engineering Department (USED) was managing all post-tsunami reconstruction efforts and needed every able-bodied man who was available for work. John joined a crew. The chain of command led up to an elite unit of the American Army, as had been the case when John worked construction in wartime Honolulu. "USED was the contractor," John writes in his *Work History.* "They were hiring heavy equip. operators, also riggers. I gone to seek this job and they hired me. My pay was now $1.90 an hr." He joined the group that was building a new breakwater in Hilo Bay.

He had a better experience with USED in 1947 than he had in 1941. The work was hard, but the pay was good: $1.90 exceeded his bus driver wages and the money the Big Five companies offered. He had a good team: "The gang was wonderful and thoughtful." USED was a federal institution and unionization was illegal; stoppages and strikes did not interrupt construction. Each man, however, was responsible for his own safety and not all men were as familiar with the deep waters of the bay as John was. One of John's "buddies" was killed in an accident. "I kept on working until December of 1947, when one of my good friends got killed by a big boulder." John quit after that, and flew back to Honolulu. "I left with all my memories of my younger days and the things I had done, also of my friends with their families. Keaukaha was changing its face and so were the rest of the places in Hilo, Waiakea and all around the islands."[25]

"A Qualified *Atomic Energy* Worker"

John returned to Liliha Street and once again began searching for work in Honolulu. He tried odd jobs—either rejecting or failing to find a job doing the construction that continued to dominate the city's landscape. Selling was the worst, he wrote, and, discouraged, he applied for Army benefits. "I lived on my Army compensation 52/20. This meant I could collect $20.00 for 52 weeks."[26] The benefit was limited; the US military provided material support to veterans for only one year. John guarded against the inevitable end of the benefit by applying for positions all over. In *Work History,* he underlines the list of jobs he applied for: "*Police officer. Fireman. Garbage trashman. Zoo keeper. Board of Water Supply.*" And he waited.

He met with the person who administered the benefits, and one day in February, she made a suggestion. "I was told by my compensation worker that if I wanted to work right away to go to Pearl Harbor and check out the jobs being offered." He took her advice. On 1 March 1948, one week before his twenty-third birthday, John began work at the Pearl Harbor Naval Shipyard. The position had not been easily won: he describes going from one shop to another, hoping to get a "job I like best." In *Life Story,* he describes the outcome: "The only thing that happened to me was that I was hired as a riggers helper. I was tired of staying at home and doing nothing. I decided to hang on."[27] He hung on for the next thirty-eight years, rejecting positions outside the Yard and following the 5 AM to 5 PM schedule the Navy required.

John was one of 4500 workers at the Yard at the end of the decade, down from the 25,000 of the war years.[28] Defined as crucial to national defense, workers at Pearl Harbor were secure, well paid, and forbidden by federal law from striking. Hard and steady work marked the day. The military aspects of that work were not always evident to men who painted and reconditioned ships—climbing masts or sandblasting hulls. John's accounts of his work disconnect his daily activities from the US build-up of its Pacific outpost, which brought more ships into the yard and more work for the men. He does mention that he joined the Territorial National Guard at around the same time he started at Pearl Harbor, but he does not remark on the reason the Guard opened more positions to kānaka maoli. In that year, 1948, President Truman promoted enlistment in the face of the "critical nature of world affairs," and locals, including Hawaiians, joined in large numbers.[29] With the outbreak of the Korean War, recruitment intensified and preparation for fighting supplemented the civilian tasks the Guard performed. John threw himself into the Guard, and he dropped out of courses he had started to take at the Honolulu Police Academy.

Disciplinary positions, both civil and military, had historically been open to Native Hawaiian men under the American regime. "My grandfather Waipa

Kealohapau`ole ... was a dedicated police officer," John reminded readers of *Life Story*. In the second half of the twentieth century, the Army National Guard filled a comparable function, building a defense force while offering Native Hawaiians a means of gaining extra pay, learning skills, and being rewarded on merit. "I was assigned to be the first Sargeant." He quit one unit and joined another, one that required disciplining: "I brought this company up from scratch to be 100 percent strong."[30] At the same time, John moved up through the ranks at Pearl Harbor, and the rewards in his work setting occupy three full chapters of the story he wrote for his `ohana.

And it is this—the acknowledgment of his skills—that dominates his mo`olelo of working for Uncle Sam. Chapters XXI, XXII, and XXIII translate the specifics of a military endeavor into the learning and working knowledge he values. Like the earlier chapters on learning in Keaukaha, the paragraphs on Pearl Harbor have the list-like rhythm of one task after another—almost a chant of activities. "From the top deck we would remove and repair anchor windlass, ships stack, ships mast, ships work boats, ships quarter deck house equipment, remove dockings and repair same, remove rudder equipment"— and a long paragraph continues.[31] In the end, he received the reward of a high prestige job. "I worked on nuclear jobs that were very delicate. Each and everyone involved must be qualified to do this type of job. These jobs were done with strict verbal instructions."[32]

Training for this job demanded the "book learning" and the facility in English that had been forced upon him in Hilo's public schools. At Pearl Harbor, the benefits were concrete: culminating, he emphasizes, in the position of *"Nuclear or Atomic Energy Worker."* In the tapes he made for his children and grandchildren, he mentions another aspect of the job: "I had all my family scrutinized for being American citizens when they were born and that they were not Communists so that I could get my clearance from the American government to work in this kind of capacity." John's family members were citizens, and he had not joined a union. He was spared censure and dismissal, unlike union members, organizers, professionals, and university faculty who were subject to HUAC Hearings.[33] The promotion came through.

Ten years after he retired, he recalled a lifetime of work at the Naval Shipyard. He notes in *Work History*: "I do love working for Uncle Sam because I had lots of friends. Also the good cooperation they gave me and the trust they had for me." And he concludes with a point he made often: "The most thing I cherish is the learning and working knowledge that I have gain." As John described the yard, it differed from the other American work settings he had known. At Pearl Harbor, teamwork and solidarity moderated the racial biases, the competitiveness, and the selfishness he perceived elsewhere.

His accounts capture one aspect of American presence in the islands: the enormous opportunities for employment the military presence offered kānaka maoli, along with other islander men. John did not dwell on the role Pearl Harbor played in US imperialism, and the bargain made with a vulnerable monarch to exchange a perfect harbor for a favorable tariff on sugar.[34] In the 1950s, with the start of the Cold War, the United States expanded its facilities at Pearl Harbor and, as well, maintained a military post on the edge of Keaukaha, in the nearby airport. For eight years after the end of World War II, the American Army held on to Hilo Airport and residents like Eleanor and her family heard the roar of military aircraft every day. The lingering noise of war and the possession of space bordering the homestead were not much ameliorated when the United States gave the airfield a new name: Albert Kuali`i Brickwood Lyman Airport, in honor of the first US Army general with Hawaiian ancestry.

When she talked with me in the mid-1990s, Eleanor returned to these issues and brought them into the present by recounting her protests against proposed expansion of Hilo International Airport. Then she condemned the policy of eminent domain that permitted the United States further intrusion into lands that rightly belonged to Native Hawaiians. She told of the letters she wrote and the marches she joined. But she also described another burden, and the "true" focus of her activities in the immediate post-war decades. With a growing family, Eleanor took on the task of bringing a younger generation to adulthood in a Hawaiian homestead while acknowledging that the "future" lay with success in an American public school. Like her mother, she taught the chores that sustained and that respected the land. Like her mother, too, she impressed upon her children the importance of "English" and all that fluency in the language meant. If Sarah Kealohapau`ole was one model, the ideology diffusing through the United States supported the gender division of labor that Eleanor described. She stayed home with the children, while Albert Ahuna earned wages on a tugboat in the Hilo Harbor.

In Honolulu, John worked his twelve-hour shift and earned the money that sustained an ever-expanding household. References to *sharing* and to *providing* form a bright thread in the writings he gave me. "I was lucky for finding means of keeping my family supplied with food."[35] At home, he added to the mo`olelo, Rosario disciplined the children—and took them to the dentist, the doctor, whatever they needed. His hard work in an American institution and Rosario's responsibilities for domestic tasks reflected 1950s gender ideologies spreading across, and from, the mainland.[36]

"Our Kind of Living"

At first Rosario kept her job at Libby Pineapple, supplementing the wages John brought home from Pearl Harbor. The house on Liliha Street filled up with kin, with friends, and with children. Relatives from both sides of the family visited, some to stay for weeks and others to take up permanent residence. In *Life Story,* John describes the conflicts, angry words, and nasty gossip that disrupt life in an ʻohana—especially one crowded with individuals of different backgrounds, ideas, and demands. John and Rosario had two more children, bringing their small unit to six. Sometime after he got the Pearl Harbor job, he began to look for another house.

The chore turned out to be more difficult than finding a job. "Housing," noted the *Paradise of the Pacific* at war's end, "continues to be a dilemma."[37] More than a dilemma, Honolulu especially faced a severe housing crisis. Despite the departure of war workers, a growing population competed for scarce and often dilapidated space. Migrants from the outer islands, Japanese from internment camps on the mainland, and veterans returning from battle swelled the urban population. In 1950, the population of the city reached 250,000, far outstripping Hilo's 27,000. Fifty percent of the island population lived in Honolulu.[38] Hundreds of barracks stood empty on Oʻahu and the Hawaii Housing Authority, a territorial agency, turned to the US military to help solve the housing crisis. One of the largest areas was across the street from the Pearl Harbor Naval Shipyard.

During the 1930s, the US Navy appropriated 15,000 acres of land from a once-profitable sugar plantation.[39] The thousands of men who came in for practice runs and "war games" needed housing, and when war was declared, the Navy expanded the former plantation facilities. Throughout the four years of fighting, Navy men and their families lived in just-adequate barracks. An article in the December 1941 issue of *Paradise of the Pacific* described the compensatory comforts offered to men about to risk their lives. The "Pearl Harbor district" contains "twelve soft ball fields, four baseball fields, ten tennis courts, six hand ball courts … and four swimming pools" among other facilities for enlisted men; officers also had "one golf course of nine holes."[40] A small brochure put out by the Navy warned residents about life outside the barracks, including overcrowded schools, the cost of bus transportation, and the "dangerous temptations" on Hotel Street.[41]

After the war, a majority of Navy personnel went home to the mainland, leaving the barracks largely deserted. Under pressure from a territorial Housing Authority that was unable to manage the demand for living space in Honolulu, the Navy agreed to recondition the barracks for new residents. Navy carpenters put up cane-board walls, dividing dormitory spaces into bedrooms and living rooms for families. The high chain-link fence stayed, while the tennis courts and baseball fields disappeared. A small yard surrounded each distinct residence. John applied for housing in the place he called *Hālawa Veterans Home.* Veteran status, however, was only one criterion for acceptance into Hālawa housing. The list of criteria the Housing Authority used opened up the renovated spaces to those "in need" and "worthy."

In the same year John applied for Hālawa Housing, he put his name on the list of applicants for a plot in a Hawaiian Home Lands area. He gathered paperwork for both applications, proving his good standing in each case; in one instance he had to document his Hawaiian ancestry while in the other he had to pass a means test. John met the welfare qualifications for Hālawa, and he met the blood criterion in his application for a homestead plot. The only, and substantial, difference was the long wait he had in the latter case. He was immediately granted a place in Hālawa.

After a brief stay in veterans housing on Kapālama Heights overlooking the city, John and Rosario settled into the reconditioned barracks. Reminders of the war filled the landscape: tunnels ran from housing to the harbor, tempting playgrounds for the children; men in military uniforms left for work, along with the civilian residents; and, not far away lay the sunken *USS Arizona*, casualty of 7 December.[42] Inside the housing area, people of diverse ethnic backgrounds lived side by side, victims of economic depression in the immediate aftermath of war. As in any jerry-built housing structure, voices and cooking smells penetrated the flimsy walls and reminded an occupant of the difference between himself and his neighbors. Trouble brewed, not entirely smoothed over by a common work experience at the Navy shipyard.

John gives short shrift to Hālawa Housing in his writings and in his talk-stories. Resigned, he notes in *Life Story:* "it was the best that we could do for our kind of living."[43] Like other residents, he could not afford better housing, and in the late 1940s his designation as Native Hawaiian accorded him fewer advantages than his status as a US Army veteran. The *best* meant low-income housing, fenced in and on barren, unyielding soil.

Hālawa shared with Keaukaha an origin in a public program devised for citizens of the Territory of Hawai'i. But as John portrayed both living areas, federal implementation was the only similarity between the spaces allotted to petitioners. In his accounts, Hālawa represented all that was "bad" in crowding people together in stingy housing, without the "surroundings" that, as Eleanor said, "complete the person." The short references to Navy housing constitute a sharp and an intentional contrast to the features John attributed to Keaukaha and to Hawaiian homestead life in general. In Hālawa, John recalled, there was no harmony of interest, no sharing, and no respect for the 'āina. His neighbors, he said, not only selfishly guarded their possessions, but they also violated the rights of other people. "Halawa Housing was not a good place to live because people would steal whatever you had on your clothesline. They would also park their cars in your gardens."[44] In Keaukaha, he writes, "no one locked their doors or hid their belongings." There was "no stealing" in the homestead, and "goods" were exchanged among neighbors.

John's descriptions of Hālawa convey a breakdown in social relations. He was not alone in this interpretation. "We didn't have a community," remarked another former resident of Navy housing. "I mean, we were on our own, like."[45]

In retrospective accounts by John and others, Hālawa serves as a microcosm for a larger post-war collapse in rules for interaction among diverse ethnic groups. Such memories pose a critique of the harmony and integration US observers insisted was characteristic of the territory. The long, rectangular barracks and the six-foot-high chain-link fence did nothing to encourage attachment or shared interests—and the "surroundings" illustrated the blatant misuse of land US authorities had instituted for decades. Hawaiian construction companies were practiced in covering the ʻāina with concrete buildings and asphalt roads, and efficiently responded to the rapid population growth of Honolulu County in the 1950s.

Another former resident remembered the bleak setting of her childhood in Hālawa. When Bette Midler visited Honolulu on a singing tour in the 1970s, she described the decrepit barracks and neglected yards of her childhood home to a newspaper reporter. "There was no romance or Moon of Manakoora," she told him, referring to a popular song.[46] Like almost every mainland depiction of the islands, the song "Moon of Manakoora" evokes a South Seas paradise: "The moon of Manakoora filled the night / With magic Polynesian charms." As she implied, Hālawa held no charms for its residents. By the time Midler visited, the housing area had vanished, and a stadium and freeway interchange stood where the barracks once dominated the landscape.

In a post-war economy increasingly based on "selling" paradise to tourists, Hālawa Housing badly disturbed the picture. Tourist brochures featured palm trees, white sand beaches, and hula girls. Navy housing displayed abandoned cars, scrubby bushes, and laundry on clothes lines strung between barracks. The city and county stepped in and through the Honolulu Redevelopment Agency began to make plans for razing the housing area. A first step involved relocating the existing residents, and to do this the agency turned to newly constructed high-rise apartments, which, according to US practice, sufficed for low-income and *needy* families.[47] The HRA instituted a means test, and only those Hālawa residents with provable low-income status were offered the opportunity to move into the new buildings.

A stadium formed the centerpiece of the projected redevelopment. Slow to be constructed, Aloha Stadium boasts a seating capacity of 50,000, on innovative movable bleachers. According to the *Honolulu Star-Bulletin*, Aloha Stadium "displaced an open-air theater, piggery, saimin stand, cane field, watercress patch and stream," in addition to housing units. Repeating the persistent American narrative of progress, the columnist concludes: "Where one lifestyle is lost, another emerges."[48] The new lifestyle sustains essential American pastimes—sports, flea markets, and driving—and three six-lane freeways cover a space in which people coped with life in a dense urban environment.

The city government, its redevelopment agency, and John converged in their view of Hālawa as a decrepit public housing complex and not a "good place to live." The standards of judgment, however, differed. The county authorities considered the place an obstacle to progress while John complained about the lack of community and condemned the selfishness of his neighbors. His benchmark was a high one, and not all residents shared his comparison of Hālawa with a homestead community guided by aloha and the principle of mālama`āina. For residents who remained in Hālawa until the bulldozers came, the story of the place exemplified the victimization wrought by US government agencies. For those residents, the powerful Honolulu Redevelopment Agency exercised a right of eminent domain in order to pursue a modernization policy that left them marginalized.

A quarter of a century later, these residents took the story back into their own hands, through reunions and on the Internet. The 2002 reunion website, for instance, presents a mo`olelo that diverges from memories of and media reports on the unsightliness and disintegration of Hālawa. According to the website, "The Old Halawa Housing was a close community where families grew together and shared with each other, until the State stepped in and decided to build a freeway and a stadium. As a result, the families were forced to move to other areas. Generations have passed but in the true spirit of ohana, the families hold reunions so that they can reminisce about the good old days in Halawa."[49] Behind the text, a photographed sign announces: "*Halawa Housing `Ohana,* a gathering of kith and kin, neighbors and family."[50]

John did not attend reunions of Hālawa residents. And for twenty or so years he did not attend reunions at all; too much else was on his plate during the 1950s and 1960s. With six children, John and Rosario again found the "walls" closing in, with little compensation in the environment of Navy housing. Good fortune intervened, and a relative of Rosario offered them a small house in Mānoa. During the next two decades, John and Rosario maintained a family of fourteen children in an ethnically mixed suburban neighborhood. During the same two decades, Eleanor and Albert Ahuna raised nine children in a Hawaiian homestead, sharing the land in Keaukaha with Sarah Kealohapau`ole. The surroundings connected Eleanor to "ancient ways" in an Americanizing setting, while John found a bridge between past and present in the lush Mānoa Valley.

A "Land of Paradise"

"In 1952, the early part, I had a call from my wife and her oldest sister, that there was a small old house for rent in Manoa."[51] So John begins a new episode in his intertwined work and family histories. Rosario's kin owned the house, which had lost its tenants and fallen into disrepair. The offer came at an ideal time, just before the Honolulu Redevelopment Agency initiated its relocation plan. John and Rosario seized the chance to leave Hālawa and to avoid the option of accepting an apartment in a high-rise block. Obligations to kin and the responsibility of improving the "old house" were the only strings attached to the arrangement. John and Rosario accepted the terms.

Mānoa Valley is ten miles from Hālawa, on the other side of Honolulu. More than distance separates the two places. Mānoa is a tropically green valley, with fertile soil that once supported coffee and sugar plantations and then in the 1950s gave way to middle class homes. In 1907, the Territorial Legislature chose the valley for a new land grant college for agriculture and mechanical arts. By 1952, when John and Rosario arrived, the college had become the University of Hawai'i, its campus dominating the lower part of the valley. The family house lay behind the university, on land that slopes up toward the Ko'olau Range, the mountains that separate Honolulu from the Windward Coast. Heavy rainfall leaves morning mists in the valley, and often a rainbow—the symbol of the State of Hawai'i

John and Rosario set about rebuilding the house. "Every afternoon my wife and I would go up to Manoa and put in the floor, walls, windows, wired the house with the same electric wires, put the old toilets back and put the doors back in," he writes in *Life Story*.[52] Progress was slow: the Honolulu Street Directory of 1953 lists "Simeona, John I. emp USNS h425d," still in Hālawa. "A little at a time, we brought our things from Halawa to Manoa," John continues his mo'olelo. "Everybody thought that I was rich and living in a dignified house."[53]

John's neighbors did live in "dignified" houses. The population of Mānoa in the 1950s consisted of affluent families, including the Japanese-Americans who prospered after the war, the haole who dominated the university faculty, and Chinese with successful enterprises.[54] Scattered among white frame houses, with front patios and spreading lawns, were residues of plantation life. A few farms remained in the valley, and at its lower end a reconditioned US military barracks survived until 1959, to the distress of neighbors.[55] Redevelopment came about through the efforts of real estate agents and residents who claimed to be protecting the valley's "history and culture." Mānoa evolved into one of the most expensive neighborhoods in a high-cost state—a status it still holds. Today a church and the upscale Mānoa Marketplace occupy the land on which John and Rosario raised a family in the 1950s and 60s.

John did not simply repair the house. He added three full bedrooms and two bathrooms, patching and painting the outside walls. He planted a garden in the front, and he cleared the backyard for more plants. Rosario's kin, still the landlords, apparently raised no objections to the changes, a combination of family feeling and recognition of the improved market value. John was much less constrained in applying his building skills to the Mānoa house than were residents in a homestead area. There, as John later discovered, even a small change to a structure involved applications, paper work, and documentation acceptable to the DHHL. In Mānoa, John had more leeway to subterfuge building codes and zoning laws than he would later have as a leaseholder in the homestead of Waimānalo.

He was caught, however, between the traditional ʻohana-style living he valued and the nuclear family model that increasingly dominated life in the Americanizing archipelago. In 1952, his job at Pearl Harbor secure, John persuaded Rosario to quit her job at Libby—none too soon, inasmuch as the company faced a severe economic decline in the mid-1950s. She took on the task of raising children, a task she performed like a "sergeant," according to her sister-in-law Eleanor. She also ran the house the way Sarah Kealohapauʻole had, with an emphasis on practical tasks. In his tape for the ʻohana, John says: "each brother and sister had their own chores. The boys were all in the yard and the girls were all in the house." In *Family History,* he adds, "they are not afraid to work hard, on any kind assignment given to them." The children learned, as *Nānā I Ke Kumu* tells of custom, "that *hana* (work) was respected; laziness was shameful."[56]

Sarah visited, and so did the two sisters of Rosario, who lived next door. John continued to support the needs of a large ʻohana. All were welcome, regardless of material circumstances: "I told my wife's Aunty that we didn't have much, but just the same, for all of them to come up to our house." And they managed. "They put up a tent in my yard," John writes, adding a feature to the landscape that distinguished his space from the house-proud conventions of middle class American life.[57]

On the side of convention he, not Rosario, held the wage-earning job. He undertook the hour-long commute from home to workplace, and he bought a flimsy "second-hand 1940 Packard sedan" for the trip. "In the meantime, my car broke down and I couldn't afford to get another one, so I started to catch the bus to work everyday. I would get up early in the morning and walk the trail to catch the Manoa bus," eventually reaching the shipyard.[58] John uses the word *trail*, verbally linking Mānoa to his childhood in Keaukaha, although the streets of the valley were paved. His writings about Mānoa reveal the persistence of the homestead as a model for good living. He and Rosario had exercised one aspect of "ancient arts" in reconstructing the house. They worked together, gathering lumber, abandoned pipes, and floorboards from construction sites to make the shack livable. They exercised another in getting the children to work, weeding and cutting back underbrush. In the end, the family turned the small area surrounding the house into a flourishing farm.

John filled the front and back yards with flowers, plants, and herbs. Then he bought a flock of Rhode Island Red chickens. But one flock was not enough: "I began to raise more animals, like pigs, chickens, turkeys, rabbits, pigeons, and a cow." Now, from his perspective, "we are in a land of paradise." Whether or not his neighbors shared that perspective, they apparently did share the products: "We had lots of parties at our house because we were raising animals."[59] Besides distributing food, the parties may well have placated neighbors, forestalling the kind of complaints Mr. Ōʻili reported to me. "Some family's," John wrote, "were not working and some needed food, so I passed whatever I had down to them and continued to raise new animals."[60]

As they grew up, the children followed John and Rosario in doing tasks that nurtured the surroundings. Like his mother, John insisted that his children get up at dawn to complete their tasks before trudging off to the eight hours of school. And like the memories he shared with Eleanor, his children remember arriving in school, tired and out of sorts. They too suffered from the perceptions of teachers that they were "lazy" and "lacked ambition." But, according to John, they also talked about the farm, and the other children "would ask permission to come on a school excursion to see these live animals. This little farm of ours were a real treat to the Manoa school children." He invited the neighbors, too, spreading a lesson in sustenance along the streets of the valley. "Also the people in the community would come with their families to see the animals too."[61]

Nearly twenty years before the establishment of the Kaʻala Farm on the Waiʻanae Coast, John anticipated the lessons in "sustainable development and self-sufficiency" with which Eric Enos and his group counteract the spread of American capitalism and consumerism. The Waiʻanae project focuses on "indigenous youth" whose "affinity for the ʻāina … can be used constructively." The project has the explicit goal of developing an alternative, holistic economic model: "we are contributing to the continuation of Hawaiian culture through practicing and developing the Hawaiian work ethic and value system."[62] In two full chapters of *Life Story,* John too conveyed the importance of the Mānoa farm for transmitting a work ethic and a value system that would sustain his children through years of American schooling. Much later he wrote to me: "I sweat my backside to raise them right and give them all the education they needed."[63]

One afternoon on the Waiʻanae Coast, Father Gigi talked with me about the efforts to teach children, and their parents, the importance of a "cultural place" where "things are preserved." His words anticipate those of Auntie Eleanor, for, he told me, he also hoped to create a "peace center" where people could exchange ideas and customs.[64] The task started for him with the children in an elementary school. For Eleanor, the task began at home, with the nine children she and Albert were raising in Keaukaha.

I do not know whether she woke the children at dawn to do chores before they walked down the "trail" to Keaukaha Elementary School. I do know that she emphasized the importance of school, and the English that for her children and grandchildren would be the "future." In post-war Hawaiʻi, English may not have been the "hardest," as Auntie Etta put it. Harder, by the time Eleanor and Albert were parents, was sustaining the Hawaiian legends, crafts, and chants their own parents had been taught to forget. In her mo'olelo, Eleanor emphasized the lei making and lauhala weaving she taught, the hula lessons she encouraged, and, eventually, the enrollment in Hawaiian studies programs she urged upon her mo'opuna.

Her first obligation—the initial duty she had, she told me—was to the children in her household. "I need to consider my family … before I do anything that's going to take me away from them. First I'm a wife, then a mother, then my work." The "work" began when Auntie Edith Kanaka'ole encountered Eleanor in the small homestead store on Kalaniana'ole Avenue. That was in the 1970s, and the Hawaiian cultural renaissance had taken hold. Hearing the Hawaiian words Eleanor knew, Auntie Edith persuaded her to extend her teachings into the community. Thinking back to those years, Eleanor added, "Albert was the only one working." Her statement reveals the influence of American ideologies in which *work* meant wages; Albert was the only one earning money for the 'ohana.

Eleanor worked hard in those decades, teaching Hawaiian language in a culture education program sponsored by Hilo County. At home, she used the *'ōlelo makuahine* (mother tongue) sparingly. Her children grew up in an era when the English taught in school did not sound unfamiliar to parents, as had been the case for John and Eleanor in the 1930s. In my presence, Eleanor used Hawaiian words when she talked of Hawaiian values and customs, or when she told stories of the "ancestors" to a listening grandchild. Like John, she discouraged the pidgin into which the children and grandchildren lapsed. I once heard her rehearse a phone conversation with a granddaughter, parroting the courtesy greetings she (and the granddaughter) learned in a public school. Through her movement from one "tongue" to another, Eleanor offered her children and grandchildren entry into a setting in which Americanization could be dented by the "language that came first."

Her mo'olelo, like John's, testify to the "beach crossing" practiced by the generation that had been subject to heavy-handed Americanization. Forty years after her own schooling in English, Eleanor practiced the Hawaiian she, and her cohort, had been forbidden from speaking. And she insisted that her children practice the Standard English that leads to success in school, while she sprinkled talk-stories around the kitchen table with Hawaiian words whose nuances or kaona resist translation. But words were not enough, and Eleanor carried into the present the crafts she learned from her mother—the modes of subsistence that lie in the shadow of an American economic system.

In a Honolulu suburb, and not a homestead, John managed the "crossing" in diverse ways. He insisted that his children "clean yard" and nurture the animals he acquired, creating a farm that lay outside the surrounding culture of capital and markets. "Our family lived with togetherness," he wrote, several sentences after describing the most American job his children undertook. "As my children were growing older, we started to have newspaper routes." All the children were involved. Up at 4 AM, the girls and the boys carried the *Honolulu Star-Bulletin and Advertiser* through the streets of Mānoa. "We delivered the newspaper to half of Manoa Valley down to the University, to Punahou School and Nehoa Street for a long time. By doing this, we got ourselves a brand new 1958 Chevrolet station wagon. The newspaper route paid it off." He drove the car alongside the girls, while the "boys would ride their bikes" up and down the early morning streets.[65]

The years in Mānoa, he told me, were like being in "paradise." Although he connected the word to the "abundance" on his land, his anecdotes suggest that the word referred to wider aspects of life in Mānoa. He opened his house to kin and neighbors, and he distributed the "fruits" of his land throughout a community. He taught his children through the chores they were assigned, and he broke his backside so they could be well educated. Rosario, he remembered, sometimes objected to his lavish generosity, but he persisted. The American holiday of Thanksgiving gave him an opportunity to blend the two cultures he negotiated in those decades. "I put a dozen turkey in the ground oven or Hawaiian imu," he once told me. "Na ke kanaka mahi`ai ka imu ōnui: the well filled imu belongs to the man who tills the soil."[66]

As anecdotes in *Life Story, Family History,* and his conversations reveal, in Mānoa John enacted the values he learned in a homestead while he pursued the routes to success an American context prescribed. In those years, he developed the wisdom and the self-confidence that allowed him to achieve the position of kupuna in an expansive `ohana. Too, John accepted the criteria for promotion at a US Naval Shipyard, he punished his children for playing hooky, and he went to court to legitimize his kinship relations.

The Force of Custom, the Virtue of Law

In *Work History* and *Family History,* sent to me in one packet, John wove together the primary threads in his image of himself as American citizen and Hawaiian *kāne* (man). He does not give much attention in these pieces to the congressional hearings that culminated in statehood, and he ignores the public celebrations of that event. Nor does he discuss the Army–McCarthy investigations that tormented several of his neighbors in Mānoa and that brought the full force of anti-communism to the islands.[67] His selective account of the 1950s and 1960s does not mean there are no politics in John's life at the time. His insistence on maintaining Hawaiian values in his family is itself a political statement. Newspaper routes, Standard English, and suburban living did not turn John into a typical American family man. He moved into the role not of patriarch but of *kupuna.*

In his job at Pearl Harbor and in his insistence that his children "speak out" in the classrooms of a public school, John followed the norms of American culture. During these years of nurturing his `ohana, too, John learned the ropes of an American legal system, with its courts, judges, lawyers, and experts. He could produce the documents, the *pepa,* that showed he had fulfilled his civic duties. To an American observer, John fit the picture of "assimilated native." He had official discharge papers from the US Army, paychecks from the Navy Shipyard, as well as a marriage license and birth certificates for his children. In the photograph albums he showed me, he had pasted these documents next to snapshots of babies, teenagers, and adults.

John and Rosario applied for a marriage license in the spring of 1948. On 23 May, a judge in a courtroom in downtown Honolulu pronounced them "man and wife," and he handed them a written document testifying to the legality of their relationship. They celebrated in the best way they could. "We did not have the kind of money to have a big party for the family. All I had enough money for was to pay the judge and also for fare for our Taxi from the judges chambers to Wo Fat Chop Sui house on Hotel Street."[68] The event had an importance beyond legalizing an existing relationship between two adults. When John became Rosario's legal husband, he also assumed permanent and exclusive parenthood of her two children. With marriage, John writes in *Work History,* "our family began."

From then on, John and Rosario maneuvered their way through the tangle of laws through which authorities govern the lives of their subjects.[69] In deciding to use US law to regulate family matters, John and Rosario enter into the politics of American intervention in domestic relations. Their choices illustrate the ways in which interpretations of intimacy can limit the hegemonic power of empire.

One hundred and fifty years before John and Rosario applied for a license to marry a small band of American Congregational missionaries arrived in the islands. The stated goal of Christianizing and (thereby) civilizing the savages led to a journey with many detours and distractions. As the good men and women from New England regarded their neighbors, however, several blatant behaviors stood out as requiring swift and certain action. Perhaps most startling to these strait-laced missionaries was the looseness of family ties. Women and men seemed to drift from one to another, often acting on their affections in a public space; children wandered from household to household, avoiding discipline by changing places. There was no attempt to maintain permanent and reliable relationships between adults or between an adult and a child—or so it seemed to the group, thousands of miles from "proper" New England life.[70]

Not for the first or the last time, the well-intentioned outsiders began at home. As a supplement to church services on Sundays and lessons on the other days of the week, the missionaries preached key signs of civilization: a stable marriage, signaled by official documentation, and permanent parenthood, represented in clear commitment of adult to child. By 1840, a short twenty years after their arrival in the archipelago, haole advisors had gotten the ear of King Kamehameha III. Concerned about the fate of his nation and attentive to the rising power of Western nations, the king accepted the proposal of a new constitution for his people. The constitution created a polity "under God," and outlined the formal competencies of the government. The 1840 constitution does not discuss domestic relations, but almost immediately afterward statutes were introduced that did. One law required that marriage be contracted, legalized in court, and approved by a judge. Another law mandated that the transfer of a child from biological to social parent be approved in a courtroom and legitimized with *pepa*. Competing agendas, indigenous customs versus imperial legislation, implicated expressions of love and of caring from then on.

The passage of laws brought a new set of malihini to the islands. Lured by the tropical landscape and by the opportunity to contribute to a civilizing mission, lawyers arrived in the archipelago bearing a strict training in Anglo-American common law. Behind their desks and in a courtroom, many of these experts struggled to reconcile their training with the values articulated by people whose cases they heard. Lawyers and judges found themselves in a tangle of interpretations. Decision making was particularly knotty in the case of defining a legitimate parent-child relationship.

An 1841 statute stipulated that the transfer of a child to a social parent had to be recorded in writing before a judge. The terms of the arrangement were supposed to be unambiguous and mutual.[71] As a law of adoption, this came well before anything comparable existed on the US mainland (or in Great Britain) and in disputes judges had no legal precedents on which to draw.[72] Seven years after the adoption law passed, with the formalization of a judiciary system, experts sat ready to hear petitions for the legal transfer of parenthood. In the second half of the century, however, when an adult came to court claiming to be a "true" child, the claim had little to do with love and much to do with land.

The cases that came before the justices reflected a major change in another domain: the privatization of land. The Great Māhele of 1848 transformed the ʻāina into property, and *possession* invaded understandings of parenthood, family, and kinship.[73] Fungible, divisible, and transferable, land disturbed agreements between individuals, brought claims into court, and made ownership a dimension of social status.

Many petitioners did not have paper to prove the legitimacy of a relationship to a non-biological parent. Verbal testimony brought little clarification in the eyes of a court often dealing with the fate of large and valuable plots. Witnesses could refer to "custom," and to the tradition of giving a child to another adult to raise. Custom ensured a transfer of care and of love, not of property as defined by the Māhele. Law prescribed a contractual agreement between adults, but said nothing about inheritance. Judges waded into a morass of custom and law, finding guidance in neither.

The increasing number of cases produced puzzlement about the entailments of non-biological parenthood altogether. In the eyes of some judges, the easy "giving away" of children by Native Hawaiians appeared unnatural and irresponsible. In their judicial decisions, "natives" are "capricious" and "whimsical."[74] A conversation started by the missionaries continued in the courtrooms. The "easy passing around of children" marked a lack of civilization in indigenous people designated to be subjects of a benevolent US empire. The failure of a Native Hawaiian to designate the future of his property only confirmed the conclusion.

Not all judges were dismissive of kanaka maoli traditions. For those who condemned whimsy, there were others who attended scrupulously to custom. A person who appeared in court to legitimize her status as *true child* might refer to one of two customary arrangements: *hānai* or *ho'okama*. Judges worried over the difference between the two Hawaiian words, initially equating ho'okama with legal adoption. But the equation did not help, inasmuch as legal adoption remained ambiguous on the issue of inheritance. Only in 1905, under territorial status, did the law of adoption grant inheritance rights to an adopted child in instances of the non-testamentary death of a parent.[75]

By then the word *hānai* had replaced *ho'okama*, and hānai remains the concept that covers the customary transfer of a child.[76] For judges who looked sympathetically upon custom, the focus on property demanded a closer look at the intentions of an adult who accepted the "gift" of a child. The concept of hānai, with its connotations of concern, affection, and nurture pushed the discourse in a courtroom away from a property consideration and toward the realm of "best interests"—or the well-being of the child. And the turn to hānai set a precedent in Hawai'i's courtrooms for including expressions of love in the designation of rightful parent. Still, as I heard in the 1990s, the choice between legal adoption and the customary transfer of a child remains entangled in property rights, as well as representing a decision about care and concern.

When John and Rosario began a family in the late 1940s, their choices included legal adoption, hānai, and keeping a biological child. John and Rosario chose each of those routes, combining the resources of tradition with the opportunities offered by the laws of an American territory and state. John took advantage of his learning and knowledge to ensure the continuity of an 'ohana he had nurtured with care and with respect for the "ways of old." At the same time, each one of these intimate decisions reflected the pressures US governance put on the subjects of rule.

"We Knew How to Raise Children"

John and Rosario began their family in 1948 when John became the legal parent of her biological children. Over the next twenty years, they added to the family: four children were born to them, four were adopted in court, three were fostered, and one was adopted according to custom, a keiki hānai.

One afternoon as we sat in his garage talking-story, John interrupted to go into the house. He brought back an armful of photograph albums. These contained pictures of the children, and each one had an album of her or his own. A visual testimony to their lives, the albums also testified to his insistence that he "always treated them all the same." As we looked through the albums, then and on other afternoons, his claim seemed just: from snapshots of a toddler to pictures of a graduation, only the personnel and, occasionally, the costumes differed. Otherwise, the collection erased the distinctions the American government imposed, leaving a sense of *aloha* to underline the "togetherness" he described in *Life Story* and the "happyness" with which he concluded *Family History*.

Fourteen children grew up in the Simeona household, and many others stayed there for days or weeks at a time. "Rosario," John's sister Priscilla told me, "would have taken in any child." At first the family shared space with Rosario's parents, but two more children and constant visiting kin stretched both the physical space and the *pono* within that space. Ululani was born on 23 August 1948. Then: "We were still living at Liliha Street when we had our second child, a son who we named John Ione Simeona, Jr. I wanted to name him Isaac Alii-olani, but my mother-in-law scolded me."[77] Soon after that, the family of six moved to Hālawa Housing. There, John writes, "we had another child. A little girl who we named Starrlynn. Then in 1952 we had another son, who we called Lynnboy, so now I had a family of eight children along with my wife and myself. Now I had to work even harder, but I was still happy."[78] An anecdote intervenes in this part of John's narrative, with a plot that brings him into Honolulu Circuit Court.

The family of ten was living in Naval housing when "one day a rigger friend from the mainland" dropped his "two babies" off. "He left our house, that was Friday, after work. I was on sick leave at the time because I wasn't feeling well. He didn't come back until either Saturday, Sunday or Monday morning." The rigger actually did not come back at all. On Monday morning John and Rosario took the children with them to John's doctor, driving through the crowded streets of Waikīkī. John continues: we were riding down Kalākaua Avenue listening to the police radio broadcast. "I told my wife that something was wrong and they were calling my [license plate] number every five to ten minutes." They drove back to Hālawa. "When I turned into the driveway to my housing area, we saw policemen all over the place." The father had posted an alarm, claiming his children were missing. John and Rosario cooperated with the police and let the children go off with a social worker from Child Protective Services.[79] The social worker returned the two youngsters to their biological father.

The return did not work out, as John came to learn. "He would take the two children and leave them all over the place until the Child Service people jumped into the picture and put his two children into Foster Parents Homes." Eventually the children "came home" to the Simeona household. Five years later, the biological mother appeared on the doorstep requesting her children. John and Rosario refused. "She called us all kinds of names," John writes. Unable to resolve the conflict through talking the matter out, he again turned to a social worker at the territorial CPS agency. She suggested they apply to adopt the children. With their agreement, she took the case to court. A judge inquired into the capacities and the situations of the competing parents.

In the mid-1950s, individuals who chose to legalize a transaction in parenthood appeared in the First Circuit Court of Honolulu. Established in 1915, the Circuit Court replaced the Bureau of Conveyances, which had formalized deeds of adoption in the nineteenth century. In the case of a dispute, the judge had the Solomonic task of deciding on the *better* parent before approving a formal contract of transfer. John and Rosario premised their claim as parents on the care and nurture they had provided the two children for over seven years. The biological mother may have claimed a "natural" bond, but the judge had his own standards.

"The judge questioned her on the reason why she wanted the children now," John wrote in his chapter on the incident. Her answer—that she needed their help—contradicted twentieth-century principles in which the well-being of the child and not the needs of an adult determine the outcome. The judge gave the mother "a good tonguelashing" and terminated her rights as a parent. Her relation with the children ended *absolutely and permanently* by the terms of US law. The next step was to designate new parents, and the judge turned to the children before making a decision. "The judge requested to talk with the children. Anyway, the judge questioned them and he liked what they said, so the worker said that we could adopt the children. This we did immediately, and we changed their last name to my last name."[80] John and Rosario signed the papers that granted them exclusive and enduring parenthood. The case was closed, and a contract cemented an arrangement that had originated in compassion and in kōkua.

In the 1970s, John and Rosario once again went to court in downtown Honolulu to settle *hukihuki* (conflict) between themselves and a biological parent. The story of the two children in this case started with a family conference. John's cousin asked for a meeting, and described a problem he faced in his household. His fourteen-year-old daughter had two babies—one just over a year and the other newborn. Would John and Rosario take the children, he asked. John responded by saying he had to talk with the mother first. And so he did. She gave her consent. "You and Aunty take care of my children and adopt them whenever time you want," John recalls in his *Family History*. "I give you and Aunty my blessing and God bless you all."

Six years later she changed her mind, and asked to take the girl and the boy back. Inasmuch as the initial arrangement originated in a family conference, John may have considered a resolution through *ho`oponopono*, setting things right within a family setting.[81] He would have called a meeting, allowing everyone to speak out, hoping to achieve a solution through the expression of feelings. When he told me the story, twenty years later, he remembered mainly the necessity of leaving the private domain and going to court. He was unable, he said, to solve the conflict the young woman caused without the intervention of "outsiders." By then, too, he knew the ropes. He had consulted with child welfare workers in the first hukihuki with the rigger's wife, and the decision in that case reflected the standards experts set for good parenthood. A stable worker and a family man, John met those standards. He had paychecks to prove one aspect and baptism certificates to testify to the other aspect of his "fitness" as a father.[82] He also had a marriage license, and together he and Rosario better fit American criteria for preserving the well-being of a child than did a young, single mother. John pasted a newspaper article describing the adoption into the photograph album he kept for Carla and Joe. "Both carry my name now."

The second adoption occurred in Hawai`i Family Court. Established in 1965, this was the first court in the nation devoted entirely to the "best interests" of children. As John and Rosario discovered, a judge considered the well-being of a child through the qualities of the adults who were petitioning to be parents. In the mid-1960s, when they brought the case to court, experts in the state of Hawai`i followed the strictures laid down by the national Child Welfare League of America, and stability, both personal and financial, was a major concern. The judge in their case went further, asking the children to comment on the adults who competed for their placement. John does not mention the reaction of the biological mother to a termination of her rights. In a case I observed, a father asked repeatedly what the word *termination* meant and then cried out, "You mean I can never see my children again?"

In both cases, the meaning of *termination* was alien to customary interpretations of kinship. For John, termination was a non-issue. The cousin was a member of the extended `ohana. Given the fluidity of relationships, she would remain "kin" to the children he and Rosario adopted. Contact was always a possibility. Similarly, though with different consequences, the man in Family Court found the idea of termination antithetical to his interpretation of fatherhood. He did not have the options John and Rosario had, since his performance had already failed to meet US-imposed standards, and he lost the point he made in his courtroom protest.

One year after John and Rosario finalized the second adoption, a new chief justice was appointed to the Hawai`i Supreme Court. William Richardson, with a background that combined haole, Chinese, and Native Hawaiian ancestors, introduced custom more firmly into the courts of the state. As he stated, "We set about returning control of interpreting the law to those with deep roots in and profound love for Hawai`i."[83]

His statement advanced existing tendencies to acknowledge indigenous custom in US courtrooms. Yet, in the twentieth as in the nineteenth century, the implications of giving a child to another person challenged entrenched cultural notions of parenthood and in recent decades, of motherhood. In the nineteenth century, uncertainties about rights of inheritance led to examination of the entailments ascribed to non-biological parenthood. In the twentieth century, the "best interests of the child" principle had an analogous impact on judicial inquiries. Vague and often subjective, the principle emerged from the Progressive movement on the mainland, which replaced consideration of the adults with attention to the child.[84] In Hawai`i, hānai provided a model. Lawyers and judges could look to the terms of a customary transfer to "measure" expressions of love, concern, and commitment in the child's interests. A keiki hānai, *Nānā I Ke Kumu* tells readers, is "a child who is taken permanently to be reared, educated, and loved by someone other than natural parents."[85]

John and Rosario had been designated "fit" parents in the best interests of four children. Not only the stability of marriage and income, but also the demonstrable care and commitment they provided to a family of six children turned opinion in their favor. Not many years after the second adoption, another three children came into the Simeona family. In the early 1970s, John's sister Winona came by with her daughter and two sons. "In the meantime," John explains in *Family History*, "I took care of my niece and brother [actually two boys] which belong to my sister Winona who gone to the mainland and left those children with me. Now I got 13 children." The three adolescents stayed, to be raised by John and Rosario. "We had no education," he wrote in a letter, "but we knew how to raise children."[86]

"Perfectly Natural to Us"

When we looked through the big batch of photograph albums John told further stories, meandering over episodes in the `ohana he had nurtured for five decades. One afternoon John stopped to contemplate a baby picture pasted in toward the end of an album. This baby was "number 14."

"She was ours, from the Hospital to Home with us. We raise her up and everywhere we go she would be with us. She was our doll."[87] The child was Kapua, born in 1979, the daughter of John's son. John called her his *keiki hānai*. Not only did he do the duties of loving and raising the child, but he also fulfilled another criterion given in the sourcebook on Hawaiian custom, *Nānā I Ke Kumu*. The person who took the child "was traditionally a grandparent."[88] Kapua was the daughter of his son—the nephew he had fostered—and in his use of the word *hānai*, John emphasized the link to custom. He does not use the word for an earlier adaptation of custom. "My baby girl's name was Ululani and she was her Grandparents pride and joy," he writes in *Life Story*. He continues, in stores "she would pick up anything she wanted and her Grandfather would pay for it."[89] Yet the language—pride and joy—and the anecdote suggesting Ululani was spoiled both evoke accounts of hānai by Native Hawaiian scholars like Mary Kawena Pukui.

When Ululani was born, he and Rosario lived in the same house as her parents. Thirty years later, he and Rosario brought Kapua home from parents who lived on the other side of Oʻahu. Furthermore, the economic situation in the islands had changed, and John's son struggled to support the three children he already had. Secure in his Pearl Harbor job, John offered more resources than his son could. "We had more to give," John told me. Her parents "couldn't give this girl the needs and wants." At the same time, his moʻolelo embed the economic motivation in an account of loving, favoring, and treating Kapua as special. "She was our pet," John unabashedly acknowledged. In her conversations with women in a harsh urban environment, Karen Ito heard a similar blurring of "petting" with the provision of resources to a child. After describing the economic basis for a transfer, one woman concluded: "It is a Hawaiian tradition to have a favorite child, who is called a 'pet,' and people are said to pet certain children."[90]

The favored child, or *punahele,* is given particular foods and accorded unique privileges. Not "spoiled" in the American reading of the custom, the pet in the family acquired responsibilities, a burden. The keiki hānai was expected to carry on family genealogies, chants, and other knowledge. As Mary Kawena Pukui, herself a punahele, writes: "The grandparents went out of their way for the punahele. Teaching, teaching, teaching, all the time." There was no time for play, she adds.[91] This aspect of keiki hānai dropped out, and as far as I know Kapua did not acquire the burden of memorizing "all the family ʻaumaka [ancestors] by name." [92] John distributed the task of carrying on family knowledge equally over the fourteen children in his ʻohana—a version of his claim, "I treat them all the same." Three years after Kapua joined the family, he composed his *Life Story,* the document that transmitted Hawaiian ways to future generations. In his words, "I put all I know about my livelihood, my knowledge, my learning" and "I hope that my family will do the same for their families."[93]

A year later, in October 1983, Rosario died. Kapua was four years old, and she was devastated. John describes the event in his *Family History*: "She was crying, what are folks doing with my Mommy." After the funeral, Kapua's parents asked for her back. "I said yes. It was a sad day for me, I couldn't say anything." He told me he was afraid he could not care for the little girl on his own. A family gathering resolved the issue, and John avoided the hukihuki that had taken him to court in earlier instances.[94] Kapua went home to John's son and his wife across the island.

She did not stay there permanently. Kapua moved back and forth from the Leeward to the Windward Coast, from one father to another. John writes: "today Kapua came home." He summarizes his welcome in a phrase that links custom to the material considerations a social worker or judge might apply: "I provided what she needed." A climax to the story came in May 1995, when the sixteen-year-old Kapua ran away and no one could find her for several weeks. John called the cops, who located the teen-ager. "I told the cops that I want a hearing." A social worker from Child Protective Services judged John the *fit* parent and, in the best interests of the child, proposed that Kapua return to his home. The official placement with John left Kapua's status as keiki hānai in tact. As long as the custom of hānai guided the arrangement, the ties between John and his son were strengthened and not severed by the exchange. Kapua is my "own," John would say, and the child of my son.

"Hānai is a traditional practice that survived," the kanaka maoli historian Kanalu Young notes. "And it continues to survive today as a traditional solution to a persistent contemporary problem—the need to provide a child with *aloha*."[95] Young offers an interpretation of hānai that recognizes its function in a society in which Native Hawaiians are denied economic advantage and educational opportunity. From this point of view, hānai is a safety net, a way of marshalling, sharing, and extending resources. At the start of the twenty-first century, hānai remains a crucial way of providing a child with security in terms broadly encompassed by *aloha*.

From John's point of view, the incorporation of children into the ʻohana under different rubrics made little difference. "We had fourteen," he said at one point, "and eleven more who were involved with our children." His stories tell of raising the children equally, of providing the necessities, and above all, *educating* them into a world of two cultures. "I want all these children here to be educated because I don't want them to be illiterate," he recorded on tape.

Stories of his role as father blur the distinctions over which lawyers, judges, child protective workers, and scholars struggle. By the time John began his family, experts had accepted a convenient parsimony: *hoʻokama* dropped out of elite and common parlance, as did *luhi*, or temporary care.[96] Hānai persists, as Young points out, an assertion of custom and an assurance of the permanent care American norms require. Like John, Young describes a mode of incorporation in which *aloha* covers everything a child needs, from "things" to the security of belonging.

Hānai continues to play a part in strategies for dealing with economic difficulties, the pressures of federal and state rules, and contradictory notions of childrearing. Like Karen Ito, I met individuals who frankly described hānai as a way of handling various hardships, from a loss of income to a recalcitrant teenager.[97]

On a sunny afternoon in the early 1990s, I chatted for several hours with Vanessa. She told me about having given her infant daughter to her mother to raise. She explained why: "My mother needed another child in order to receive AFDC (Aid to Families with Dependent Children) money." Throughout the story, she referred to her daughter as a keiki hānai. Vanessa had no more thought of raising her daughter than of denying her own parenthood. The transfer constituted a way of gaining benefits from a federal program, and it worked because Vanessa and her mother shared an understanding of Hawaiian custom. In her conversation, the term *keiki hānai* called up tradition and adapted to contemporary circumstances the value a child had for her grandparent.

Elena told me another story of putting a traditional custom to use in an American state. We were sitting in a high-rise apartment in downtown Honolulu, and she explained how she got the space. It was "Section 8" housing, she said, and she had to meet the means test that qualified her for a government program. Under Section 8, the federal government pays a portion of rent to landlords for tenants deemed in need and worthy.[98] Elena satisfied the criteria by taking in her sister's child, so that she had more children than her income supported. Like Vanessa, she referred to the arrangement as hānai, the child as keiki hānai. References to customary notions of love and "special care" threaded through her story. Elena assumed that the administrators of Section 8 accepted her interpretation of the transfer.

A judge in Family Court supported Elena's assumption that some officials sympathized with the instrumental use of custom. In his chambers, the judge told me he attended to interpretations of hānai in his decisions about the best placement for a juvenile. When a delinquent stood before him, he continued, he might take advantage of hānai in order to find a "safe" home and to avoid the risks that came with "institutions." In those cases, he listened to the oral testimony of friend or kin, and did not ask for documents proving "parental fitness." A haole who had grown up in Hawai`i, the judge was familiar with the kind of stories Vanessa and Elena told me. "I let them exploit the system," he said to me, contrasting his opinions with those of some of his fellow justices. Like judges who preceded him in Hawaiian courtrooms, he appreciated that the entanglement of custom and of law allowed him to attend to the particular best interests of the individual who stood before him. In his role, he treated both custom and law as subject to interpretation—not a strict but a loose interpretation of practice and of "letter."

His approach extends a story that began in the 1840s, when judges who were sympathetic to kānaka maoli accepted oral testimony as proof of a committed parent-child relationship. Nor were those early judges any more hesitant to acknowledge the material dimensions of commitment. Hānai, like legal adoption, could provide the child with material resources. If in the nineteenth century reference to custom focused on the inheritance of property, in the twentieth century, hānai responded to the restrictions imposed by federal and state programs designed to benefit Native Hawaiians. The oscillation between law and custom opens a way of compensating for the marginalization and discrimination US policies enforce. When family is a site of imperial control, persistent acts that redefine kinship break down the uniform impact of hegemony. Moreover, as John, Rosario, Vanessa, and Elena demonstrate, taking control of "intimate relations" issues in a critical redistribution of material resources.

Vanessa and Elena, like John and Rosario, had arranged the transfer of a child outside a US courtroom, but within the boundaries of an American economic and political system. In the mo'olelo they shared with me, use of the term *hānai* played against the constraints that system imposes. For each one, the customary practice offered a response to an economic crisis while steering away from the accusation of welfare dependency ready at hand for officials and experts who did not share the viewpoint of the Family Court judge with whom I spoke.

In the last decades of the twentieth century, the practice of hānai became part of heated debates over Native Hawaiian identity. While the custom persisted, its relevance to contested entitlements, to the significance of blood quantum, and to "what kine Hawaiian" preoccupied legislators, experts, and persons around a kitchen table.[99] Behind these specific issues lay a divergence between treating hānai as a sign of *being Hawaiian* in an American state or regarding practice of the custom as an indication of allegiance to Hawaiian nationhood.

The autobiography of Queen Lili'uokalani provides a foundation for the significance of hānai in debates that continue in the twenty-first century. Banished from her throne by American military action, Queen Lili'uokalani wrote the history of Hawai'i through her own life.[100] She describes her childhood: "But I was destined to grow up away from the house of my parents. Immediately after my birth I was wrapped in the finest tapa cloth, and taken to the house of another chief, by whom I was adopted." She adds: "This was, and indeed is, in accordance with Hawaiian customs. It is not easy to explain its origin to those alien to our national life, but it seems perfectly natural to us."[101] In deeming the custom *natural,* she implies its endurance outside the economic and political institutions forced upon her people. Carried into the present, her story evokes a further split in interpretations of hānai. A member of the royal family, the transfer to another parent emphasized her sacred status and protected the privileges that were hers by birth.

A century later, in conversations I had, class and status influenced discussions of hānai. Far from the situation faced by John and his unemployed son, or Vanessa and Elena, a kupuna in a wealthy ʻohana echoed the words of Queen Liliʻuokalani: "Hānai is just natural and normal, no one talks about it." She told the story of raising the first child of her daughter, and the special privileges she granted the child. "Natural," she repeated, meaning a matter of culture. Her account emphasized the education, the privileges, and the honor accorded a keiki hānai—the child who was the *pet* and held in high esteem. The details she offered resonated as closely with the entry in *Nānā I Ke Kumu* as had John's anecdotes. In her ʻohana, however, the "naturalness" of acting Hawaiian had nothing to do with economic necessity.

Abraham Piianaia, director of the Hawaiian Studies Program at the University of Hawaiʻi, talked with me in the late 1980s. Recalling his childhood, he described himself as a "classic hānai." He was, he said, expected to be the "carrier of grandparental wisdom" and the "custodian of the family genealogy." Piianaia distinguished the "classic quality" of his upbringing from practices "today" that are often "the outcome of some unfortunate circumstances." These changes, he continued, resulted from the move away from subsistence to a wage-based economy, and the American ideology that condemned a mother who did not raise her own child. Once "natural," in his view, the practice of hānai had been fractured by the "loss of close living."[102]

His comments indicate that Piianaia does not any longer share the belief Queen Liliʻuokalani expressed one century earlier. Faced with the loss of her nation, the queen turned to custom to ensure the continuity of the Hawaiian people. Hānai, she wrote, produces a "community of interest and harmony," and this community symbolizes the endurance of kānaka maoli as a *people*. A century later, the community had further fractured, according to Abraham Piianaia, and hānai lost its original function. No longer a source of unity, the custom accentuated economic and political differences under an American regime.

John and Eleanor offer a different, more hopeful perspective. In their stories, the homesteads stand for the place of custom, where the interpretations of and actions premised on kinship survive. The suppression of Native Hawaiian modes of living in general and of childrearing in particular threaten the purported pono of hānai, but the ʻohana provides a bulwark against encroaching Americanization.

A plethora of uses as well as conflicting interpretations of "giving a child" expose the fault lines in a projected community of interests. John's stories display the range of possibilities, from the bitter struggles that took him to court to the ho'oponopono that determined Kapua's place in the family. He and Rosario took advantage of the "discipline" imposed on kanaka maoli families by a child welfare worker, a lawyer and judge, and, once or twice, the cops. Equally, they drew on the values all fourteen children learned at home, so that his son agreed to the transfer of a child to her grandparents.

Even the arrangement between John and his son got entangled in ideologies American-trained child welfare workers imposed. The death of Rosario prompted John to question his ability to care for the little girl on his own. He had acknowledged the "standards" of experts, and these did not include giving parenting responsibilities to older children. That had worked during the Mānoa years, when his first daughter took on parental duties. He writes in *Life Story*: "Ululani was the mother and father of our house. She saw that everything was done in the house right."[103] He may, too, have accepted the gender component in child welfare standards. There was, in effect, no mother in his household in 1983.

Growing attention to the significance of biological bonds between mother and child began to intrude into childrearing practices in Hawai'i, as elsewhere in the last two decades of the twentieth century. The emphasis on *natural* bonds had a particular impact on hānai, and on the role of the practice in the event of an unplanned pregnancy. This was the case for a woman I met in Wai'anae, whose conversation dwelt on the knots she encountered between "Hawaiian custom" and American values. Peaches worked for a social service agency, and her specialty was "children and family." She was well versed in the standards of parenthood authorized in an American state and enforced in her social work training. She was equally articulate about the conflict with Native Hawaiian interpretations of kinship. She described her own experience.

"I was pregnant at fifteen," she told me, and "I gave my baby to my mother to raise. I wanted to be a teenager." When we talked fifteen years after the event, she said that her coworkers in the agency were urging her to "get your son back." They insisted she should be the mother of "*my own child*." The arrangement could have been undone: no court papers documented the transfer. In Peaches's view, the boy was her mother's own, a true keiki hānai. "He calls her Mom," she said, the kinship term she herself used. The story wandered, as Peaches wondered out loud about a custom that contradicted the lessons in parenthood she applied in her job—and the pressures toward "natural motherhood" those lessons contained. The afternoon we talked, on the beach, Peaches struggled to hold on to an "ancient custom" in a world of US law, Americanized social work training, and advice from her non-Hawaiian colleagues. I do not know how she resolved her dilemma.

Half a century earlier, sixteen-year-old Eleanor gave her first daughter to her mother to raise. Lonna was, she assured me, keiki hānai, and she added, "I don't think I would have let her [mother] adopt her." There was, however, an adoption in the family.

In the 1970s, Eleanor and Albert went to court to adopt the first child of their third daughter. In her handwritten genealogy, on yellow-lined paper, Eleanor recorded: "Shanna Kealohapau`ole Ahuna" next to the name of her daughter Aloha. A tiny, barely legible arrow points to the parenthetical "(adopted by Albert and Eleanor)." The choice of legal adoption rather than hānai occurred when Shanna was still an infant. "We adopted her," Eleanor said in another conversation, "to give her security." The security extended to inheritance of the house and yard in Keaukaha. A commissioner for the Department of Hawaiian Home Lands, Eleanor knew well the tangle of rules about passing down a lease to property in a homestead. And she concluded that hānai was more vulnerable than legal adoption. An unwritten, oral agreement between adults did not hold much power compared with the law, especially when it came to disputes over possessions. "Property," as Eleanor said, compels a person to choose the virtue of law over the force of custom. She and Albert decided on the heir to their homestead plot, and they protected the decision by legitimizing their parenthood in an American court. Daughter of their daughter, Shanna met the requisite blood quantum.

People only go to court, Eleanor repeated, when there is an issue concerning land. In this she echoed the origins of the court cases that followed the Māhele in the mid-nineteenth century. She knew, too, the limitations of American law under the tighter restrictions imposed by the DHHL. In addition to the court paper testifying to an adoption, she and Albert gathered documents attesting to the Native Hawaiian ancestry Shanna acquired from her biological kin.[104] After Eleanor's death, Shanna stayed in the Keaukaha house with her children, and she hung family pictures on the living room walls. I looked at those pictures with her, and she pointed to one in particular: the whole family was gathered around Auntie Eleanor. Lonna stood in the group right next to Eleanor, the ninth child, first-born daughter, and keiki hānai.

Custom and Law, Collective Rights and Equal Rights

Like her brother, Eleanor went to court to legitimize a kinship relation in the terms set out by American statutes. And like her brother, she made the decision for pragmatic reasons—in her case, not to resolve a dispute with a biological parent but to acknowledge that a legal arrangement held more weight under the US regime, and in state agencies like the DHHL, than an oral agreement. A decade after she adopted Shanna, when she began her protests against DHHL policies, one of her strongest complaints involved the lack of recognition paid to the terms of legal adoption by the agency. DHHL policies, she wrote, contradict the letter of US law, which grants an adopted child full rights of inheritance.[105]

Eleanor and John do not describe their encounters with American law as compulsory or oppressive. Choosing the contract, the paper signed and sealed in a courtroom, served a particular purpose. In the case of a child, adoption gave her a status in the eyes of the state, confirmed—if not completely honored—by bureaucrats in state agencies. At the same time, hānai gave a child a place in the long continuity of Native Hawaiian tradition, assuring her full incorporation into an ʻohana. The distinction between adoption and hānai was instrumental, reflecting the changing economic and political circumstances under which Native Hawaiians negotiated life in an Americanized setting. In the domestic arena the distinction faded, as John's "I-treated-them-all-the-same" and the portraits in Eleanor's house showed. Affections and actions at home, like stories at a kitchen table, mark a movement against the hegemony of imperial control. Kinship perpetuates culture in the shadow of the law.

In order to "make a way" and "build a family," John and Eleanor alternated between law and custom, and thereby negotiated *being Hawaiian* in an American context. Over a century earlier, the men who made decisions in the courts and counsels of the kingdom similarly saw opportunity in the coexistence of law and custom, if not always with perfect clarity or comprehension. However, then as now, coexistence does not mean shared interpretation or equal implementation.

Moʻolelo about adoption and hānai comprise one thread in the increasingly complicated and contested relations between Native Hawaiian customs and rights and the US legal system. At home, hānai and adoption equally brought a child into the ʻohana. In the legal realm, the status of adopted and of hānai child differs dramatically. The difference does not have to do with original incorporation into the family, but with biological identification: what sets a child apart in John's family, and in many other Hawaiian families, is *blood quantum*. It does not matter in this context that biological identification as full or part Hawaiian, 50 percent or 25 percent blood, is used legally mainly for positive discrimination: granting a child access to schooling, for instance, or designating a successor to a homestead lease. In view of the longstanding categorical refusal of the Unite States to acknowledge collective rights, government and trust programs for Native Hawaiians remain bound by a biological identification of the "native subject." Consequently, these programs can never overcome the racism that has characterized the colonial regime for over two centuries.

In John's view, the style of upbringing he embraced and the values he taught assured the Native Hawaiian identity of his fourteen children. When he claimed "100 percent Hawaiian," he summarized a cultural calculation that had nothing to do with blood quantum. When he designated an heir to the homestead, however, he chose a child whose blood quantum could not be disputed by the

DHHL. Eleanor, too, validated the qualifications of her designated heir with papers that documented the race-based Hawaiian ancestry demanded by the state agency. In Eleanor's family, moreover, a second and a third generation have attended the Kamehameha Schools, meeting the academic requirements and the *proven* ancestry necessary for acceptance into the prestigious private school.

For John, Eleanor, and other members of the `ohana, race symbolizes a bureaucratic imposition, and an exploitative distortion of the meaning of genealogy through which individuals identify as "Hawaiian."[106] That race plays an even more important role in political debates in the post-Hawaiian renaissance era is due to vociferous arguments non-Hawaiians make. By alleging reverse discrimination and violation of the US constitution equal-protection clause, web activists, lawyers, and ideologues of conservative think tanks attack all programs that grant special rights to Native Hawaiians. Challenges in the courtrooms of the state and the nation to the Kamehameha Schools admissions policy are typical.

In the summer of 2003, a plaintiff filed a lawsuit that at first glance seems to refer to a clash between "Native blood and custom," as the *Honolulu Star-Bulletin* put it.[107] In that case, the mother of a boy, Brayden Mohica-Cummings, declared he was Hawaiian on the basis of her status as keiki hānai in a Native Hawaiian family. Kamehameha accepted him at first, but rescinded later when the mother could not produce documents that proved his Hawaiian ancestry. School officials did not question the equation of hānai with legal adoption. They argued, rather, that the boy failed to fulfill the crucial criterion of a longstanding policy: written documentation of a biological—blood—link to Hawaiian ancestors. The *Star-Bulletin* article concluded with a provocative statement: the hānai custom that defines Hawaiian culture does not define a person of Hawaiian identity.[108]

For the attorney, *Mohica-Cummings v. Kamehameha* was little more than a side show, settled when the Schools admitted the boy.[109] His actual goal of challenging the admissions policy became clear in a second lawsuit he filed at the same time. He took on the terms of a policy that stemmed from the original bequest made by Princess Bernice Pauahi Bishop. Under the bequest, the Schools have the sole and exclusive purpose of educating children of Hawaiian ancestry, determined by genealogy and not blood quantum. According to the attorney for the unidentified plaintiff, however, the policy violates federal law prohibiting racial discrimination in private contracts.

In its journey through the courts, *John Doe v. Kamehameha Schools* prompted various responses on the part of judges. Some argued that the Kamehameha Schools' admission policy was racially exclusionary, while others perceived the policy as a legitimate means of improving "the educational disadvantages suffered by Native Hawaiians and their marginalized status," in the words of the en banc panel of the 9th Circuit Court in 2006. The outcome of the 9th Circuit Court ruling upheld the admissions policy of the Kamehameha Schools, but the decision did not resolve the issue of legitimate Native Hawaiian rights. As John and Eleanor insisted, without referring to the lawsuits, those rights are not equivalent to minority rights that offer disadvantaged individuals compensation and relief.[110]

In her analysis of *John Doe v. Kamehameha Schools*, Trisha Kehaulani Watson argues that the whole conflict is not about minority rights. The case concerns the special rights of an indigenous people who were dispossessed and displaced by the United States. "Kamehameha Schools' admissions policy is not an affirmative action program—it is an exercise of beneficiaries' rights and cultural rights. Native Hawaiians have legal rights that are unique to Native Hawaiians."[111]

In 2008, joined by other lawyers the attorney in *Doe* appealed to the US Supreme Court, only to withdraw the case abruptly after the Kamehameha Schools paid $7 million dollars in settlement. The enormous amount distressed many Native Hawaiians and alumni of the Schools. "One march included more than ten thousand people, many wearing red shirts with the saying 'Kū I Ka Pono'—Justice for Hawaiians."[112] But for Kamehameha administrators, the 2000 *Rice v. Cayetano* decision in the Supreme Court loomed large in the background. In that case, the plaintiff, Harold Rice, won his bid to overthrow the "Hawaiian only" voting rule for trustees of the Office of Hawaiian Affairs.[113] In view of *Rice*, and a legal-political atmosphere in which all differences, even those between corporation and person, evaporate into "equal rights," the settlement may have been the most realistic strategy for the Kamehameha Schools. The consequence, however, is that all programs for Native Hawaiians remain under the threat of being labeled *racially discriminatory*.

What happened in the new millennium makes the perpetual ambiguity in American policy toward Native Hawaiians only more evident. Native Hawaiians were defined as different but not *alien,* and then integrated as American citizens without having the chance to define themselves as an indigenous people or a nation. Given the colonial situation, kānaka maoli have had to develop and defend their own interpretations by constantly fighting against, subverting, manipulating, or accommodating to the ambiguous policies offered by a supervisory federal government.

When John applied for a homestead lease and when he designated an heir, he had to adhere to laws that racialized his identity and that of his child.[114] In both cases, he had to collect the documents that traced biological relatedness back to a Native Hawaiian ancestor. When, however, he talked to me about bringing up fourteen (and more) children in a house in Mānoa, and the chores they learned in order to maintain a farm, he chose *custom* as the foundation for "100 percent" Hawaiian identity. His passages on Kapua in *Work History* and the letters he sent me reiterate the attachment to "ancient ways" that pervade his accounts of life in Mānoa, the living he called "paradise."

He echoes the description of hānai in *Nānā I Ke Kumu,* calling Kapua his pet and his doll, and mentioning that she was "always with us." But she was not the designated heir to his homestead plot in Waimānalo. He gave that legacy to his adopted daughter Carla. He left *all* his children another legacy, in *Life Story.* Written after he retired from Pearl Harbor and his work for Uncle Sam, the sixty-four-page document tells of *being Hawaiian* under the laws of the United States. By then head of the ʻohana, John transmitted his learning/knowledge on paper and in the English he encouraged his children to practice at home as well as in school. *Life Story* told his children how to maintain Hawaiian values even if denied a plot in a homestead or entry to a school for children of Hawaiian ancestry. Not naïve, his gesture recognizes the precariousness of American practices regarding land and property, and instead presents the stability of customs upon which an individual can draw in order to survive without depending on material wealth, accumulation, and consumerism.

Eleanor also transmitted the knowledge it was her duty to pass on. Through her writings, teaching, and meetings, she delineated the elements of Hawaiian culture with a special emphasis on language. In her case, she took her role of kupuna outside the household and into the institutional settings of a classroom, a commission meeting, and a district court. By the time I met her, Eleanor's talk of *raising* a younger generation referred to a broad swath of moʻopuna, keiki, and ʻōpio. She told stories of "boys" who were caught in the American judicial system, of restless youngsters to whom a Hawaiian Cultural Center offered opportunity, and of homestead neighbors lacking "knowledge" of homestead rules and American laws. She determinedly brought her brother under her wing, and in his last years he carried the wisdom and knowledge he had acquired beyond his doors to the *people* he designated as bearers of tradition—the elderlys I met at his Senior Citizens Club one day in 1989.

Notes

1. The House of Representatives had approved statehood for years; the Senate balked, fearing the disruption of American interests caused by a large, racially diverse population. See Lawrence H. Fuchs, *Hawaii Pono,* chapter 17; Roger Bell, *Last Among Equals.*
2. Rich Budnick, *Hawaii's Forgotten History,* 139.
3. See Ann Laura Stoler, "Tense and Tender Ties," 829–865. Adria L. Imada offers another interpretation of intimacy and empire: "A fantasy of reciprocal attachment, this 'imagined intimacy' made it impossible, indeed unimaginable, for Americans to part from their colony"; "Hawaiians on Tour," 114. In fact, it worked both ways, and an "imagined intimacy" gave John and Eleanor a mode of responding to the workings of empire.

4. John Simeona, *Life Story,* MS., 35 (in the author's possession).
5. Ibid., 37.
6. US. Census Bureau, *Census of Population,* Vol. II, 52-8, Tab.6, and 52-28, Tab.27.
7. Gwenfread Allen, *Hawaii's War Years,* 371. According to the US Office of Business Economics, Income of Hawaii, the number of unemployed in 1946 was 2132 and in 1949, 21,436; figures from Thomas Hitch, *Islands in Transition,* 176. Clearly the change after the war was vast.
8. Budnick, *Hawaii's Forgotten History,* 121.
9. Center for Oral History, *An Era of Change,* 1081.
10. Fuchs, *Hawaii Pono,* 388–389.
11. See Ulla Hasager, "Localizing the American Dream"; Edward Norbeck, *Pineapple Town.*
12. Simeona, *Life Story,* 38.
13. "Native Hawaiian girls have higher rates of teenage pregnancies"; S.K. Kanaʻiaupuni, N. Malone, and K. Ishiboshi, *Ka Huakaʻi,* 204.
14. Simeona, *Life Story,* 37.
15. John did not talk about the rise of unions in the 1940s or the importance of strikes to workers rights; see Lowell Chun-Hoon, "Labor."
16. Noel J. Kent, *Hawaii,* 72.
17. *Paradise of the Pacific* 57, no. 9 (1945), 27.
18. Simeona, *Life Story,* 37.
19. See Ron Takaki, *Pau Hana,* and the description throughout of plantation managers, some of whom established and exploited ethnic enclaves, others of whom saw ethnic groups as dangerous and subversive. See also Edward Norbeck, *Pineapple Town.*
20. Andrew W. Lind, "Trends," 1, 3.
21. Edward D. Beechert, *Working in Hawaii,* 170.
22. See Jonathan Y. Okamura, *Ethnicity and Inequality in Hawaiʻi.*
23. Simeona, *Life Story,* 37–38.
24. Founded in 1946, Trans-Pacific soon became the friendlier Aloha Airlines.
25. Simeona, *Life History,* 39.
26. In an effort to keep veterans off the bread lines, the US government instituted a companion act to the GI Bill—financial support to aid the reentry process for those who did not qualify for college courses. "The national veterans readjustment allowance, which paid $20 to unemployed veterans for a maximum of 52 weeks, went into effect in September 1944," and the number of checks continued to rise through 1948. Allen, *Hawaii's War Years,* 371.
27. Ibid.
28. http://www.phnsy.navy.mil, accessed 8 October 2010.
29. *Honolulu Star-Bulletin,* 23 March 1948, 23, C1.
30. Simeona, *Life Story,* 41.
31. Ibid., 47.
32. Ibid., 48.
33. "The first major congressional investigation took place in Honolulu in April 1950, when a total of sixty-six residents of the islands were called to testify before the House Un-American Activities Committee"; Fuchs, *Hawaii Pono,* 369.
34. In 1887, David Kalākaua ceded use rights to Pearl Harbor to the United States in exchange for lifting the tariff on sugar.
35. Simeona, *Life Story,* 44.
36. In "Re-membering Panalāʻau," Ty P. Kāwika Tengan describes the "production of masculinities"; 29. Simultaneously, and with a similar goal of disciplining an indigenous people, the United States engaged in the production of "femininities."

37. *Paradise of the Pacific* 57, no. 9 (1945), 27.
38. Robert C. Schmitt, *Demographic Statistics,* 116.
39. Budnick, *Hawaii's Forgotten History,* 113.
40. *Paradise of the Pacific* 55, no. 12 (1943), 103.
41. Beth Bailey and David Farber, *First Strange Place,* chapter 3.
42. In 1958, Dwight D. Eisenhower designated the *USS Arizona,* whose badly damaged hull lay visible in the harbor, a national memorial. In 1980, the US National Park Service took over, running one of the most popular tourist spots in Hawai`i.
43. Simeona, *Life Story,* 42.
44. Ibid.
45. Oral History Interview with Janet Matsumoto, Honolulu, O`ahu, 5 May 2005. Transcript at http://nisei.hawaii.edu/object/io_1156239437015.html, accessed 22 October 2009.
46. http://www.betteontheboads.com/boards/magazine-27.htm, accessed 22 October 2009.
47. "The first high-rise apartment building was the 12-story Rosalei, 445 Kaiolu Street at the Ala Wai Blvd., opened in 1955." Schmitt, "Some Construction," 101.
48. http://archives.starbulletin.com/2003/09/28/special/story8.html#jump2, accessed 12 September 2009.
49. http://www.aieahighalumni.com/Halawa percent20Reunion.htm, accessed 22 October 2009.
50. Ibid.
51. Simeona, *Life Story,* 44.
52. Ibid.
53. Ibid.
54. "Although 52 percent of the residents [sic] in the older subdivision tracts of the lower section of the valley are occupied by Caucasians, occupancy of the remaining residents here and in other parts of Manoa is diversified among racial groups"; Byron E. Emery, *Intensification of Settlement,* 78.
55. Mānoa war housing included: "501 duplex units, 50' apart, on 55' by 68' lots, consisting of 3740 square feet"—bigger than the spaces in Hālawa. The buildings were finally shut down in 1959. Mānoa Valley Residents, *Mānoa,* 141–142.
56. Mary Kawena Pukui, E. W. Haertig, and Catherine Lee, *Nānā I Ke Kumu* (II), 51.
57. Simeona, *Life Story,* 51.
58. Ibid., 45.
59. Ibid.
60. Ibid., 46.
61. Ibid.
62. "Welcome to the ahupua`a of Wai`anae," brochure in author's possession.
63. John Simeona to the author, 30 August 1995.
64. Interview with Father Gigi, 7 May 1990.
65. Simeona, *Life Story,* 55.
66. "Welcome to the ahupua`a of Wai`anae," brochure in author's possession.
67. See, among others, Fuchs, *Hawaii Pono,* chapter 15.
68. Simeona, *Life Story,* 40.
69. Sally Engle Merry writes, "In the end, ironically, the weapon of the weak is law"; "Law and Identity," 150.
70. In *Paths of Duty,* Patricia Grimshaw provides a thorough account of missionary response to Hawaiian natives.
71. Judith Schachter, "'A Relationship Endeared to the People,'" 215.

72. A Massachusetts law passed in 1855 is considered the first American adoption law. England did not pass a comparable law until 1926.
73. See Lilikalā Kameʻeleihiwa, *Native Land and Foreign Desires*.
74. In re Mellish, 3 Haw. 123. Schachter, "'A Relationship Endeared to the People,'" 211–231.
75. In the United States, domestic—or family—law is state based; inheritance rights of an adopted child vary from one jurisdiction to another.
76. See Alan Howard, et al., "Traditional and Modern Adoption," 21–51.
77. Simeona, *Life Story*, 41.
78. Ibid., 43.
79. Under a federal government mandate, all states have a child protective agency to handle abuse, neglect, and abandonment. The Territory of Hawaiʻi maintained a Child and Family Service agency; after 1959, the State of Hawaii Department of Human Services was established to oversee an array of child and family services. John refers to the agency that handles abuse, neglect, and abandonment.
80. Simeona, *Life History*, 49.
81. Hoʻoponopono is the "specific family conference in which relationships were 'set right' through prayer, discussion, confession, repentance, and mutual restitution and forgiveness"; Pukui, Haertig, and Lee, *Nānā I Ke Kumu* (I), 60. For a detailed account of the use of hoʻoponopono in the late twentieth century, see E. Victoria Shook, *Hoʻoponopono*.
82. All fourteen children were baptized in the Church of Latter-Day Saints.
83. Quoted in Melody Kapilialoha MacKenzie, *Tribute*, 6
84. See Schachter, *A Sealed and Secret Kinship*.
85. Pukui, Haertig, and Lee, *Nānā I Ke Kumu* (I), 49.
86. John Simeona to the author, 3 June 1995.
87. *Family History*. John does not mention Kapua in the 1982 *Life Story*.
88. Pukui, Haertig, and Lee, *Nānā I Ke Kumu* (I), 50.
89. Simeona, *Life Story*, 42.
90. Karen L. Ito, *Lady Friends*, 28.
91. Pukui, Haertig, and Lee, *Nānā I Ke Kumu* (II), 55.
92. Ibid.
93. Simeona, *Life Story*, 64.
94. See Shook, *Hoʻoponopono*.
95. G. Terry Kanulu Young, *Rethinking the Native Hawaiian Past*, 129.
96. See Howard, Heighton, Jordan, and Gallimore, "Traditional and Modern Adoption," 21–51.
97. Ito, *Lady Friends*, 12.
98. Section 8 of the US Housing Act of 1937 (amended in 1974) authorizes the payment of rental housing assistance to private landlords on behalf of low-income residents. The US Department of Housing and Urban Development manages the program.
99. J. Kēhaulani Kauanui, *Hawaiian Blood*, 1; Jonathan Osorio, "What Kine Hawaiian Are You?"
100. In 1896, three years after the US military facilitated the conquest of her throne, Liliʻuokalani was under arrest. A year later, her civil rights were restored under the US-controlled Republic of Hawaii.
101. Liliʻuokalani, *Hawaii's Story*, 4.
102. Interview with Abraham Piianaia, 4 September 1989.
103. Simeona, *Life Story*, 57. Ululani died of leukemia in 1964.
104. See Rona Tamiko Halualani, *In the Name of Hawaiians*, chapter 3.

105. That guarantee is provided only state by state.
106. See Kauanui, *Hawaiian Blood,* chapter 1.
107. http://starbulletin.com/2003/08/24/news/story5.html, accessed 1 September 2008.
108. Ibid. See also Judy Rohrer, *Haoles in Hawai`i,* 90.
109. "Strong Native Hawaiian opposition to the Mohica-Cummings lawsuit and the boy's acceptance by the trustees was evident in the more than 84,000 signatures collected by the Na Pua Ke Alii Pauahi (The Children of Princess Pauahi) organization"; Oka-mura, *Ethnicity and Inequality in Hawai`i,* 103.
110. See chapter 5.
111. Trisha Kehaulani Watson, "Civil Rights and Wrongs," 9.
112. Rohrer, *Haoles in Hawai`i,* 91.
113. See Rohrer, "'Got Race?' The Production of Haole and the Distortion of Indigeneity in the *Rice* Decision."
114. Halualani, *In the Name of Hawaiians,* chapter 3.

5

"Stand Fast and Continue"
Homestead Generations and the Future

In 1972, John and Rosario acquired a plot in a homestead area. They had waited for a quarter of a century for their land. A decade later, John retired from Pearl Harbor Naval Shipyard, and he turned his attention to new activities. In clubs, associations, and at meetings, he extended his experiences as kupuna to a wider circle of kindred outside the borders of an ʻohana. In that decade, too, John fully assumed the role of ranking senior in the ʻohana, the hānau mua, "accepted source of wisdom … and the custodian of family history."[1] Stretching his obligations, John joined his sister Eleanor in her quest to "improve" the lives of her "people." The two kūpuna shared moʻolelo, lessons in political action, and the means of transmitting knowledge to a younger generation.

The 1970s and the 1980s saw the fruition of a Hawaiian cultural renaissance. The embrace of culture by Native Hawaiians clashed with the reluctant (and often two-faced) responses of state and nation to demands for recognition and protection of that culture. Throughout these decades, Eleanor and John examined the meaning of "transmitting knowledge" in a variety of ways, including writing, organizing a constituency, and, above all, working to conserve the ʻāina—hard won and precariously assured to the Native Hawaiian people. An engagement with law and custom that at once transcended and remained intricately connected with building a family propelled changes in their interpretations of hānau mua, elder, and community leader.

Eleanor and John engaged in activities and in reflections against the background not only of the cultural renaissance but also of three federal administrations—those of Reagan, the senior Bush, and Bill Clinton, who "apologized" to the Hawaiian people—and for Eleanor, a fourth under George W. Bush. Each administration offered a distinct concept of "native" and of "indigenous rights," yet all upheld the significance of race in decisions made for a specified ethnic group within a nation-state. Eleanor and John assumed the burden of translating the speeches, the statutes, and the solutions proposed by public actors into resources for the kānaka maoli.

This chapter brings John and Eleanor to the last years of their lives and to the beginning of a new century. At the end of the nineteenth century, an armed force took over the independent nation of Hawai`i. A century later, demands for sovereignty and indigenous rights shift the balance from a policy of forced assimilation to a renaissance of cultural practices and Hawaiian nationhood. During this period, John and Eleanor redirected their activities. Their engagement with Hawaiian culture became more politicized, and they developed stringent tests for the worth of legislative decisions, court opinions, and presidential apologies. These official declarations must, the siblings asserted in writings and in talk, address the deprivations and disadvantages Native Hawaiians face in their daily lives: lack of jobs, restricted educational opportunities, and a sharp shortage of affordable housing. In applying the measure, John and Eleanor encircled a wide group of people, enhancing the meanings of `ohana, laulima, and mālama`āina. Hānau mua, ranking seniors, they also accepted the burden of passing on responsibilities to a new generation. Eleanor said: "Ku pa`a! Be steadfast in what you desire to do and stay together as Hawaiians and as citizens of Hawaii."[2]

Challenges to Sustaining Hawaiian Community

John looked back to Keaukaha when he envisioned the future of Hawai`i. In depicting the homestead along the lines of a traditional ahupua`a, he advocated not a return to the past but an extension of aloha, of sharing and sustaining, into the present—an era he called "modern times." Eleanor stayed in Keaukaha, and she envisioned a future that would redeem the original intentions of the 1921 Homes Commission Act. In her vision, this future was literally and figuratively built on the farm lots of Pana`ewa, the homestead area that for her demonstrated the failures of the act. Yet Keaukaha remained the touchstone for Eleanor as well as for John, the place of pono, and the template against which to cast proposals for sustaining a way of life.[3]

Keaukaha is a distinctive place not only in the memories of Eleanor and John. Even today Keaukaha represents "the Hawaiian place indeed" (Keaukaha nō e ka wahi), as the well-known singer Israel Kamakawiwo`ole put it. When it was designated as a homestead in the 1920s, with its settled population of kānaka maoli, Keaukaha already differed from other places. That difference became more pronounced over the subsequent decades.

In the 1930s, Keaukaha was one of seventeen districts, as Davianna Pōmaika`i McGregor writes, "on the fringes of Hawai`i's economic and social life."[4] The large majority of residents in the district were Native Hawaiians, who created a community of "close living" while working in the industries that supported Hilo's sugar plantations. In the homestead, in contrast to other places—like Waimānalo on Oʻahu—the "indigenous ecosystem" was sustained.[5] When the sugar industry lost its significance in the 1940s, the Hilo district became a "backwater," the position it would hold for the rest of the twentieth century. Hilo never became a prime tourist destination, and it never attracted large-scale industry. From 1930 to 1970, the Hilo district gained less than 7000 inhabitants.

Growth of the Keaukaha Homestead was also limited, not only by the decline of Hilo's role in the archipelago but also by encroachment on the acres allotted to the homestead. Just as the first 205 allotments filled up in the late 1920s, the territorial government exercised the principle of eminent domain and appropriated land that belonged to the trust. The land was deemed essential for the nearby airport, which expanded first under military control and then in the fifties as part of the network of airports for Hawaiʻi's developing tourist economy. In the end, the Hilo Airport occupies 650 acres, while the homestead comprises 295 acres. As a result, the allotments in the homestead became smaller and the number of leases increased only incrementally, from 239 in 1929 to 472 in 2009.

Small and on the fringes of Hawaiʻi's economy, Keaukaha kept its social cohesion and its sense of identity as a Native Hawaiian community. The residents were in a strong position to fight for their collective interests. Compared with other homesteads, the Keaukaha Association was especially "vigorous," according to a report on Hawaiian homesteads in 1964.[6]

When John moved to Waimānalo in 1972, he came to a quite different homestead. The second residential homestead in the territory would evolve in close, continuous, and conflictual relations with the "outsiders" who controlled the terms of its existence. Waimānalo was implicated in American imperialism in ways that Keaukaha was not.

A year after the founding of Keaukaha, the commissioners designated a homestead area on the Windward Coast of Oʻahu. A lush valley between the Koʻolau Mountains and the Pacific, Waimānalo had long been entangled in the relations between a kingdom and the representatives of an American regime. In 1848, then reigning King Kamehameha III claimed the valley as a portion of Crown Lands. Two years later, his resources depleted, the king leased 7000 acres to Thomas Cummins, an Englishman. Cummins signed a fifty-year lease, at $350 per year, and he "imported fine bulls and heifers from California and brought in Southdown Sheep around the Horn from Boston."[7] A decade later, his son inherited the lease. John Adams Cummins was linked to an American president by name and to Hawaiian royalty by birth—his mother was a distant relative of King Kamehameha I. Like his father, the younger Cummins used the land primarily for pasturage.

In 1876, King David Kalākaua negotiated a Reciprocity Treaty with the United States. Eleven years later, under the "bayonets" of haole elite, he renegotiated the treaty.[8] Under the new terms, Congress eliminated the tariff on sugar in exchange for acquiring Pu'uloa (Pearl Harbor) for the United States. Cummins soon realized the profit to be made from turning his rich land to sugar, and he planted 7000 acres in cane. The Waimānalo Sugar Plantation flourished through the overthrow of a queen and the incorporation of Hawai'i as an American territory. It flourished, too, despite Cummins' protest against the illegal Declaration of a Republic of Hawaii in 1894, and his (temporary) arrest. The company lasted through the Second World War, and closed in the economic downturn of 1947.[9]

Two decades earlier, when the Homes Commission selected Waimānalo for a residential homestead, the decision left Cummins' land—and his profits—intact. Like sugar cane lands all over the territory, his were exempted according to Section 203 of the Hawaiian Homes Commission Act. Cummins had not, however, been able to prevent the appropriation of land by the US government, owner of the *public* (no longer Crown) land he leased. In 1917, President Woodrow Wilson took 1500 acres for the Waimānalo Military Reservation, "nearly three miles of Oahu's finest beach."[10]

In 1925, the US government stepped in again, through the office of the Commissioner of Public Land in the territory. Needing revenue, the commissioner proposed to auction off beach lots in Waimānalo, land that was not used by Cummins or for small local farms. The highest bids for these lots came from residents of Honolulu, well-off city residents who could afford the price of desirable ocean front lots. Luxurious homes built on private property stretched along the bay, between road and water. On the other side of the road, under the shadow of the Ko'olau Mountains, the Homes Commission claimed land reserved for the Hawaiian people. In 1925, the commissioners offered eighty-eight leases to qualified Native Hawaiians. The acres reserved for homestead plots included: 1400 acres of "barren and steep mountain ranges unfit for human habitation"; 700 acres that are "waste and unproductive"; 372 acres that are "habitable" and "productive."[11]

Over the next seventy years, the territorial and the state governments added acres to the homestead—eighty acres here, twenty-eight acres there—and made plans for further transfers. The list for getting a plot in Waimānalo remains long, and applicants wait for decades to move in. The lengthy list makes for good media material, and the basis for human-interest stories. An article in the *Honolulu Advertiser* is typical: "Retired landscaper Edward Kaanehe is a patient man. He's been waiting since 1951 for a Hawaiian Home Lands lot in Waimanalo and at 66, after nearly 40 years, he's still confident he'll get one."[12]

Waimānalo is "choice," in the word Eleanor applied to Keaukaha. And like the homestead on the Big Island, Waimānalo survived through its close connection to the industries in an expanding American economy. Waimānalo homesteaders commute in and out of Honolulu, traveling the thirteen miles to shipyards, construction sites, and commercial enterprises. Travel had improved during the nineteenth century, thanks to the demands of the royal family and of wealthy residents of the beach lots. In 1862, the government approved an expansion of the "ancient steep and winding trail that served as a passage through the Koʻolau Mountains between Nuʻuanu Valley on the Honolulu side and the fertile windward side of Oʻahu."[13] In 1933, the territorial legislature supported improvement of the ocean route, naming the roadway *Kalanianaʻole* after the prince who brokered a homestead policy.

Then in the 1950s, the territory hired one of the most prominent urban planners in the United States, Harland Bartholomew, to draw up blueprints for the further development of the archipelago. The Honolulu branch of his company introduced the same plans for Hawaiʻi as they had in cities and counties all over the mainland.[14] According to Bartholomew, urban development depends on a transportation system linking suburban areas to central cities, and he proposed an elaborate freeway system for the islands. In this vein, too, he collaborated with the healthcare tycoon, Henry J. Kaiser, to construct a new suburb between Waimānalo and downtown Honolulu. Hawaiʻi-Kai attracted real estate investment, and high rise buildings now obscure the view of the Koʻolau Mountains.

Bartholomew and Associates delivered a comprehensive zoning plan for the whole territory, and the company drafted the Land Use Law passed by the state in 1961. The Hawaiʻi law is one of the earliest to reflect a dominant planning philosophy that is heavily imbued with ideas of modernization and regional planning. Among its regional plans, Bartholomew and Associates presented a vision for Waimānalo Valley. The plan proposed a form of development that left the agricultural lands of the valley in tact, but aimed to "expand urban facilities to accommodate the increasing population of the island ... and to alleviate the present unsanitary conditions within Waimanalo village."[15]

Native Hawaiians were of no consideration in the plans submitted to the state government. Harland Bartholomew made plans not only without the input of kānaka maoli living in the valley, but his vision also ignored the homestead area and its needs altogether. For this reason, it is no loss that the plans never materialized. The only impact of Bartholomew's plan was the building of new highways, on which the whole project of overcoming the "drabness" of the Waimānalo Valley through urban development was based in the first place.[16]

The improvement of roads linking Waimānalo to Honolulu had a major impact on the day-to-day lives of homestead residents. The trip around the coast or over the Pali Mountain pass became easier and commuting to work a smoother process. Reconstruction of the scenic coastal road also made it easier for tourists, visitors, and campers to reach Waimānalo, and heavy traffic now separates homestead residents from the beach. Eventually, too, fast food restaurants and a small shopping center appeared on the sides of Kalaniana`ole Highway.

Despite these environmental and commercial onslaughts, the Waimānalo Homestead remains "choice" for residents and for applicants. Dependent on an urban economy and not on farming, residents still embrace an image of the place that evokes the old ahupua`a of Waimānalo. In 1978, a local historian wrote in *The Nalo News:* "Waimanalo was a beautiful and peaceful Hawaiian settlement, heavily populated with hundreds of grass huts dotting the valley floor. It was green and lush, with forests of breadfruit trees, mountain apples, kukui, coconut trees, taro patches and sugar cane."[17] The article goes on to "treasure" the residue of old days, including the large polo grounds left by the Cummins family.

The Nalo News came out intermittently in the 1970s and early 1980s. Written by residents of the area, articles in the paper constitute a mo`olelo that appropriates and reinterprets the language in reports on the valley prepared by various state agencies. The masthead reads: "A community newsletter published by Waimanalo Council of Community Organizations," and the content testifies to a unified and "harmonious" community. The Native Hawaiian residents of a homestead are not distinguished from the rest of the population, although Hawaiian culture is accorded recognition in articles describing a canoe race or a King Kamehameha Day celebration. *The Nalo News* repeatedly calls attention to laulima, to working together, and to shared interests in the future of the land. The *Honolulu Star-Bulletin* and *Advertiser* eagerly took up these descriptions of solidarity and energy in the coastal community. An image publicized throughout the state, in its most popular newspapers, thus erased the distinctive history of the valley under US administration.

The Waimānalo Homestead also fell off the radar of the Department of Hawaiian Home Lands during the 1960s and 1970s. The DHHL staff paid little attention to homesteaders who apparently fulfilled the federal and state goal of creating a peaceful and assimilated indigenous people. Disregard came in the face of an increasingly long list of applicants for a place in the desirable location. The state agency dragged its feet about demanding acreage from the trust lands for new housing. Unlike other homesteads—particularly those on the parched Leeward Coast, Waimānalo seemed to require little to no attention.[18] Householders fit the picture US observers had painted in the 1920s: orderly, docile, and hardworking. Or so it conveniently seemed.

In 1979, a reporter at the *Honolulu Advertiser* introduced a new note into stories about Waimānalo. His article described a protest by residents of the valley against the proposal to build a new commercial airport in the area. The language offers a startling—and rare (at least in the media)—perspective: "Then the Hawaiians of Waimanalo, boxed in on three sides by progress, their backs to the Koolaus, found themselves threatened by assault from the air."[19] While the protest engaged residents from all parts of the valley, the reporter distinguishes the homestead area—and provides a critique of the proposed destruction of a way of life under the rubric of progress. "Boxed in" and subject to "assault," his words evoke the decades-long experience of Native Hawaiians in their homeland. This time around the state withdrew and discarded the airport plans.

The reporter captured a movement in the homestead itself. The Hawaiian cultural renaissance prompted not only the restoration of custom but also a pointed reiteration of issues directly relevant to the lives of kānaka maoli. In Waimānalo, John's friends and neighbors forced the homestead back on to the radar of the Department of Hawaiian Home Lands and demanded accountability on the part of DHHL staff. On 27 January 1983, during Eleanor's term as commissioner from the Big Island, the Home Lands Commissioners acknowledged that Waimānalo had been "mistreated." The minutes for that day record: "Over the years the Waimanalo area has received the least amount of planning, funding, and implementation of projects."[20] Three years later, the Department compensated for years of mistreatment by enlarging the land area occupied by Blanche Pope Elementary School, at the entry to the homestead. Still, more names remained on the list for a plot than there were plots to go around.

"The Whole Person is the Surroundings"

After twenty-five years, John's name reached the top of the list, and he received notice of an available plot. He accepted with alacrity, and he brought two daughters with him to choose the exact place. "They pick a nice place and I submitted my land area [to the DHHL]," he recalls in *Family History*. The choice fit into the DHHL category of "fully improved lots with new homes on them." He rejected the other possibilities: a fully improved vacant lot or a vacant lot with minimal improvements. "It was 1972 I move in my new home with no children and big 4 bedroom house," he continues in *Family History*. The two youngest children remained in Mānoa, to finish high school. Complete in the eyes of DHHL, the house did not suit John's vision of a home for an ʻohana. He shared his sister Eleanor's precept: "The whole person is the surroundings, the house and the yard."

John began with the yard. He built a fishpond near the front door and he filled it with golden carp. In the backyard, he planted new trees and cut back the thick kiawe weeds that spread from the ditch behind his lot. When I met him in 1989, he talked about his next home improvement plan. He intended to enclose a cement patio on the side of the house, and turn the area into a large parlor. First, he explained, he had to take his plans to DHHL for approval. And not just plans, but the contractor drawings, structural details, and proof of compliance the agency demanded. He had to bring papers testifying to his income and to his ability actually to make the improvements.[21] John gathered up the requisite documents and then, accompanied by a daughter, went to the downtown Honolulu offices of DHHL for a series of appointments with staff members. In the end, after an afternoon of interviews, his proposal won approval.

In talk-stories when I visited and in letters, he narrated a long tale of getting the deed done. He no longer had the freedom he experienced in Mānoa, when he and Rosario collected leftover lumber and discarded pipes to complete the "shack" they acquired from kin. Unlike some of his neighbors, John did not risk his place in the homestead by running his own wires or water pipes into the house. He acknowledged his responsibility as a leaseholder and he simultaneously enacted his role as head of an ʻohana. His first contractors were family members, cousins and uncles who worked for local construction companies. The decision, as he described it, was not a matter of money but rather of obligation and concern. In caring for his surroundings, John supplied sustenance to men whose economic lives were precarious. In turn, he expected his relatives to conduct business like any other construction firm.

At the end of 1992, he was ready to move forward. "I'm going to extend my patio, my bedroom, my roofing repair, and little minor things in the house," he wrote to me in December.[22] Four months later the contractors were ready to begin, but the weather was bad, rainy and wet. A year later he described an even bigger delay, with more ramifications than a rainstorm produced. "I didn't start on my house as yet because all those involved in my contractor [company] went on the strike. At the end of the strike those who was handling my paper and process work got layed off. No job for them. I guess they were down on the totem pole."[23] Still hopeful, he added, "But now there are new persons handling my contracting case, so I'll be having those people ready to go to work."[24]

In September 1994, the four walls were up. "My inside of the house is completed, with new rugs, all bedrooms and the parlor. When the rest of the house is completed, then they will carpet my patio floor. Then I will have a house warming for good luck."[25] He was waiting for the roof over the enclosed patio to be completed. He had hired a cousin to do the work, and the cousin passed the job on to another member of the ʻohana, an uncle. The uncle shirked his responsibilities. Not only did he fail to come to work, but he also kept asking for money in advance. John refused to pay: "if he spent it all and don't fix my house, I would have to finish with what the bank will give me as additional loan."[26] At the same time, John continued to fulfill his role as elder in the ʻohana and he passed the job on to yet another relative. "I thought giving the roofing job to my Grand Daughter's husband, to help him out. It turned out to be sour."

Sourness came once again from a demand for money in advance of work. "My Grand Daughter's husband wanted all his money up front, before he can do his job," John complained at the end of September. "I told him the law does not work that way."[27] John referred to laws imposed by the state in order to manage a family arrangement that had gone sour. He did not have to go to court, as he had in the adoption cases, since his granddaughter's husband simply quit. John hired yet another crew, this time with a clear contract for payment upon the completion of work. In his Armistice Day letter, in November 1994, he informed me: "my house is finally finished," and he added: "I believe that my house is well blessed and good luck for me that it is completed."[28] A year later he added: "There is so much space in my house now that I can house many family and friends."[29]

In contrast to his complicated entanglement with kin, John managed the thicket of American laws and bureaucratic regulations with ease. Not every homesteader negotiated the DHHL rules with equal aplomb; some made their improvements "unofficially," while others treated the process like a theater of the absurd. Humor was Gordon's way of responding to agency rules when he narrated the story of the reconstruction he did, a few blocks down from John's house.

Gordon intended to build a new house for his daughter on the plot he had given her when, in the mid-1990s, he moved to an extension of the homestead. He knew the ropes. He gathered the required papers, picked up his mother, and drove into downtown Honolulu. Together they went from one staff member to another, down the corridors of a typical administration building. "They insisted," he told me, "that I provide detailed specifications on a wall that was going to be torn down." He protested, called friends, and sent his mother to put more money into the parking meter. Finally, he prevailed, and with permission in hand (on paper), went out to the car—where he found a ticket on his windshield. His mother, it seemed, put money into the wrong meter. "We paid for someone else's time."

The DHHL *Residential Lessee Handbook* reminds homestead residents of the services the agency performs. These include examining construction plans and building permits for homesteaders who then have to apply to the county for final approval. DHHL staff members check that documents meet the regulations stipulated by county authorities. Phrasing the examination as a benefit, the DHHL ends up creating the kind of obstacle course Gordon described. He reserved much of his scorn for the interview by a DHHL staff member, who had little idea of the land that Gordon knew like the back of his hand.

John accepted the process without complaint and with the end in mind. Gordon tolerated the bureaucratic tedium by extracting humor from the situation: someone else had gotten a "free ride" while he sat in an office for hours. Eleanor expressed neither tolerance nor humor when she talked about the DHHL. She was highly critical of agency staff, who exacerbated the demands put on a leaseholder to produce "proofs." Not only did a petitioner have to gather hundreds of pages to prove his qualifications in the first place, but after "winning" a lease he also had to establish a weighty paper trail if he intended to improve his surroundings. The necessity of providing contractor specifications, financial documents, and building permits hampered the homesteader. "The funnel," said Eleanor, "grows narrow."

Eleanor was less troubled by the constraints on home improvement than by the failure of DHHL commissioners to act when the state used eminent domain to appropriate homestead land. She described staff passivity as yet another betrayal by the agency established to *kāko'o* and *kōkua* the people. Her eight years as commissioner taught her politics, and showed how strong the temptation was to compromise, to give in, and to forget the duties of leadership. When she retired she applied the lessons to DHHL administrators, who in her view were responsible for the fate of her people. In letters and talk-stories, she urged DHHL staff to honor their kuleana to "Hawaiians and citizens of Hawaii." She penetrated into the heart of the agency's two-pronged mission: to represent Native Hawaiians and to implement the terms of a congressional act.

A state agency, the DHHL inherited the enduring tangle over land policy in Hawai'i, exacerbated in the last decades of the twentieth century by close scrutiny of "race-based" programs on the one hand and by attention to Native Hawaiian rights on the other hand. DHHL is caught in a crossfire. Pressures from a state in need of revenue and from a federal government claiming land for "national security" bump up against calls for responsibility by homestead residents who stand in front of bulldozers, hold meetings, and work together to protect the resource Prince Kūhiō acquired after a decade of bringing his people's demands to Washington, DC.

"For Generations to Come"

DHHL brochures and websites explain, justify, and defend the rules staff members impose on petitioners and on lessees. From first to last, regulations limit the use of trust land by Native Hawaiians. Petitioners have to meet explicit requirements—first of all to prove a quantum of 50 percent or more Hawaiian blood, but also to be older than eighteen and to demonstrate financial stability. The applicant also must fulfill distinct standards of behavior: be frugal and delay gratification, the welcoming booklet *Lo'a Ka 'Āina Ho'opulapula* instructs. Once awarded a plot, the lessee must apply to the DHHL for permission to improve the land or to renovate the house.

Moreover, according to the rules, a leaseholder cannot dispose of a lease in any way she or he sees fit. Lessees like John and Eleanor could not simply designate an heir. Like every other occupant of homestead lands, they were confined to a narrow list of relatives in the choice of successor. Until 1986, the designated successor had to prove he or she could meet the same criterion as the original leaseholder: a blood quantum of at least 50 percent Hawaiian. This rule created a constant nuisance, and a blunt intrusion into private life; protests ultimately led to a relaxation of the rule. In 1986, spouses and children with at least 25 percent Hawaiian blood were acceptable as successors.[30] In 1997, the modification was extended to grandchildren and in 2005 to brothers and sisters.[31] But the complications and absurdities of the original strictures did not vanish.

A year before he died, John intervened in a problematic succession faced by a cousin. He described the problem in letters throughout the spring of 1995 and in conversations when I arrived in Waimānalo that summer. His cousin was dying of cancer and John worried about the fate of his widow. "#1 she is not a 50 percent Hawaiian to live on the land or in their house that they now [live in]. My cousin is a pure Hawaiian, married his wife, a pure Filipino and [she] has no say when he pass away. She could not understand what he is trying to do. His oldest son lives with my cousin and wife, #2 this son has 50 percent Hawaiian blood. His dad don't want him to handle this problem because he doesn't trust him to care for his wife." John's anecdote illustrates the ways in which internal domestic problems get entangled with DHHL rules. "His wife don't understand the rules and regulations of Hawaiian Homestead laws. This is where I come in to help comfort his family. I know the laws."[32]

In the situation of his cousin, the wife lacked the requisite blood quantum and the son who did meet the measure was, according to John, unreliable and untrustworthy. John proposed a solution: "So I told my cousin to have his second son to stay in the house and take care of their mother until she pass on. She would be in good hands. I hope that I did what is right." The second son, with the required 50 percent, demonstrated familial responsibility in John's eyes. "I hope all the talk I had with him and his wife was settled down," he wrote to me a month after he began the story.[33] He never told me the outcome.

John signed his name on the Home Lands waiting list in 1948, the year of his marriage to Rosario. I do not know whom he designated as a successor on his application or when he decided on the heir to the plot he acquired in Waimānalo twenty-four years later. At the time of applying he would have been instructed to appoint a successor to the application rights, and that person had to prove 50 percent blood. In the (obfuscating) words of the DHHL pamphlet, "As an applicant, you are encouraged to designate a qualified successor to succeed your application rights upon your death. This is done by completing a Designation of Successor to Application Rights for Homestead Lease form. It is important to give a copy of the Designation of Successor to your designated successor."[34] The choice he made then at least secured a place for a member of his `ohana on the long list of applicants. To achieve "continuity," DHHL urges all applicants to provide documentation not only of their own blood quantum but also that of the designated successor to application rights.

In *Loa`a Ka `Āina Ho`opulapula,* the DHHL offers a rationale for the many restrictions on homestead leases beyond the general 99-year limitation (or 199 years, in the case of an approved succession). The Hawaiian Home Lands program is designed to "provide sustenance for generations to come." While this might be interpreted as addressed to the leaseholder, the sentence actually justifies the DHHL policy of maintaining control over the disposal of plots: preserving the trust for the people and preventing loss through the transformation into family land.

After John was awarded a lease, he could name a new successor to the land—to the house and the yard. Once again, there were rules to follow. "The successor is your spouse, child*, grandchild, father or mother, widow or widower of a child, brother or sister, widow or widower of a brother or sister, or niece or nephew," as long as the individual can meet the blood quantum requirement. The asterisk expands the definition of *child*. "Child successor," as interpreted by the Office of the Attorney General for the State of Hawai`i, includes a legitimate, biological child and a legally adopted child—as long as that child can document Hawaiian ancestry. "If you are adopted," the pamphlet further instructs, "you must establish proof of your native Hawaiian ancestry through your biological parents, not your adoptive parents."[35]

The bureaucratic requirements did not pose a problem for John when he decided to designate his daughter Carla as heir to the Waimānalo plot. He was able to present documents testifying to her legal adoption. Nor did a problem arise over her Hawaiian ancestry: papers existed to prove her blood quantum.[36] If he had lacked the correct documents or if the adoption had been a conventional American one, with anonymity between the biological and social parent, the pamphlet also offered guidance. The last pages contain a list of agencies that can help an adopted person open records that are sealed by Hawai`i state law in order to trace her or his "blood" ancestry.

The restrictions listed in *Loa`a Ka `Āina Ho`opulapula* present a picture of a bureaucratic regime of clear rules and regulations, of accountability, and of responsibility to clients. In fact, the restrictions create a broad space of ambiguity and leave a great deal to administrative discretion. In cases like that of John's cousin, the person who qualifies by blood to inherit may disqualify him or herself by improper conduct. Within an `ohana, several members may claim to be qualified, disputing the right of the chosen heir either at family meetings or, ultimately, in a courtroom. And finally, legal adoption is not the only way in which a person becomes a "true" child in a family. For over a century, the status of keiki hānai has troubled both formal and informal rules of succession. *Loaʻa Ka ʻĀina Hoʻopulapula* uses "legitimate biological" and "legally adopted" to define *child successor*. A keiki hānai, adopted in a customary arrangement, does not satisfy the definition.

Eleanor argued that people choose legal adoption in order to make sure a child can inherit property. She was explaining why a Native Hawaiian might go to court rather than simply maintain the hānai arrangement long validated by custom. Her opinion came from years of experience on the Hawaiian Home Lands Commission, when disputes over homestead leases and leaseholder rights filled the meeting agendas. While most of these disputes involved the loss of Hawaiian land to a government institution asserting the principle of eminent domain, others directly addressed the right of a homestead resident to ensure the continuity of land within hisʻohana. When Eleanor left her position as commissioner, she turned her attention to the conditions under which a Native Hawaiian could preserve, care for, and bestow land on a chosen heir.

In her role as president of Hui Hoʻomau Keaukaha-Panaʻewa, she confronted the issue of inheritance directly. "Issue #4: THE SPOUSE SUCCESSORSHIP." She writes: "There should be a protection for the surviving spouse to protect his/her interest in the life interest invested in the homestead lease. This loss would otherwise lose his/her security of a home at a very vulnerable time and age." In one sense, this statement comes out of empathy and respect for elders who, like the wife of John's cousin, can be cast aside by the rigid imposition of DHHL rules. In another sense, the statement reflects Eleanor's ongoing protest against the blood quantum rules, which may result in the dismissal of a spouse as legitimate heir.

The issue regarding successorship is one of seven in a document she prepared in 1990. The opening statement tackles the blood quantum rule, and then Eleanor goes on to detail, issue by issue, the ways in which DHHL staff members betray the interests of the Hawaiian people and fail to protect the land for beneficiaries. In between Issue #4 and the closely related seventh issue, ADOPTION OF A PERSON, Eleanor takes the agency to task for bowing to "public use" (#5) and for ignoring the availability of sugar cane lands, no longer planted in cane (#6). Issue #7 points to the discrepancy between DHHL policies and "the law"—American law. "The law says that an adopted person does inherit all that his adoptive parents leave him—and the Commission says no. How very controversial—if the court cannot and will not impose the constitution at all times, then the court should not be involved with DHHL issues. This gives the beneficiaries great STRESS!!!"[37]

Adoption brings her critique closest to an exposure of the blunt discordance between the DHHL and state and federal laws. Issue #7 is itself tangled, caught in a tension between acknowledging the *legal* establishment of a child's identity through adoption and the *genealogical* verification of ancestry in Hawaiian tradition.[38] Inasmuch as a homestead lease can be construed as property, claims of legitimate status as child successor become more heated, recalling the dilemmas faced by nineteenth-century judges after the 1848 land division. Like a number of those opinions, DHHL rules regarding inheritance effect a conversion of ʻāina into individual property, despite the official emphasis on land as a collective source of sustenance for generations to come.

Instructions on successorship spell out an unintended consequence of Prince Kūhiō's negotiations: the disempowerment that results from denying a person the right to determine the fate of his property. The prince's compromise, to protect the land held in trust from the buying and selling that brutally devastated Native Hawaiian ʻāina, ended in depriving his people of leverage over the disposition of a valued resource. Implemented by agency bureaucrats, the rules tie the hands of those who receive land they are owed. The ensuing stress is palpable, and Eleanor looked to federal and state law for its reduction.

Legal changes initiated by the Hawaiʻi State Legislature and approved by the US Congress broadened the category of beneficiary. But those changes were not enough, in Eleanor's perspective. She continued to object not only to the rigidity of DHHL rules but also to the contradictions and confusions that further narrow the pool of potential recipients of a lease, either as original applicant or as designated successor. Her writings extract the most significant of the agency's betrayal of the people: a definition of *child successor* that ignores the custom of hānai, the imposition of a burden of proof that puts a surviving spouse at risk, and, overall, the demand for hundreds of pages of paperwork on the part of a lessee and a designated heir.[39]

State and congressional amendments regarding the transmission of leases only indirectly address the core problem to which Eleanor referred: how to balance the interpretation of land as collective property of the Hawaiian people with demands for the power of disposal by individual Native Hawaiians. Her 1990 document, with its seven "controversial" issues, accepts the rationale for a leaseholder policy. She does not argue that homestead land should be granted on a fee simple basis, which establishes private ownership. Eleanor recognized the very real risk of privatization: "Hawaiians have throughout our history lost our ʻāina to everybody who had the money to pay taxes and buy land at prices out of reach of Hawns—and it still goes on."[40] With that loss in mind, she considers the leaseholder policy crucial to the maintenance of ʻāina—property of the people—and argues for a change in the terms of a lease. When Governor Waiheʻe extended the period of a lease by 100 years when a homestead had been passed on to an approved successor, Eleanor expressed a measure of satisfaction. The lengthened term ensures continuity over generations and the perpetuation of a leasing policy ensures that land remain in trust, reserved for Native Hawaiians as a whole—except in cases where the government decrees the sale of land for commercial or multipurpose projects.

These decisions sparked Eleanor's wrath, and she condemned the DHHL for not intervening in the "stealing" of Native Hawaiian land by the government. From her point of view, the agency at once trapped applicants and residents in a chaos of bureaucratic rules and depleted the trust for all sorts of dubious ventures. Eleanor did not mince words in her criticism of the Department's surrender to claims by county, state, and federal authorities to the *productive* use of land. Up until the end of her life, she argued against the seizure of homestead land for endeavors deemed more valuable to the public, like an airport runway, a sewer line, or a new shipping company office. She protested on her feet as well as in her writings. And she urged the members of her hui to follow suit by constructing a community center on homestead land, thereby keeping the area in the hands of homesteaders. Her vision of the Peace Center, too, kept Pana`ewa-Keaukaha under Native Hawaiian care.

John and Eleanor tried to adhere to an interpretation of the `āina in their private interactions, as well as in public statements, protests, and plans. In 1996, they had to make a decision about the title on their mother's plot in Keaukaha. John apologized for not writing to me: "I know that I have not written to you this month because I did have lots of things to do in Hilo pertaining to my mothers old land in Keaukaha," he wrote in March. "The day you left, I've gone over to my sisters and now its all done. The new owner don't have to worry of anything because it is cleared by the Hawaiian Home Stead Dept [DHHL]."[41] John and Eleanor followed the rules set by DHHL in order to ensure the *righteous* preservation of "house and yard."

Their decision reflected a conviction that in the homesteads lay the source of a resilient Hawaiian culture. "I know the families and neighbors that we had known lived in a community of love. Everyone was close. They would gather for anything that needed to be done."[42] For John, Keaukaha was always the model for the future of his people. Eleanor similarly emphasized the importance of homesteads, but with a political cast: "it is still the DHHL and the Commissioners" through which the Native Hawaiians can achieve well-being.[43] For John and for Eleanor, the decision about the house and yard in Keaukaha was part of a broader effort to reconstitute the surroundings that perpetuate proper kanaka maoli living.

Beyond the Four Walls

On an afternoon in the summer of 1991, John told me that "some boys" had trashed the fishpond in his front yard. All that remained were the bodies of the carp he had nurtured and treasured. Later still he wrote in a letter that his dog had been "stolen" from the back yard. On yet another visit, I learned of the theft of the brand-new van his daughter parked in front of the house. In Keau-kaha, John remembered, "no one locked their doors. There was no stealing."

Reports of problems on the Hawaiian homesteads emerged in the 1960s, fueled by the perception of intensifying urban crime, dysfunctional families, and dilapidated neighborhoods on the mainland. Were the homesteads comparable to a ghetto, asked an observer in 1963?[44] A year later, in his State of the Union address, President Lyndon Johnson introduced his plan for the Great Society. He proposed a dual approach, a "war on poverty" and a "war on crime."

The federal programs showed mixed results in general, and they left the Native Hawaiian population largely unaffected. According to an analysis by Dana Tagaki four decades later, the "war" did not change the social ecology of poverty in Hawai`i, "which matches closely the geography in which native Hawaiians live."[45] Her inquiry reiterates the findings in a study funded by Congress in the early 1980s. The Native Hawaiian Study Commission presented a devastating report to the Senate Committee on Energy and Natural Resources and to the House of Representatives Committee on Interior and Insular Affairs.[46] Bleak and appalling, the Commission report demonstrates that Native Hawaiians have shorter life expectancy and higher infant mortality rates than other ethnic groups, high absenteeism and school dropout rates, higher unemployment rates—with 27 percent of the population below the poverty level—and the litany continues: "Native Hawaiian youth constitute the largest percent of juveniles arrested for several crime categories."[47]

The media spread news of the report. The picture Prince Kūhiō painted of a "dying race" had not substantially altered in six decades. Raw statistics on poverty, disease, and dysfunction confirmed the persistent marginalization of a people. The Commission report points to the emptiness of a political rhetoric of rights that glosses over actual conditions on the ground. Representatives to the 1978 State Constitutional Convention had drafted four new amendments designed to protect Hawaiian language, culture, sacred sites, and traditional modes of subsistence. While the amendments mark a response to the cultural renaissance, implementation does not address the problems publicized by the Commission.

From a kanaka maoli perspective, a restoration of cultural resources is crucial for moving Native Hawaiians out of dependency as welfare recipients and postcolonial subjects. But that is not enough. Kānaka maoli struggled in the 1980s not only for recognition of Hawaiian culture but also for distinct programs that address poverty, evictions, denial of educational opportunities, and lack of health care.

The reform of the federal welfare system under Bill Clinton in the 1990s did little to lower rates of poverty among Native Hawaiians. But the grassroots protests of the previous decades provided fresh impetus to efforts to mobilize

Native Hawaiians to defend their legitimate rights. Scholars at the University of Hawai`i joined the efforts, supplying further data to supplement (and sometimes contradict) government reports.

In 1987, the University Urban Planning Program sent a research group to Waimānalo, where 50 percent of the population was classified as Hawaiian in 1980 (55 percent in 1990).[48] The group gathered residents of the village, the beach lots, and the homestead together to discuss conditions in their area. The agenda listed topics on which the Commission report focused: education, employment, housing, and crime. The proposed solutions resemble those in the federally funded study: improving schools, providing job training, establishing recreation programs for teenagers, and building affordable housing. At the same time, the community plan places a burden on the people, counting on a form of activism that has a legacy in the past.[49] What is crucial, the authors of the study insist, is the capability and the resources of Native Hawaiians to act on their own, to "stand fast." "For many years to come there is the opportunity for Hawaiian community building, organization, enhancement and empowerment which should be concomitant with the land management aspect of getting the Hawaiian Land back."[50]

The shift from "receiving welfare" to "empowerment" has not substantially altered material conditions for kānaka maoli. In 2000, "The Hawaii State Department of Health found that 19.1 percent of Native Hawaiians were living in poverty."[51] Data collected over the next decade show continued economic marginalization. However, changes have occurred on another level. Over the last decades, more and more kānaka maoli participate in activities that lead to empowerment and self-determination—practicing traditional modes of subsistence, transmitting arts and skills, and teaching the Hawaiian language to a younger generation. And it is exactly this low-keyed path of grassroots activism, political in consequence if not in name, that John and Eleanor adopted as their interpretation of a Hawaiian renaissance.

The group of urban planners from the university selected John as one of the representative citizens of Waimānalo. "John Simeona—Waimanalo Senior Citizens Club" is listed as a "resource" on the back page of the report.[52] John was a kupuna, a respected elder in the community, and a member of several organizations, not just the Senior Citizens Club. "I'm still involved with all my Clubs, Seniors of Waimanalo, Alu Like, Hawaiian Homes Community Association, the Military Community Association, Neighborhood Board, Helping the Homeless people and church work," he wrote to me in 1991. He added, "I cannot sit and look at four walls."[53] Each club played a different part in his view of his responsibility and of the people for whom he bore a burden. In fact, he did not engage with all clubs equally, and his stories negotiate the relationship between the actions required of a kupuna and the behaviors expected from a community leader. As head of household, John mediated conflicts, taught a younger generation the Hawaiian values he learned as a boy, and sustained an incorporative `ohana. As a leader in his clubs, he attempted to mobilize others—the elderlys—into bringing their needs to the attention of state and federal officials.

In Keaukaha, Eleanor accepted the luhi her position as senior member of an `ohana required. When neighbors dropped in for lunch, she fed them generously and with equal generosity offered advice on problems—from designating a successor to correcting a rebellious mo`opuna. One afternoon, a young man joined us at lunch. Victor had come to garner Eleanor's support for his claim to the Hawaiian throne. He showed her his notebooks, with handwritten pages that traced his genealogy back to the Kamehameha line, and he asked her to "confer" with other kūpuna on the Big Island to support his bid. Eleanor was intrigued by Victor's claim, and she talked with him about the ancestry he had recorded. But, in the end, she declined the role he asked her to take as a kupuna whose wisdom the people honored. Not the restoration of a monarchy, in her view, but a collective, concerted program of action to tackle the deprivation and discrimination in the state would preserve the "life of the land." Eleanor took on the burden of leadership in organizing this effort.

She belonged to an association called Hui Makakilo, and she invited her brother John to join the group. In the early 1990s, the association had the primary goal of holding the Office of Hawaiian Affairs accountable for the revenues it received from lands held in trust for Native Hawaiians. John explained the name to me: Hui Makakilo means "ever watchful eyes."[54] Eleanor monitored the selection of the officers in the hui. John was president, she told me, and, "my cousin was vice president." She continued her mo`olelo: "They challenged OHA. They filed suit against OHA for using trust monies. And they sued OHA to look at the records. And the judge allowed them, because they were natives. They went everyday, dressed like missionaries in white shirts and suits. They read the records and they found that OHA had breached the trust. And I believe that." John's story of Hui Makakilo runs through the letters he wrote to me from 1989 until 1995. Like his sister, he concentrated on the case against OHA, sometimes giving me details of the process and sometimes excusing a tardy letter because of "the time I took with my association."

The Constitutional Convention of 1978 established the Office of Hawaiian Affairs to serve the interests of Native Hawaiians in the state. The list of agency responsibilities includes: "The betterment of the conditions of native Hawaiians as defined in the Hawaiian Homes Commission Act of 1921," to be accomplished through the "fair" distribution of funds garnered from leased *public* lands.[55] The agency prompted controversy from the beginning, and by the mid-1980s, the media, activists, and various associations criticized its structure, its policies, and its decisions.[56] Critics claimed that OHA trustees pocketed income that belonged to the people, leased lands without concern for

Native Hawaiian claims, and ignored the responsibility for well-being in the original mandate. Eleanor's assertion that the "people" were owed thousands of dollars in back rent was a thinly veiled condemnation of OHA.

Governor Benjamin Cayetano responded to the complaints Eleanor, with Hui Makakilo, was not alone in making. In June 1995, he signed a law to provide $600 million to settle land claims and he proposed the transfer of 16,000 acres of state land to the Home Lands Trust.[57] But demands for the return of land and the fair distribution of revenue rightly belonging to OHA continue. In April 2012: "After nearly 30 years of working towards an agreement with the Office of Hawaiian Affairs (OHA), Governor Neil Abercrombie today signed into law a measure that settles OHA's unresolved claims to income and proceeds from ceded lands. Senate Bill 2783 conveys contiguous and adjacent parcels in Kaka'ako Makai valued at $200 million to resolve this dispute."[58] And this will not be the end of the story. The legacy of Hui Makakilo, and other associations, lasts.

In the 1990s, I attended meetings of Hui Makakilo, held in the open garage of John's house in Waimānalo. At a typical meeting, the older generation gathered: Henrietta with her notebook; Uncle Billie with an oxygen tank; Auntie Mary—and a few younger cousins. (John's children did not participate.) Eleanor usually did not make the trip over from Hilo, and John took charge. The young cousins wandered off, smoking and chatting. The group covered a range of subjects, from state politics to comments on a cousin who had "again wasted money" on a new van. John held back from interfering, letting the talk proceed anecdotally and digressively. After one meeting, he said to me: "did you see how I kept them in order?" He also expressed his disappointment in the failure of the younger generation to take the burden of leadership he was giving them. "No one follows in my tracks."

"Be Active!" Eleanor instructed the 'ōpio through the high school student who interviewed her in 1975. "You have a hand in shaping the community."[59] John offered a similar message in the tapes he made for his 'ohana in 1994. Addressing "you folks," he told the children and grandchildren: "Now you can go ahead and see where we coming from. I feel that we got more to offer you now for you folks. Now you folks have to discuss this among yourselves."[60]

Enacting Custom, Displaying Culture

At the same time as John served as head of Hui Makakilo, he was also president of the Waimānalo Senior Citizens Club. These leadership roles, he said, kept him out of the house and hard at work.

The Waimānalo Seniors group belongs to a network of organizations that stretch across the state. The Department of Parks and Recreation established the clubs to serve the graying population, offering time and space for activities, performances, and discussion. An occasional visitor brought her or his expertise, and an anthropologist from the university invited me to accompany him to a meeting. The Waimānalo group met in a community center behind the village, in an open space close to the Ko`olau Range. The center served multiple purposes, and youngsters played baseball and soccer outside, on green fields, during the meetings. John treated the group like an extended `ohana, occasionally comparing the members to recalcitrant and restless children. He took charge there in several ways, not least by managing my incorporation, explaining my work, and telling his story into my tape recorder at the end of one meeting.

He was active, too, in another senior club. "I also belong to another club for Elderly Hawaiians to relive their old Hawaiian Culture as in the olden days with Hawaiiana, culture speaking, quilting, sewing pandana leaves or lau hala weaving, music, learning, and many others."[61] He called it a club, ignoring the fact that this group belongs to a social service agency that defines the purpose and sets the agenda for meetings. Alu Like, Inc., is an organization that originated in the "vision" of a group of social workers, scholars, and community leaders. The Hawaiian scholar Mary Kawena Pukui provided the name, Alu Like, which means *striving together*. Auntie Edith Kanaka`ole, the kupuna who encouraged Auntie Eleanor to teach Hawaiian language, gave the motto: "Let us work together, natives of Hawai`i (E alu like mai kākou, e nā `ōiwi o Hawai`i)."[62]

Alu Like receives funding through the 1974 Native Americans Programs Act (Title VIII of the 1964 Economic Opportunity Act).[63] But not directly: the congressional act designates a "governing" body to disperse funds, and in the case of Native Hawaiians the Office of Hawaiian Affairs fills the role. Alu Like applies to OHA, among other sources, to fund its programs, asserting its commitment to expanding its "service to Native Hawaiians" through the provision of job training, educational opportunities, and health and nutrition plans. And while OHA does not impose the 50 percent definition of Native Hawaiian for funding, Alu Like does restrict some of its programs to those with "Hawaiian ancestry."[64] Ke Ola Pono No Nā Kūpuna, the program for seniors that John joined, "is available to independent individuals of Native Hawaiian ancestry 60 years or older and their spouses. A birth certificate is required for proof of age and ethnicity."[65]

In 1989, soon after he met me, John wrote about losing weight through the Nutri System plan then popular on the mainland.[66] He lost "42 pounds," he reported, and was "picked out from the Honolulu State senior to portrait a Health Program for public commercial [TV] for only 60 second."[67] In the early 1990s, he enrolled in the "Hawaiian Culture and Diet program" supervised by Alu Like. "The mission of the Kumu Kahi Department is to advocate for and support Native Hawaiian elderly in enriching and enhancing their lives by preserving and restoring their health and well-being, sense of dignity, self-respect and cultural identity."[68] Concern with health crossed borders for John, and he wrote: "I'm reading medical history and diet food books because I love to follow up on new methods to help sickness."[69]

John refers to the Alu Like group as a club to which he belongs, diminishing the difference between a social service program and the Waimānalo Seniors. He blurs the distinction between the groups by stressing the generational criteria—the kūpuna both groups served. And he dwells on goals the two groups had in common: drawing from an older generation the knowledge and experience that contribute to the well-being of a younger generation. Moreover, in reflecting on the senior clubs, John minimizes the difference between the explicit political engagement of Hui Makakilo and the cultural activities his new clubs endorsed. Thinking back on the hui, he adds a piece to the court case against OHA he had frequently recounted. "We had people cover education, hospital, medical, housing, social service, welfare, legislature, environment."[70] For John, these activities were as political as litigation. In the senior citizens group and in Alu Like, he pursued a political agenda by finding ways to mobilize his fellow elderlys through the "performance" of traditional practices. He insisted on the significance of enacting custom for obtaining redress from state and federal programs.

John concentrated his efforts on restoring the confidence of his fellow seniors in the arts and skills an American imperial regime had suppressed. "Boy, I wish you could be there with me," he wrote about an Alu Like event. "Their show was fabulous, all the elderlys participating in hula, singing and playing instruments of different kind."[71] In another letter, he wrote: "Full house, lots of talents, music, ladies dancing and culture items which every one had made by hand and the showing it off to the public and it really was very beautiful."[72] That was the Waimānalo Seniors.

"Culture display" covers the activities of both groups in John's accounts. The details he provided, often in several pages, reveal the meaning he gave that phrase. Whether sponsored by Alu Like or by the Waimānalo Seniors, events engaged the elderlys in practicing arts their ancestors knew, from weaving to dancing to speaking with each other in Hawaiian—for those who had managed to retain the native language. At one event I attended, seniors acted out the story of the US takeover of Hawai`i, interpreting a moment in history their schoolbooks had obscured.[73] John attended these events mainly, as far as I could tell, in the role of advisor. In that role, he attempted to implement the connection between the two groups through collaborative events, shared activities, and mutual celebrations. I try, he said, "to bring them together." And he sometimes succeeded. "We had a bang up day. Lots of entertainment by both clubs and when it was over the other club [Alu Like] did not want to go home."[74]

John's commitment to unifying the two groups had several sources. One was a conviction, learned from his sister and practiced in their shared hui, that a collective presence would garner more attention, attract larger audiences, and influence the decisions made by state authorities. The other source was his interpretation of Hawaiian values, and the beneficial outcome of acting together and curbing individual ambition. His actions reiterated, too, the points made by the urban planners who met with the residents of Waimānalo and advised the group "to establish the type of collaboration which are [sic] appropriate with outside Hawaiian groups to mobilize needed resources."[75]

The advice given by academic advisors suited John, and he applied the notion of collaboration generously. In the spring of 1995, he persuaded the seniors to join with other groups in supporting a legislative bill to gain back acres. "I did a bang up job with the Elderlys last Saturday. We had hundreds of people attending the legislature, voting on a good bill, and they pass it, so I'm happy to search and find facts on the program for our Hawaiian people and non-Hawaiian people also."[76] He expressed satisfaction in his ability to mobilize neighbors, friends, and kin, and to expand headship of an ʻohana into a wider arena. "I'm number one in the Simeona Ohana," he claimed.[77] And he added: "I represent hundreds of people."

Over time, the collectivity broadened even further. In the process of concentrating on culture displays, John effectively circumvented the classification of "Hawaiian" by blood quantum or race imposed by US agencies. Partly, this was a result of membership: Waimānalo Senior Citizens Club included individuals living in all parts of the village—haole from mission families, newly settled Japanese, a few Puerto Ricans, along with the homesteaders who came with John. However, he set the same terms for his participation in Ke Ola Pono No Nā Kūpuna, with its membership criterion of "Hawaiian ancestry." As he narrated details of the displays to me, he made it clear that the performance of Hawaiian culture did not depend on an identity ascribed by a government agency, but was the choice of a participant—an acquired art.

Eleanor, too, stretched the meaning of *Hawaiian* when she condemned race-based policies, and especially the 50 percent rule, in her statements about implementation of the 1921 Act. Like John, she rejected the premise that Native Hawaiian identity could be defined by an externally prescribed blood quantum or by documented proof of "pure" ancestry. "Hawaiians are all colors of the rainbow," Eleanor wrote in her proposals for a Hawaiian Cultural Center. The center, she continued, will contribute to the "long awaited ability to determine and accomplish a real sense of self-sufficiency for ourselves."[78] Both Eleanor and John detached Native Hawaiian values from the bitter debates over nationhood raging in the state in the last decades of the twentieth century.

"The Party Did Not Continue, but the Plans are Still There"

"The Hui Aloha club, we dissolved that club," John recorded in the taped stories for his `ohana. In our conversations, Eleanor filled in the background of his brief reference. "We wanted to create the Aloha political party," she told me in 1997. "We were in the process of creating another political party in Hawai`i. We went to the Lieutenant Governor's office to get the forms"—for the required number of signatures—"but we never finished."[79]

Only after she left her position as Department of Hawaiian Home Lands commissioner did she directly confront the politics of an American state. Moreover, her entry into the political arena fit into an atmosphere of increasingly vocal movements for Hawaiian nationhood, sovereignty, and independence. Eleanor had spent the 1970s and 1980s engaged in reviving the `ōlelo makuahine (mother tongue), sustaining homestead lands, and passing down "traditions" to members of her `ohana. In the early 1990s, she translated these activities into an explicit rejoinder to decisions made by state and federal authorities.

In an American state, Eleanor recognized the significance of building an effective voting bloc. She envisioned the Aloha Party as a mechanism for pulling Native Hawaiians together as a constituency that would have a voice in the political arena. "A cousin suggested we call it the Aboriginal Party." No, she told him, "you would kill it. We need to welcome everyone. Give them a reason to leave the Republican and Democratic party." She prevailed, with the name that represented the "spirit" of Hawai`i. In contrast to vocal nationalists who identified self-government and sovereignty with a nation-state, she and John saw a source of empowerment in the exercise of the rights American citizens have. Neither sibling denied the importance of the United States, and resources that included education, economic opportunities, and the enfranchisement that had been accorded to Native Hawaiians in the nineteenth century. At the end of the twentieth century, voting rights were no longer circumscribed by property requirements, only by the reluctance of people to go to the polls. A new party, in Eleanor's view, could increase kānaka maoli voter participation.

John should be president, she told the gathering group. "My cousin," she remembered, wanted to be president, "but I told him, 'your life is not clean. Give it to brother [John], his personal life is above-board.'... He worked for the Federal Government and his life is good. They would have a hard time shooting him down." The cousin protested. "I told him, in politics you have to ask, am I vulnerable? Can they shoot me down?" Eleanor had learned politics, and she knew the dangers of "scandal" in the American political system. In the fall of 1990, John complained about the "mud slinging that hurts the Hawaiian candidates."[80] He maintained his integrity—and in the words Eleanor used, people *listened* to him because he spoke "with common sense." She chose him to lead the party, she said, because he had become "very visible."

Eleanor tried the route of party politics, leaning on the power of a voting bloc to achieve an end. But it was a brief attempt, soon relinquished in the face of failure to gain support and her strong intuition that politics on an American model threatens grassroots efforts to regain self-governance. In the end, the Aloha Party did not materialize. Both John and Eleanor had come to harbor doubts about a process that exhausts itself in maximizing votes instead of mobilizing individuals to act. Respecting their cultural roots, they advocated a traditional mode of gaining consensus through sharing stories and constructing a moʻolelo of Native Hawaiian concerns that did not depend on the political system of the United States. This perspective influenced their responses to the demands made by activists for sovereignty and an independent nation-state. Assuming the roles of kūpuna, John and Eleanor considered their activities in senior clubs and homestead hui the best way to participate in and influence the rapidly changing landscape of Hawaiian politics in the 1990s.

John maintained his commitment to his clubs, and to an approach to problems through talk, even when he grew impatient with the gossip and chatter of the elderlys. As a former land commissioner, Eleanor was less reluctant to operate in a political sphere and in the 1990s, she transferred her goals for the Aloha Party into the work she did as president of Hui Hoʻomau Keaukaha-Panaʻewa. The "party did not continue but the plans are still there," Eleanor explained to me, moving on to her new idea. "But I'm excited about these other plans, for a Peace Center." In her descriptions, the Peace Center transcended the entanglements of party politics and yet carried the significance of Hawaiian homesteads beyond the level of local concerns. Replacing the idea for a Hawaiian Cultural Center, the Peace Center left behind the emphasis on entrepreneurial activity, on participating in a tourist economy, and on offering the health and welfare benefits the state neglected to provide for Native Hawaiians. Her neighbors and kin had "stubbornly" refused to support a Hawaiian Cultural Center, and, like Father Gigi on the Waiʻanae Coast, Eleanor turned to the prospect of bringing Native Hawaiian values to a global arena. Yet the heart of her proposals—and John's activities—lay in the values Keaukaha represented.

Homestead associations, including Hui Hoʻomau Keaukaha-Panaʻewa, are informal and voluntary. On virtually every homestead, these associations have never had a formal administrative role, neither in the territory nor in the state. Eleanor and Albert established Hui Hoʻomau together, a fresh site of activity in Keaukaha, which possessed competing homestead associations.[81] In Waimānalo, the primary homestead association began in a similarly informal way. A decade after the first leases were accorded, the few families on homestead land got together and founded the Waimānalo Hawaiian Homes Association (WHHA) in 1938. Like Hui Hoʻomau, WHHA depends on the skills of leaders to act as mediators between diverging functions: to discuss and implement the policies of DHHL on the homestead, and to organize residents of the homestead as a community that can represent its interests to an array of state and federal agencies.

When I knew him, although he listed the Hawaiian Homes Community Association as one of his clubs, John did not attend meetings. The debates at the meetings I attended focused on Honolulu County zoning laws and on United States educational policy, and put aside the perpetual problems of long applicant lists, inadequate infrastructure, and irresponsible rulings by the DHHL. The proposals that emerged from WHHA meetings addressed state, city, and county policies that had to be implemented on Hawaiian homesteads. These bureaucratic approaches did not engage John, inasmuch as such solutions did not draw on the experiences—and the knowledge—his generation of kūpuna shared. At the same time, he appreciated the work a younger generation undertook in the homestead hui.

Eleanor stayed with Hui Ho'omau Keaukaha-Pana'ewa for nearly a decade. However dissatisfied she was with her neighbors—who did not invest in or agree to her proposals—the hui itself represented a communal effort, the collaboration among residents that potentially formed a power base. She expended her efforts as president of a homestead association, and in that role she declared the centrality of DHHL to the well-being of Native Hawaiians. At meetings, in conversations, and in writings, she insisted on the importance of enforcing accountability to the people by a staff appointed to serve the people. Throughout, she was adamant about the obligation of Hui Ho'omau to keep "watchful eyes" on the state agency.

In 1992, Eleanor pulled Hui Ho'omau out of the State Council of Hawaiian Homes Associations (SCHHA). In her letter of withdrawal, she accused SCHHA of demanding sovereignty and independence from the United States.[82] "The manner in which your self-governance chair addresses us in her report was *unacceptable*. If that was any indication of her manner of reigning as the Queen she set herself up to be in her Ohana O Hawaii Document, I want no part of that—and you indicated that Ohana O Hawaii's Sovereignty model was going to be SCHHA's also." The return to monarchy in the reference to a "Queen" further alienated Eleanor, beyond the implication of haughtiness. From her perspective, the goal of the homestead associations was to gain leverage by operating within the context of federal and state laws, not to reclaim the kingdom as a (fictitious) political sphere. She finished her letter of resignation in no uncertain terms. "You see, it is still the DHHL and the Commissioners in spite of and with whatever imperfections there are in the system—they are still the servants of the people."

What informs Eleanor's view of the relationship between homestead associations and the DHHL is her firm belief in accountability on both sides. On the one hand, the state agency owes responsibility to the people, a replication of the relation between ali'i and maka'āinana. On the other hand, the people have to assume responsibility by addressing the needs of the ʻāina to the state agency. And for Eleanor, especially in the face of the failure of the Aloha Party plan, this included the duty of kānaka maoli to exercise their voting rights collectively. The homestead associations can "get the voting mana for our beneficiaries and betterment," she writes. As she reveals elsewhere, she is referring to the opportunity homesteaders have to influence DHHL practices by electing good governors and legislators in the state. Because land commissioners are political appointees, a change in the state administration can bring about an overhaul of DHHL. "The Department of Hawaiian Home Lands is a blessing for its beneficiaries," she wrote after she left the department. "However, it does pose to be a troublesome, unfair and controversial pain to some beneficiaries. Herein lies a truth of life for all beneficiaries. But like everyone else, we enjoy the freedom and the restrictions of the same laws of the land." [83]

Eleanor did not object to the existence of DHHL or deny its value to the Hawaiian people. She criticized the Byzantine rules and regulations, and she condemned staff members for further narrowing the "funnel" by a rigid implementation. The rightful beneficiaries suffer, she wrote, first under the restriction of *Hawaiian* to those with "pure" ancestry and a Hawaiian surname and then under restrictions on disposal of a lease. She saved especially severe denunciation for the principle of eminent domain, and the DHHL failure to keep trust lands out of the grasp of outsiders—real estate developers and the military in particular.

Essentially, her brief against DHHL held that presumed beneficiaries are betrayed by bureaucrats who see themselves not as advocates of the Hawaiian people but as enforcers of federal laws and state regulations. "There is a very adverse position being placed on Native Hawaiian beneficiaries by HHL staff." What happens when Hawaiians are required to provide written proof of 50 percent blood, she asked in 1990: "Are staff members there to help encourage or are they there to harass and added heartaches and 'kill' the Hawn who holds this document?" Administrative rigidity and unresponsiveness, she concludes, deprive Hawaiians of the "little lands we have as beneficiaries of Prince Kūhiōʻs luhi and kaumaha [heaviness]." [84]

Her whole critique of DHHL in the 1990s raises the question of how the category of *beneficiary* can be defined fairly, legally, and generously. Prince Kūhiō responded to cross pressures in his 50 percent designation and in his compromise with the landowners Eleanor clusters together as "Sugar barons." She rejected the 50 percent blood quantum and favored the original 1/32nd as representative of Hawaiian history and culture. From her perspective, the broader category acknowledged the mixed ancestry of a majority of Native Hawaiians while retaining the importance of genealogy—of continuity to past generations. Her definition of *beneficiary* counters the implication of race in the classification imposed by the 1921 Act and restores the identification of

"Native Hawaiian" through genealogical reckoning. Like the prince in his original proposal, Eleanor supports a criterion that is faithful to the people.

The congressional act is designed to rectify the conquest of one nation by another through the compensatory mechanism of "returning" land to the people. Like other such federal acts, the HHCA skirts over interpretations of identity by the people who are subjects of the policy. As Eleanor suspected, the act manages the distribution of a valued resource to indigenous people without recognizing the autonomy and the history they possess. The act leaves in the hands of the US Congress the power to decide who "indigenous people" are. This so-called plenary power to grant status as *sovereign* places kānaka maoli in the same relation to the federal government as American Indian tribes and Native Alaskan villagers. However, unlike its practice toward many Native American *tribes,* Congress never granted the status of a nation to the Native Hawaiian *people.*

The way the United States judges the original conquest of Hawai'i has changed dramatically in the last hundred years. Yet the federal government still holds on to its power to define the people of a once independent nation and to measure out the terms of compensation for an illegal takeover.[85]

The Apology: A Foundation for Reconciliation?

In November 1993, President Bill Clinton apologized for the illegal overthrow of the kingdom in 1893; his speech became known as the "Apology." Congress approved the points the president made and enacted Public Law 103-150, with an emphasis on *reconciliation* between Hawai'i and the United States.[86] But reconciliation through an apology is at best a rhetorical surrogate for granting indigenous rights and supporting the self-government of Native Hawaiians. It is no surprise that the Apology was more or less a non-issue for Eleanor and for John.

John did not mention the Apology in his letters that fall. He had other things on his mind: he was in the hospital with heart problems. In his later letters, he expressed sharp disapproval of responses to the speech that culminated in competing proposals for political sovereignty and full independence. Activists, in his portrayal, lost kuleana in individual ambition: "All clubs want to be chiefs."[87] In 1994, a piece in *The Contemporary Pacific* testified to the multiplicity of players on the field: "there are at least ten positions, some advocated by only a handful of persons."[88] Eleanor did not talk about the Apology either. She had long recognized that rhetoric does not address *real* problems and only encourages more speeches on the part of self-interested leaders.

Clinton gave his speech ten months after parades throughout the islands marked the 100th anniversary of the armed takeover of an independent nation. Between the January protest marches and Clinton's response, Governor John Waihe`e established a Hawaiian Sovereignty Advisory Commission (HSAC) to mediate various proposals for a reorganized relationship with the United States. Waihe`e charged the committee with planning a convention whose main agenda item would be the unique status of Native Hawaiians in an American state. While John recognized merits in the governor's proposal, he did not agree with the details. Too much, he implied, was top down. "As of now I'm still active in my community association activities, hussel and a bussell to give people better knowledge of Hawaiian issues, laws of the land and also be on committees to regulate proper procedures in implementing state laws for a Hawaiian convention, which is run by the governor, which I don't agree. But I will hang in there to see how far we will move and how the convention comes out."[89]

The committee proceeded slowly, negotiating the intricacies of state and national politics. In 1994, Waihe`e revised the committee, changing both its name and its charge. The newly conceived Hawai`i Sovereignty Elections Council promised a plebiscite on nationhood. Two years later, in September 1996, the plebiscite was held, and the outcome was a Native Hawaiian Constitutional Convention (NHCC). In 1997, delegates to the NHCC voted to support a proposal for a Native Hawaiian government. Senator Daniel Akaka took up the cause, reformulated the demand, and introduced a bill for "Native Hawaiian Government Reorganization" into Congress in 2000.[90] The bill became, and over a decade later remains, a fierce provocation to debates in Congress, in the Hawai`i State Legislature, and around kitchen tables throughout the islands.

John died three months before the 1996 plebiscite. However, he already expressed his doubts about the proposed convention and plans for Native Hawaiian self-government. He rejected a convention that did not stem from the will of the people, and he distrusted an agenda drafted so that the governor and state legislature played a decisive role. From his point of view, self-government from the top down does not empower Native Hawaiians or provide the cultural and material resources the people need in order to determine their own future. In one of his few comments about statehood, he refers to the inadequacy of the statehood plebiscite in 1959. "I don't like what they did in making our Island a 50th state because we did not have enough information of what's going on," he wrote in the winter of 1995. "All we knew when everything was over and how they did it, I believe through Proxy and no testimony by people like us."[91]

He was equally doubtful about the proposals for sovereignty and self-government articulated by Native Hawaiian leaders. In those cases, too, he detected neglect of the voices and the needs of kānaka maoli. His opinion was clear. "As for sovereignty, I don't buy it."[92] A few months later, anticipating the state convention, he continued to reflect on the several public versions of sovereignty. "Now they want to have their own government in a government." The nation-within-a-nation model, adapted from the US policy for American Indians, would not work. "How can we do that, we don't have the Federal funding and we don't have any thing to bring us money. So you see where we stand, because we have to be on our own legs to get ahead."[93] The governor's proposal for a convention did not provide those legs.

Eleanor did not talk about the convention, and she was not very much interested in a formalized Native Hawaiian government. At the end of his term, she praised John Waihe`e for a decision more closely related to the homesteads: "Mahalo for the expanded 100 years in our Homestead leases. Mahalo for the 16,000 acres of land that fulfilled the 20,000 more or less in HH Lands inventory." She ends the letter, "Mahalo, especially, for making the DHHL a full partner of the State of Hawaii as a full fledged Department of the State of Hawaii with the Budgeted Funds for its full operation."[94] She shared John's critique of bids for sovereignty that came from self-appointed spokespersons and his distrust of a resolution of Native Hawaiian demands through state-organized conventions.

Instead she focused attention on the existing institutions whose designated mission was to insure Native Hawaiian sustenance and survival. Eleanor perceived in the Department of Hawaiian Home Lands and the Office of Hawaiian Affairs the key battlegrounds on which Native Hawaiians could achieve the material and cultural resources that allow a people to be sovereign. For Eleanor, land was at the heart of the struggle and living on the land the mode of achieving a self-sustaining and self-determined lāhui.[95] The official return of acres in 1995, small as the allotment was, constituted an important step in satisfying a series of claims for acreage rightfully belonging to Native Hawaiians and wrongly sold by the state.

"The Legs to Stand On"

A year before Waihe`e agreed to the transfer of 16,000 acres, a parcel of land was given back to kānaka maoli under quite different circumstances. In the summer of 1994, the state accorded nearly seventy acres to a group of Native Hawaiians through the "Save A Nation Foundation, Inc., a non-profit organization under a Hawaiian group called the Ohana Council."[96] The group initially occupied the beach at the foot of the Makapu`u Lighthouse and across the street from Sea Life Park on the coast road between Waimānalo and Honolulu. John and I often sat there to talk-story, and one afternoon he pointed out several small shrines across the sand in front of us. Those were the only sign of an occupation that had lasted for months, defying the state law against "permanent" camping. In mid-summer 1994, the Department of Parks and

Recreation threatened to arrest the illegal campers. By August, the group had gained enough public attention to induce the State Board of Land and Natural Resource Management to offer acreage in the agricultural lands behind Waimānalo, in the foothills of the Koʻolau Mountains. I asked John if we could drive up and look. "No," he said, "they have a right to their privacy."

Rather than driving me to Puʻuhonua O Waimānalo (place of refuge), John started to talk with respect about the project and its leader, Dennis Puʻuhonua "Bumpy" Kanahele. Bumpy had established a community based on Hawaiian values, where residents spoke Hawaiian, relied on Hawaiian "arts and skills," and revived the old taro *loʻi* (terraces). As part of the aloha spirit, the group offered refuge not only to Native Hawaiians but also to homeless, disenfranchised, and displaced individuals—housing for people in need. An article in the *Honolulu Advertiser* gave a positive cast to the undertaking: "All are welcome, stated Kanahele, 'if they're willing to work.'"[97]

Puʻuhonua O Waimānalo represented a version of sovereignty John supported. Bumpy's politics of institutionalizing mālamaʻāina and restoring traditional modes of subsistence appealed to John and distinguished the group from the activists he criticized. Bumpy's plan gave people "the legs to stand on," through hard work and care for the land.

John praised the model Bumpy set up in the back of Waimānalo because it offered a solution to the problems Native Hawaiians face without entailing dependency on the US government. Living on the land, decision making through consensus, cooperation and aloha—these components of Bumpy's plan allowed Native Hawaiians to exert self-governance in the here and now, and in the given political context. No more than his sister did John look to the restoration of the monarchy; nor did he trust claimants to the throne, laughing, one day, at the "bum" who claimed a royal lineage. The way John presented Bumpy's plan to me, the group had autonomy, premised on culture and not on an act signed by the US Congress. He compared the Native Hawaiians to the American Indians, who, he said, suffered and deteriorated under a federally approved system of self-governance. "We are worse than the Indians," he explained in a letter. "The Hawaiians are mostly poverty families."[98]

Poverty, and its impact on the lives of his kin, neighbors, and fellow workers, was much on John's mind during the summer and fall of 1995. "Lots of unforeseen things is happening in our country," he wrote. "As long as they don't hurt our Poor People and Elderlys I be satisfy."[99] In fact, *they* were hurting the poor and the elderly. "I do believe the Congress we have now is trying to satisfy themselves and not helping our poor people or elderly people."[100] John and Eleanor had grown up during a Great Depression, and both appreciated New Deal policies that shored up the territory through concrete programs, including the CCC. In the mid-1990s, John observed the breakdown in such policies, and the dismantling of a welfare system without any concern for the people. And while he admired President Clinton, he had only harsh words for members of Congress whom he accused of "making war" on the poor.

The fact of extreme poverty among Native Hawaiians led to opposing solutions in the political debate about indigenous rights and just demands. For nationalists, the only way to overcome poverty is by establishing an independent, sovereign Hawaiian nation. For John and Eleanor, the problem of poverty extended across ethnic boundaries. Yet the manifestations of extreme deprivation vary. Sharp income disparity topples the myth of a "melting pot" and accentuates differences in mobility and in access to resources.[101] Filipinos, Samoans, and Native Hawaiians share the brunt of an unequal distribution of wealth in the state. Displacement, exploitation, and racism marginalize *certain* members of the "racially integrated" society proclaimed by the United States, and reveal the dark side of American governance. So, as John often mentioned, does the condition of Native American tribes on the mainland. His stories, like Eleanor's, suggest a model for action in the capacity of Native Hawaiians to gather and to pose legitimate collective demands. From this perspective, the solution to poverty lies in inclusive action, a poor people's movement, and not in exclusive nationhood.

The viewpoint did not mean that either John or Eleanor ignored the distinct features of Native Hawaiian poverty. American settlers had seized and divided the 'āina, crushing indigenous means of self-subsistence. Kānaka maoli lost a way of living on the land to colonial usurpers—to the "sugar barons" Eleanor blamed and the "rich" John conglomerated into one category. These were the executors of "foreign desire," in the title of Kame'eleihiwa's mo'olelo.[102] Given the devastation resulting from unbridled greed, the United States owed "rehabilitation" and compensation ("back rent") to the indigenous people of the islands. According to John and Eleanor, the debt to kānaka maoli was unique, but the obligation a governing authority owed to people in need was not. They detailed the nature of the debt: the United States had an obligation to help an impoverished people, and in particular to restore to Native Hawaiians the resources through which they flourish *as a people* culturally, economically, and politically.

"Creating Communities Instead of Housing"

Actions like sitting in front of bulldozers, writing letters to politicians, and signing a petition to the governor enlist thousands of anonymous individuals, who, like Eleanor and John, confront everyday hardships resulting from betrayal by state and federal agencies. The significance of homesteads and the broken promise of "return" place OHA and DHHL at the core of grassroots protests.

In the 1990s, the agencies with kuleana for the people began to respond to intensifying grassroots demands. DHHL staff organized community meetings, asserting the agency's role as an accountable bureaucracy and, equally, an institution for and of Native Hawaiians. "Our mission," DHHL stated in the preamble of its *General Plan* at the beginning of the new millennium, "is to manage the Hawaiian Home Lands trust effectively and to develop and deliver lands to native Hawaiians. We will partner with others toward developing self-sufficient and healthy communities."[103] The broad objectives of the *General Plan* are refined in the DHHL's strategic plan for the next five years, and completed by twenty regional plans that focus on homesteads like Keaukaha and Waimānalo. The agency set its goals: effectiveness, being a responsible trust, accountability, support of applicants, and community building.

Questions arise concerning the actual implementation of these goals. The *General Plan* is imbued with the language of public–private partnerships that emerged in an era of deregulation as a route to "efficient" governance in the United States. What *partnership* really means depends on the particular circumstances. In many cases, the phrase simply covers a shift to private contractors who can offer a public service as a profitable business. In the *Keaukaha Plan* virtually everything is accomplished through "partnerships with other government agencies, the private sector and community organizations"—developing the land, building public facilities, renovating the infrastructure, offering houses to low-income applicants, and improving community life.

When the plans address the homesteads themselves, and the Native Hawaiians living in a homestead, the language indicates the distance of DHHL from actual problems on the homesteads. The plans reveal an asymmetric relation under the guise of partnership, taking a top-down—one might even say patronizing—approach. "Waimānalo is a long standing Hawaiian Homes community which has evolved organically over many decades," begins one section of the *Waimānalo Plan*. "Within this context the Department of Hawaiian Home Lands' recently articulated policy of creating communities instead of simply housing guides the policy for the area."[104] No irony lies in the agency's intention of "creating communities" in a plan that responds to the collective grievances of residents, expressed for decades through a hui.

The plan proposes the construction of a village center, to be located in the area behind Blanche Pope Elementary School and alongside Kalaniana'ole Highway. The village center would anchor newly reorganized residential and recreational spaces; concentric circles "map" the design for readers. Persuasive as it may appear, the plan sidesteps the harsh facts of unemployment, poverty, and homelessness that are conditions of Native Hawaiian life. Instead, the 2008 proposal bows to the findings of a marketing survey conducted in the same year.[105] "The Waimānalo Homestead," claims the DHHL plan, offers a picture of "contentment," with its "friendly, family oriented" atmosphere.[106] The rosy

picture rationalizes a strategy of caution and delay. The plan concludes: proposals should not spoil the "country setting" and the "laid back local lifestyle"
of this essentially suburban homestead.[107]

The DHHL planners know very well that they cannot simply walk in and
create communities—even in choice homesteads like Waimānalo and Keaukaha. Their strategic plan for the years 2007–11 explicitly acknowledges the
necessity of attending to demands from homesteaders for more autonomy and
participation in decisions about Hawaiian trust land. Among a list of initiatives
in the plan is: "'*Elua*: Support capacity building programs to assist Homesteaders to effectively govern their affairs within their respective Homestead
communities."[108] Whether assistance from the DHHL can be credited when
residents become active in governing the homesteads is dubious. In the years
since John and Eleanor began urging their kin and neighbors to act, a change
has come about in the thrust of activism on homesteads. Eleanor lived to see
the change; John did not.

Today, Hawaiian community advocates can be found in most homesteads.
They petition, they organize neighborhood meetings, and they campaign for
appointments on the Hawaiian Homes Commission or for election to the Office of Hawaiian Affairs Board of Trustees. In an extension of Eleanor's work
through an association whose plans originated in Keaukaha-Pana'ewa, advocates now can participate in statewide associations, like the Sovereign Coun-
cils of the Hawaiian Homelands Assembly (SCHHA) or the newer Association
of Hawaiians for Homestead Lands (AHHL).[109] Along with local homestead
associations, these organizations take up the task John and Eleanor defined as
crucial—to inform, advise, and instruct petitioners for land, to guide lessees
through their rights, and to ensure successors of acquiring what is rightfully
theirs. Statewide organizations negotiate the dual aims homestead associations
have dealt with for over a century, at once to protect the collective interests of
the lāhui and to help individual beneficiaries gain their ends. Like the associations at the start of the twentieth century, whose decisions lay behind Prince
Kūhiō's proposal, twenty-first-century associations are the building blocks for
"true" leaders.

Community advocates in the twenty-first century turn to kūpuna like Eleanor and John for the knowledge that comes from decades of experience in a
US territory and state. In these experiences lie the most effective challenge to
legislators charged with implementing the laws that determine Native Hawaiian "life on the land," starting but not ending with the 1921 HHCA. Like the
thirty or so homestead associations, the statewide SCHHA and AHHL lack
official status and administrative standing. Their ties to OHA, DHHL, and the
state legislature remain murky, circumstantial, and unreliable. The power of
homestead associations, of networks and centers, and of neighborhood boards
in the end depends upon the engagement of residents, the persuasiveness of

kūpuna, the leadership of social activists, and the consensus-building members of a hui demonstrate.

"We Already Have Sovereignty"

In June 2009, my friend Gordon gave the graduation speech at Kailua High School. Many, but not all, of the students in his audience were Hawaiian or part-Hawaiian and he knew many of them from the streets, yards, and houses of Waimānalo. He was shy, he told me, and he took on the "burden" of public speaking for two reasons: the first was to carry forward Helene's work with the younger generation, and the second was to speak directly to the adolescent boys in the audience. Helene had died the previous September, and Gordon took on her kuleana at home in the homestead of Waimānalo. Speaking in public was not his "thing," he said, but he accepted the duty the school administration handed to him; he knew it was "right."

He started by telling his own story. And he did that with the boys in mind, the group of students he saw both as at risk and with the potential to benefit from the lessons in Hawaiian culture and history his own mo'olelo contained. Telling it personally was his way, and the way of his ancestors. He described growing up in a homestead, being disaffected with school, meeting Helene, and "coming to understand" the importance of education broadly defined. He emphasized the importance of truth and of spirituality. Those were words he used to refer to integrity and to bravery, and to remind the boys that courage did not mean being aggressive or warlike, but as Tengan writes, "being courageous enough to look at your spirit."[110]

His attention to growing up male did not leave the "girls" out. For Gordon knew, and he talked stories about, relationships that were spoiled by the lack of confidence, the unemployment and discrimination, and the demoralization faced by Hawaiian and part-Hawaiian men.[111] He attributed his own courage and ability to kōkua to Helene, and to the many years she had spent trying to change the school system in Waimānalo. Her insistence that Native Hawaiian children were being "cheated" in American public schools led her to work outside the classrooms, to talk with parents, and to engage in the canoe races through which generations learned to cooperate, respect one another, and "take care." She passed on to Gordon the lesson she taught the parents, the teachers, and her neighbors in Waimānalo: the need "to apply Hawaiian cultural concepts and terminology" to all aspects of life.[112]

Gordon reminded his audience at Kailua, the "Home of the Surfriders," to ride the surf not as tourist or guide, but as ali'i—the model for the behavior of a true Hawaiian person, kanaka maoli.[113] He had ridden canoe with some of their fathers, and he had watched a few of the boys learn to paddle themselves.

He also recognized a few members of his audience from the meetings he held in Waimānalo, in the Blanche Pope Elementary School, where his wife and his mother had spent hours of their days. Gordon conducted his lessons in the physical space of the school—the building that had opened with the playing of American patriotic tunes by the United States Air Force Band—and he broke with the haole-style teaching usually imposed in that space.

He invited the men and boys who were "interested" to come and talk-story. He opened the meetings at 5 AM, just as the sun was rising, and he prepared an abundant breakfast, with plenty of coffee for the sleepy participants. His idea was scrupulously attentive to the "ways" of his neighbors and kin. Those who wanted to be there would get up, he said, and make their way down the several blocks to Pope. The dawn hours of talking-story did not, then, intrude on the rest of the day. The men, he told me, chuckling, might go back to bed; the boys, well, he did not dwell on that. Gordon was not rigid, and he delighted in the different stories the men—some as young as sixteen, others as old as eighty—told about their lives. What they did after breakfast was up to them. His goal of providing confidence and a new interpretation of "being a man" to the participants fits one major thrust of the new agenda for transforming a colonial, hegemonic, and oppressive history into a vital and concrete restoration of Hawaiian cultural values. "The processes through which men in the group come to define, know, and perform these kuleana," Ty Tengan writes, "articulate with the larger projects of cultural revitalization, moral regeneration, spiritual/bodily healing, national reclamation, and the uncertain and ambiguous project of mental and political decolonization."[114]

At the start of the twenty-first century, Pope Elementary School instituted a "Hawaiian word of the month" program: the word for May 2011 was *kamaehu*, translated as "resilience, survival, and recovery." These concepts thread through the speech Gordon gave at the large, crowded, suburban high school—a speech in which he depicted the resilience, survival, and recovery of Hawaiian culture through an adaptation of the courage and bravery of kānaka maoli of the past.

Like Helene, and John and Eleanor in an older generation, Gordon recognizes the importance of bringing courage to day-to-day problems: the continued failure of schools to meet the needs of Native Hawaiian youth, the inadequacy of an American health system for offsetting the high rate of disease in the indigenous population, the inequitable distribution of resources by a state that, impoverished itself, further abandons the "poor and needy" of whatever ethnic background. The residents of Waimānalo are "working and winning, not whining," wrote a reporter for the *Honolulu Star-Bulletin*.[115] The article praises modifications in the school curriculum, the opening of health clinics, and the development of recreational programs for children—the hard work done by individuals like John, Eleanor, Helene, and Gordon. The four are not alone. In the footsteps of the farmers who protested against eviction in the 1960s, the ʻohana that fought the US Navy over bomb testing on Kahoʻolawe, and the women and men who sit in front of bulldozers all over the archipelago, "thousands of people, faceless and unnamed" work to alter the conditions under which Native Hawaiians experience the twenty-first century.[116]

"We already have sovereignty," Eleanor told me, and her moʻolelo call for putting that cultural autonomy to good use. Concrete and specific actions, in Eleanor's case through a homestead association and in John's through his several clubs, offer a route to the outcome Prince Kūhiō projected when he called for the "rehabilitation" of his people.[117]

The meetings I attended and the talk-stories I heard indicate that in the daily lives of individuals who identify as Native Hawaiian the political topics of sovereignty and nationhood, as well as the Akaka Bill, remain abstract. The bill becomes a remote and often divisive screen against which everybody involved projects a vision of the future for Native Hawaiians beyond an impossible (and imperialist) reconciliation. Fading into the background, the screen becomes irrelevant for individuals who engage in initiatives in the homesteads, in community organizations, in the public schools, and in an array of economic, environmental, and educational programs. The self-confidence and perseverance of those who define themselves as 100 percent Hawaiian, or kanaka maoli, or ʻōiwi stretches from conversation around a kitchen table to the halls of a state legislature and the corridors of Congress. These qualities spread to a new generation, the first to grow up Hawaiian in a setting where the ʻōlelo makuahine and cultural values can prevail.

Notes

1. Mary Kawena Pukui, E. W. Haertig, and Catherine Lee, *Nānā I Ke Kumu* [I], 126.
2. In Rhea Akoi, ed., *Kuʻu Home I Keaukaha*, 70.
3. Like other concepts, *pono* cannot be translated with one English word: it refers to a condition that is right, correct, proper, true, and harmonious.
4. Davianna Pōmaikaʻi McGregor, *Nā Kuaʻāina*, 10.
5. Jeff Corntassel, "Toward Sustainable Self-Determination," 119; see also Hokulani K. Aikau, *A Chosen People*, 177.
6. Allan Spitz, *Social Aspects*, 52.
7. Harland Bartholomew and Associates, *A General Plan*, 13.
8. In 1887, faced by an armed group of men, Kalākaua was forced to revise the constitution; the resulting document is known the Bayonet Constitution.
9. The company "sold the remaining six years of the lease and its fee simple [owned] lands to the newly-organized Waimanalo Agricultural Development Company, thus ending over seventy years of sugar's domination of the Waimanalo scene"; Bartholomew, *A General Plan*, 15.

10. Ibid., 16.
11. Department of Hawaiian Home Lands, Waimanalo Land Inventory Report, Honolulu: 1989, *23*, http://hawaii.gov/dhhl/beneficiary-consultation/Waimanalo percent20Land percent20Inventory percent20Report.pdf, accessed 12 March 2011.
12. *Honolulu Advertiser,* 6 August 1989, G-2.
13. http://Files.usgwarchives.net/hi/keepers/koc58.txt, accessed 1 June 2011.
14. His plans were not always greeted positively. See http://urbanreviewstl.com/2009/12/harland-bartholomew-negatively-impacted-many-cities/Steve Patterson, accessed 23 June 2012.
15. Harland Bartholomew and Associates, *An Action Program,* 11. The vision of urban development with low-, middle-, and high-income residents in a green valley with one of the best beaches of Oahu already informed the *General Plan* of 1958–59. After Hawai`i gained statehood, the new government, urban planers, and citizens hoped that the federal government would follow through with John F. Kennedy's promise to start "the return to the people of Hawaii of those military installations no longer being used." Quoted in Harland Bartholomew, *An Action Program,* 3. Bellows Field—the planner argued—"constitutes what is probably the largest and best single site available for urban development in the island of Oahu," 2. However, the return of Bellows Field to the state did not materialize, and neither did the plans of Harland Bartholomew.
16. Bartholomew, *An Action Program,* 23.
17. *The Nalo News* 2, no. 10 (November 1978), 3.
18. On the Leeward Coast, Nanakuli and Wai`anae face economic difficulties—the land is too dry for agriculture and employment in Honolulu industries is lower than that of Waimānalo residents.
19. *Honolulu Advertiser,* 6 August 1979, A-14.
20. Minutes of the Hawaiian Homes Commission meetings 1980–88, Department of Hawaiian Home Lands, Series 239, Hawai`i State Archives.
21. See Rona Tamiko Halualani, *In the Name of Hawaiians,* chapter 3.
22. John Simeona to the author, 3 December 1992.
23. In April 1994, the Hawaii Government Employees Association went on strike, and it is possible that John's kin either belonged to the union or went on a sympathy strike. Rich Budnick, *Hawaii's Forgotten History,* 222.
24. John Simeona to the author, 18 May 1994.
25. John Simeona to the author, 8 September 1994.
26. John Simeona to the author, 15 September 1994.
27. John Simeona to the author, 23 September 1994.
28. John Simeona to the author, 11 November 1994.
29. John Simeona to the author, 4 July 1995.
30. J. Kēhaulani Kauanui, *Hawaiian Blood,* 5.
31. http://hawaii.gov/dhhl/lessees/questions-and-answers-for-designating-successors, accessed 8 July 2008.
32. John Simeona to the author, 19 January 1995.
33. John Simeona to the author, 20 February 1995.
34. http://hawaii.gov/dhhl/applicants/appforms/applyhhl, accessed 8 July 2008.
35. Ibid.
36. Halualani details the many problems that can arise in the designation of an heir: besides lack of written documentation, frequent name changes, for instance, can "rob" a person of Hawaiian identity in the eyes of DHHL; *In the Name of Hawaiians,* 118–119.
37. Memorandum by Eleanor Ahuna, Controversies on DHHL Policies and Administration Rules, Memorandum, 6 December 1990 (in the author's possession).

38. As long as adoption law prescribes anonymity and the DHHL demands proof of biological ancestry, the two are incompatible. Facing this situation, *Loa`a Ka `Āina Ho`opulapula* does provide a list of agencies that will help an adoptee open her court records.
39. Documentation may involve gathering as many as "thirty notarized documents"; Kauanui, *Hawaiian Blood,* 4.
40. Memorandum by Eleanor Ahuna, Controversies.
41. John Simeona to the author, 15 March 1996.
42. John Simeona, *Life Story,* 6.
43. Eleanor Ahuna to the Honorable Trustees of the Kamehameha Schools and the Bernice Pauahi Bishop estate, 29 September 1992 (in the author's possession).
44. "Given the historical difficulty of maintaining neatness and cleanliness in homestead areas, does the uniform building guarantee a uniform slum area?" Allan A. Spitz, *Organization,* 40.
45. Dana Tagaki, "Native Hawaiians," 494.
46. Native Hawaiians Study Commission Report on the culture, needs, and concerns of Native Hawaiians, Pursuant to Public Law 96-565, Title III. Washington, DC: US Department of the Interior, 1983.
47. http://wiki.grassrootinstitute.org/mediawiki/index.php?title=NHSC_Conclusions_ And_Recommendation, accessed 23 March 2010.
48. http://www.census.gov/population/www/documentation/twps0076/twps0076.html, accessed 25 April 2010.
49. Noenoe Silva uncovers the story of persistent kanaka maoli activism in *Aloha Betrayed.*
50. University of Hawaii Department of Urban and Regional Planning. Waimanalo Planning Issues: A Community Based Reconnaissance. University of Hawai`i, Honolulu, 1987.
51. S. Rep. No. 109-221, at 2 (March 2006). See, for a more detailed discussion, Seija Naya, *Income Distribution.* In addition: "Hawaiians/part-Hawaiians have had the shortest life expectancy of all major groups since 1910"; *Health Trends in Hawai`i. A Profile of the Health Care System,* sponsored by the HMSA Foundation, 7th ed., 2006, http://www .healthtrends.org/status_life_expect.aspx, accessed 8 April 2010.
52. So is Haunani-Kay Trask, soon to become an outspoken proponent of Hawaiian sovereignty.
53. John Simeona to the author, 18 November 1991.
54. In his letters, John occasionally wrote, "Maka Kilo, Inc.," perhaps emphasizing the corporate/cooperative nature of the hui.
55. "Among provisions incorporated into the new state constitution was the establishment of the Office of Hawaiian Affairs as a public trust, with a mandate to better the conditions of both Native Hawaiians and the Hawaiian community in general. OHA was to be funded with a pro rata share of revenues from state lands designated as 'ceded.'" About us/OHA website at http://www.oha.org/index.php?option=com_content&task =view&id=25&Itemid=118, accessed 22 June 2012.
56. Haunani-Kay Trask has been openly and fiercely critical of OHA. In the mid-1990s, she wrote: "This article touches on one collaborationist organization, the Office of Hawaiian Affairs (OHA), created by the state of Hawai`i to short-circuit our drive toward sovereignty." Trask, "Kūpa`a `Āina," 87.
57. Budnick, *Hawaii's Forgotten History,* 224.
58. http://hawaii.gov/gov/newsroom/press-releases/governor-enacts-bill-to-resolve-ceded-lands-claims, accessed 24 June 2012.

59. Akoi, *Ku`u Home I Keaukaha,* 72.
60. John Simeona in a tape recording, September 1994.
61. John Simeona to the author, 2 October 1990.
62. http://www.alulike.org, accessed 31 January 2009.
63. "OBJECTIVES of the Act: To provide financial assistance to American Indian non-profit Native Tribes and Villages, and for Native Hawaiians and Native American Pacific Islander organizations for the development and implementation of social and economic development strategies that promote self-sufficiency. These projects are expected to result in improved social and economic conditions in Native American communities and to increase the effectiveness of Tribes and Native non-profit Organizations in meeting their social and economic goals." http://www.cfda.gov/pls/portal30/CATALOG.PROGRAM_TEXT_RPT.SHOW?p, accessed 8 October 2009.
64. OHA "requests separate funding for the 'less than fifties'"; Kauanui, *Hawaiian Blood,* 195.
65. http://www.alulike.org, accessed 31 January 2009.
66. John Simeona to the author, 19 September 1989.
67. John Simeona to the author, 8 October 1989.
68. http://www.alulike.org, accessed 31 January 2009.
69. John Simeona to the author, 11 October 1995.
70. John Simeona to the author, 21 April 1995.
71. John Simeona to the author, 4 August 1991.
72. John Simeona to the author, 19 January 1992.
73. See Amy Ku`uleialoha Stillman, "'Nā Lei O Hawai'i.'"
74. John Simeona to the author, 20 March 1991.
75. University of Hawai`i Department of Urban and Regional Planning, *Waimanalo Planning Issues,* 8.
76. John Simeona to the author, 5 April.1995.
77. John Simeona to the author, 29 July 1995.
78. Eleanor Ahuna to all elected members of the Hawaii County Administration and Council, The Hawaii State legislators (and nine other institutions), 31 January 1993 (in the author's possession).
79. Not to be confused with the Aloha `Āina Party, founded in 1997, which still exists, though not on the ballot. http://en.wikipedia.org/wiki/Aloha_Aina_Party_of_Hawaii, accessed 1 June 2009.
80. John Simeona to the author, 9 October 1990. John Waihe`e, who would become the first elected governor with Native Hawaiian ancestry, campaigned in that year.
81. The Keaukaha Community Association, for instance, had a long history, under different names. "For the past 29 years," states the website, "we have been called the Keaukaha Community Association"; http://www.keaukaha.org/welcome.html, accessed 2 August 2009.
82. This was not a false, if a somewhat exaggerated accusation. The SCHHA did demand self-governance for the homesteads in the early 1990s; Chieko Tachihata, *The Sovereignty Movement,* 205.
83. Memorandum by Eleanor Ahuna, Keaukaha Hawaiian Homeland Homestead, 30 September 1993 (in the author's possession).
84. Memorandum by Eleanor Ahuna, Controversies.
85. See T. Alexander Aleinikoff, *Semblances of Sovereignty.*
86. Congress "apologizes to Native Hawaiians on behalf of the people of the United States for the overthrow of the Kingdom of Hawaii on January 17, 1893 ... and the deprivation of the rights of Native Hawaiians to self-determination; expresses its commitment

to acknowledge the ramifications of the overthrow of the Kingdom of Hawaii, in order to provide a proper foundation for reconciliation between the United States and the Native Hawaiian people; and urges the President of the United States to also acknowledge the ramifications of the overthrow of the Kingdom of Hawaii and to support reconciliation efforts between the United States and the Native Hawaiian people." A joint resolution to acknowledge the 100th anniversary of the 17 January 1893 overthrow of the Kingdom of Hawaii, and to offer an apology to Native Hawaiians on behalf of the United States for the overthrow of the Kingdom of Hawaii. S.J. Res. 19, 103rd Congress, became Public Law No: 103-150.

87. John Simeona to the author, 18 May 1994.
88. Chieko Tachihata, *The Sovereignty Movement,* 203. See Judith Schachter and Albrecht Funk, "Sovereignty, Indigeneity, and Identities."
89. John Simeona to the author, 24 May 1993.
90. Akaka supported Native Hawaiian claims, and he introduced the bill year after year—winning approval from the House of Representatives but not from the Senate. In April 2011, the Senate Committee on Indian Affairs approved the bill, which was scheduled to go to the full Senate in fall 2011. Nothing has happened, as of this writing.
91. John Simeona to the author, 9 February 1995.
92. Ibid.
93. John Simeona to the author, 12 June 1995.
94. Eleanor Ahuna to the Honorable John Waihe`e, 21 January 1995 (in the author's possession). The next governor, Benjamin Cayetano, actually signed the bill that assured the 16,000-acre return.
95. See Jennifer Noelani Goodyear-Ka`ōpua, "Rebuilding the `Auwai."
96. *Honolulu Advertiser,* 24 August 1994, A-12.
97. *Honolulu Advertiser,* 25 July 1994, A-8.
98. John Simeona to the author, 24 August 1995.
99. John Simeona to the author, 5 August 1995.
100. John Simeona to the author, 12 September 1995.
101. See Jonathan Y. Okamura, *Ethnicity and Inequality in Hawai`i.*
102. See Lilikalā Kame`eleihiwa, *Native Land and Foreign Desires.*
103. Department of Hawaiian Home Lands, *General Plan,* Honolulu, 2002.
104. DHHL, *Waimānalo Regional Plan,* Honolulu, 2008, 14.
105. Through survey questions, the marketing firm discovered that "most residents" on homesteads are content with the way things are going. *DHHL Lessee Survey,* SMS Research and Marketing Inc., March 2009.
106. Ibid., 8.
107. DHHL, *Waimānalo Regional Plan,* 8. This characterization also contrasts with the alarmed and urgent descriptions of troubled homesteads like Nanakuli and Wai`anae, on the Leeward Coast.
108. DHHL, Strategic Plan 2007–2011, Goal 2, Objective 2. The plan was presented and distributed widely, but is offered now only in a truncated version on the DHHL website, http://hawaii.gov/dhhl/publications/strategic-plan/Strategic percent20Plan percent202007-2011.pdf, accessed 3 September 2011.
109. The SCHHA has been in existence since 1987, and the AHHL since March 2011.
110. Ty P. Kāwika Tengan, *Native Men Remade,* 77.
111. Notes from *Indigenous Rights Symposium,* 11–12 February 2011. See, in addition, Tengan, *Native Men Remade.*
112. Helene K. Mattos and P. H. Medeiros, *A Survey,* 11.

113. See Isaiah Helekunihi Walker, *Waves of Resistance*, 2–3.
114. Tengan, *Native Men Remade*, 8.
115. *Honolulu Star-Bulletin*, 28 September 2003, http://archives.starbulletin.com/2003/09/28/special/story, accessed 1 October 2010.
116. Jonathan Kay Kamakawiwoʻole Osorio, "Hawaiian Issues," 16.
117. As the indigenous scholars Jeff Corntassel and Cheryl Bryce write, "Overall, one sees that grass-roots efforts … do not rely heavily on rights as much as they do on community responsibilities to protect traditional homelands and food systems"; "Practicing Sustainable Self-Determination," 160.

Epilogue

On 3 January 2004, Eleanor and I exchanged New Year's greetings over the phone. The turning of the year and time passing set her to thinking about death, and she talked about the funerals of various kin. Mostly she talked about her husband Albert and his death in 1995.[1] I had heard accounts of the way he died, sitting peacefully in a chair next to her. I had not heard much about the funeral until that January phone call. "There are stories told at funerals," Auntie Eleanor said over long distance, "that reveal more than you knew before."

These stories reveal the constitution of a person in a kindred, attached to the ancestors and to the ʻāina. The symbol of the ʻohana, a taro plant, links people to the "staff of life" for kānaka maoli—and indicates the "rootedness" of individuals in common soil.[2] The entry in *Nānā I Ke Kumu* reads: "Members of the ʻohana, like taro shoots, are all from the same root."[3] In her moʻolelo, Eleanor stressed the intricate connection between person, ancestor, and ʻāina when she reminded me, "a person is *good* when his house and yard are in order."

Our January phone conversation deepened the meanings of a phrase I had heard over the years. Her talk-story placed Albert in the natural and social surroundings they shared: raising nine children in a homestead, participating in the hui they had founded, and keeping a "watchful eye" on US institutions that enforce the terms of "life on the land." The anecdotes she offered long distance convey the person Albert was through his interactions with others, in an ʻohana, in a Big Five shipping company, and, in later years, in the Church of Jesus Christ of Latter-day Saints. The details Eleanor retrieved from memories of his funeral expanded her interpretations of *being Hawaiian* in an American context. And they told of the politics of that process.

Her memories of Albert completed a kind of narrative triptych, complementing reflections on her own life and the stories she told about her brother in a eulogy that dwelt on his kuleana to the ʻohana. The moʻolelo about Albert began with his genealogy, and the ancestors whose names we had traced one day in the Mormon Archives in Lāʻie, on Oʻahu—the Chinese laborers who came to Hawaiʻi in the nineteenth century: "not Chinee!" her granddaughter teasingly protested. Eleanor chuckled over stories of Albert's "wild partying" after a day pulling a huge freighter or a luxury liner into Hilo Harbor. And she described Albert's oscillation between obedience to officers in the Matson

Navigation Company and his protests against a state agency as vice-president of Hui Ho`omau Keaukaha-Pana`ewa.[4] Labor for a corporate entity and work for the Native Hawaiian residents of a homestead constituted the condition under which a person of his generation managed the imposition of an American regime. Eleanor's account of Albert's life corrects a history of complete hegemonic control and, as well, it mirrors the ongoing political contest between the United States and a culturally sovereign people.

In the eulogy she gave for her brother in 1996, Eleanor similarly portrayed a person through his "relational history" to land and people.[5] She dwelt on the years John spent in Keaukaha and the lessons of kūpuna that sustained a "100 percent Hawaiian" person through his life in an American territory and state. The phrase is John's, in the subtitle of his *Life Story*, and not Eleanor's. However, she filled out the constituents of his self-identification when she talked of her brother's goodness, his integrity, and the wisdom he transmitted to generations that "come after." She offered us a portrait of a man whose care and concern for others persisted in a context of competing demands—"foreign desires" versus the enduring "sources" of custom.[6] The eulogy, her memories of Albert, and her own mo`olelo interweave, together illustrating the "beach crossings" that provide strength, stamina, and survival to the Native Hawaiian people.[7] Ultimately, Eleanor's stories convert unequal and unjust encounters into an occasion for rebalancing relationships.

Stories are told around the kitchen table, on beaches, in courtrooms, at funerals, and during the long days of a wake. The setting changes but the outcome is the same. Various as they are, storytelling occasions elaborate the means of appropriating a past in order simultaneously to create a template for the future. Talk-stories are exchanges, and the eulogy Eleanor offered John's mourners acknowledged the wisdom (and the opinion) each one of us had. The stories told, in whatever setting, combine, cohere, clash, and, sometimes, diffuse—opening rifts that cannot be bridged. And so the occasion of talk-story, too, reveals more than a participant or an observer knew before.

There was another funeral, a few days after Albert's. Eleanor's talk of that event, soon after it occurred, exposed the unraveling that a death can bring. The stories told at the time severed the "relational histories" of participants and obstructed expressions of *kaumaha*, grief and sorrow. The moment, the second funeral, displayed in microcosm the conflicts that can threaten the collectivity in a larger sense. But, as John knew, there are always stories to tell, and the bleak discordance of a funeral is only one episode.

Entangling and "Setting Right"

John's son died a week after Albert, in mid-September 1995. The letters John wrote then, and for several weeks afterward, describe the anger and bitterness the event produced. His story of his son's funeral depicts the fraying of a fabric he had woven through the years of becoming hānau mua in an expanding `ohana. The funeral brought problems and difficulties into the open, and John filled his letters with reflections on the causes and consequences of a severe disruption of harmony.

The day of the "viewing" had been a bad one, he wrote. When he arrived, his daughter-in-law came out and stood in front of the church. Arms akimbo, she blocked his entrance. He tried several times to override her "stubborn" refusal to let him in, and he failed in his attempts. And so: "I called in three of my hanae [hānai] boys" to break the stand off. The three were "cops," and they arrived in full blue uniform. Under those conditions, John entered the church to pay his last respects to his son.

The story did not end there, or that day. John continued to mull over the impact and to reflect on the sources of the disruption. In between these pained and puzzled reflections he interspersed comments on the sovereignty movement, then at its height in the state. The breakdown signaled by the blocked church door prompted a reiteration of lessons he had practiced all his life, and which for him represented the "100 percent" in his subtitle. Unity, responsibility, and interdependence—these traits of an `ohana stood in stark contrast to his construction of the positions activists were taking in the state.[8] As he contemplated the break represented by the funeral, he also dwelt on the fracturing, divisiveness, and hostility that, in his view, colored discourses on sovereignty at the time. In his view, activists forgot traditional sources of sustenance and well-being in their rush to establish an independent political entity. The letters John wrote during and after the funeral cross between the core elements of an `ohana and the content of movements in the public arena. Such crossing had been John's way all along.

He had worked hard to raise fourteen children, on the arid soil of Navy housing, the fertile land of Mānoa Valley, and finally on the "choice" homestead plot in Waimānalo. He imposed pre-dawn chores (which his children still remember), insisting on the Hawaiian tenet *I ka nānā no a `ike*—by observing one learns.[9] Then he punished the child who played hooky, corrected the one who spoke like a tita, and urged each one of them to achieve in the American public schools they attended. The son who died had enlisted in the US Army and had spent months in Germany, perhaps visiting the town John remembered when he named the boy. Family lore is that John gave this son, Lynn-Boy, and a daughter, Starr-Lynn, names adapted from a small German town he went through during the Second World War.

John did not write about the choice of name. He did write about the return of Lynn-Boy from Germany. His son came back "home," and he moved his wife and child into the house in Waimānalo. The homecoming posed problems John did not expect. His letters describe incidents, moments in the life of the `ohana that undermined the values he had conveyed to the younger generation. He told me: the three had "marked the food" they put in the refrigerator; they had refused to kōkua—to help—with household tasks, and they had "spent all their money" on "useless stuff." Every detail pointed to its reverse: the generosity, cooperation, and solidarity John attached to life in Keaukaha.

The anecdotes fill page after page in among the longest letters he wrote to me, and they evoke John's harshest condemnation of American culture: the consumerism and the greed that a landscape of box stores perpetuates, along with an ideology of private property and of wealth as a sign of status. He linked the accumulation of "stuff" to self-indulgence and selfishness. His son and daughter-in-law did not spend lavishly, but in John's view they clearly put themselves ahead of the well-being of the ʻohana. The scene at the funeral exposed the precariousness of aloha in the face of an American mode of life and, too, dramatized the gap between generations competing values could produce.

As Eleanor said, funerals "reveal more than you knew before." For John, the funeral of Lynn-Boy cast new light on the efforts he had made to preserve the meaning of being 100 percent Hawaiian. And he juxtaposed the components he transmitted—"we knew how to raise children," he said—to the notions of indigenous identity current in political discourse in the mid-1990s. In the time I knew him, and in the letters he wrote, John stuck with the word *Hawaiian*. He did not adopt contemporaneous terms like kanaka maoli or ʻōiwi. *Hawaiian* evoked a collectivity, the *people,* and a relationship with ʻāina. *Hawaiian* offered an interpretation of nationhood that he considered distorted by, lost in, the competing claims of chiefs—the pithy word he applied to leaders of the sovereignty movement. Moreover, he added to his use of *Hawaiian* an inclusiveness, the possibility of belonging, that in his view the nationalism of activists eliminated.

The story of the funeral also represented a stage in John's life story. His examination of the lessons he had taught, and the inevitable impingement of a non-Hawaiian way of life, brought his reflections full circle. The arc of his life, as I would put it, flowed from the deep immersion in Hawaiian culture he remembered from days in Keaukaha through intense involvement in American institutions—public school, the CCC and the Army, and decades at the Pearl Harbor Naval Shipyard—and culminated in the dissemination of wisdom during his years in Waimānalo. Living on the land in Waimānalo did not represent a return to the past but rather a turn to the future, and an anticipation of the flexibility with which the next generation could negotiate Hawaiian values within an American state. Two full pages in *Life Story* describe the adult accomplishments of fourteen children, and he concludes the tape he made in 1994: "I'm proud, I'm very proud of you folks. I always brag about my family." These moʻolelo convey the fruits of learning and working, and form a counterpart to the distress Lynn-Boy's funeral prompted.

The arc of Eleanor's life, as I knew it through her stories, differed from that of her brother's. With the exception of two summers and one fall during the Second World War, she stayed in the Homestead of Keaukaha. From that *home* place, she extended her activities through the archipelago, directing her attention to the policies and practices that still today constitute the relationship between the United States and Native Hawaiians. Her assessment of the impact of American imperialism on Hawai'i circulated around land—the *stealing* of acres under the rubric of development and progress, the militarization of the 'āina by an American nation continually at war, and the tangled give and take of an act that established Hawaiian home lands. In her role as Department of Home Lands commissioner and as president of Hui Ho'omau Keaukaha-Pana'ewa, Eleanor worked hard to apply the lessons she learned from her ancestors.

These lessons were multiple, nuanced, and, from time to time, boldly counter to the American culture that she, like her brother, constantly negotiated. And for me, these lessons were most clearly articulated in her proposals for a Hawaiian Cultural Center and in her vision of a Peace Center. The two projects embodied her interpretation of Native Hawaiian identity, the first in response to the policies of an American state and federal government and the second with a view to the world stage. The projected Hawaiian Cultural Center contained the sources of cultural autonomy, from language teaching to the "entrepreneurial" marketing of crafts that provide material sustenance for a people. Perhaps most significantly, she set the Cultural Center on Pana'ewa, the agricultural homestead that exposed the failure of the 1921 "return" of Hawaiian land to the Hawaiian people.

The Cultural Center did not materialize, and Eleanor's subsequent vision marked a turn in her interpretation of *Hawaiian*. The Peace Center displayed the "heart" of a nation, the aloha spirit that constituted the core of Native Hawaiian values. Moreover, the representation of the nation of Hawai'i in a Peace Center was a deliberate response to the "identity" of the American nation. Through the Peace Center, Eleanor depicted the United States as a military power, whose bases stretched across the 'āina and whose wars crossed the world. In both the Hawaiian Cultural Center and the Peace Center, she constructed a view of nationhood that was premised in culture and not in the political sovereignty demanded by activists. As she would say, one way or another, "We already have sovereignty."

Eleanor recognized that the sovereignty she asserted was at risk under the intrusion of state and federal policies. To respond to the risk, she prescribed concrete action—take a stand, she urged the 'ōpio, and you can have a hand in the future of your community. Words have a force, in writings and in talk-stories around a kitchen table. The words Eleanor used, over her lifetime, were inseparable from the doing she modeled for generations to come. In *Ku'u*

Home I Keaukaha, the name of her homestead is translated as "time of writing." A variant translation is "the passing current."[10] For Eleanor, the definitions coincide, for to write is to pass on to the people the power to act.

Moʻolelo: Coming Back to Talk-Stories, Stories, and Histories

At the end of our afternoon together, Mr. Ōʻili gave me two gifts. One gift was a lauhala hat he had woven, intricate and tight, which is now hanging in my office. The other gift was a small Hawaiian flag—also in my office. Mr. Ōʻili's stories were as multilayered and nuanced as any I heard, full of the kaona that Marshall Sahlins and others say make it impossible for a malihini fully to understand Hawaiian. I think Mr. Ōʻili knew how I might understand his story, which culminated in the vision of a Native Hawaiian "community" sailing around the islands in a cruise ship. Or maybe it is fairer to say that his story culminated in the two gifts he gave me: the hat that stood for a traditional craft, but that also might be said to represent the "weaving" of two histories, the tight entanglement of the United States and kanaka maoli lives. The flag, handed to me at the same time, was another version: the symbol of a Hawaiian nation his cruise ship account critically penetrated. In return, he asked for my "book," for the moʻolelo I would tell and that he unfortunately did not live to receive.

The moʻolelo John and Eleanor shared with me structure the content and the approach of this book. Hours of conversations, reams of paper, and stacks of tape recordings comprise their gifts to me. In return, they expected to read the moʻolelo composed by an anthropologist to whom they offered counsel: listen and observe; don't be *niele niele*—nosey with questions. Completed only after their deaths, my moʻolelo must be a gift to the younger generation upon whom they pinned hopes for the future.

The concept of moʻolelo is difficult to translate. The Hawaiian dictionary defines one word with many: story, tale, myth, history, tradition, literature, legend, journal, log, yarn, fable, essay, chronicle, record, article. In the Introduction, I quoted Jonathan Osorio's comment that all kanaka maoli stories are moʻolelo and all have a purpose behind the telling. Eleanor phrased a similar interpretation in a different way, when she told me, "all books are a person's opinion," the place where a person takes a stand. She placed a burden on me, as I am sure she knew, to consider the thrust of the story I would tell and the goals I set in telling that story. And while her moʻolelo and John's, accompanied by the ones other people offered to me over two decades, form the heart of the preceding account, they are filtered through my genealogy, both academic and personal. Moreover, I remain the visiting (malihini) anthropologist, resident of the country that illegally took over an independent nation.

Composing moʻolelo is an ongoing process, as John and Eleanor conveyed in the diversity of stories through which they negotiated competing identities. From casual chats at a McDonald's to extensive reminiscences recorded on tape, the two kūpuna shared the work of making and remaking cultural ways of *being Hawaiian*. Eleanor taught and learned the Hawaiian language; John did not. John created a farm in the suburb of Mānoa, his way of passing on malamaʻāina—a language of attachment to land. Both inscribed their learnings in words—in *Life Story* John wrote for anʻohana, in the grammar Eleanor prepared for a new generation of Hawaiian speakers, and in the hui through which they both delineated Hawaiian values within the terms set by a "foreign" government. In the force of their words lay resilience and optimism about the future. In the last letter John wrote to me, he looked forward to a family reunion in Keaukaha. The gathering, he estimated, will include "500 people or better, give or take."

Private Stories, Public Histories

The line blurs between talk-stories around a kitchen table and the stories presented in the public domain of a Home Lands Commission meeting, a protest march, or a congressional hearing. In my account of US–Hawaiʻi relations, I have juxtaposed one story to another in an effort to show the intertwining of interpretations and the bearing of a casual reference on a legislative debate and the other way around. Stories are always exchanges and not monologues, and assembled they compose a foundation for the future John and Eleanor envisaged.

In 2000, Senator Daniel Akaka introduced his Native Hawaiian Government Reorganization Bill to an American Congress for the first time. The Akaka Bill is too a kind of moʻolelo, interrupting the political discourse of the federal government with references that reflect the senator's personal attachment to the Native Hawaiian people. Introduced year after year, the text of *Akaka* changed in response to comments made in the Senate Committee on Indian Affairs and in the House Committee on Natural Resources. While the House ultimately passed the bill, the Senate has not. Chair of the Senate Committee, Akaka took the model of American Indian tribes as the basis for a "reorganized" Native Hawaiian government. Abbreviated as *nation-within-a-nation*, the model places American governance into a particular framework that, for a portion of activists, distorts the situation of kānaka maoli. In contrast, for supporters of the bill the model is the only workable possibility for political self-determination.

Arguments and strife between politicians and chiefs obstruct the creation of an integral story for the future, whether in Washington, DC, or in the state of Hawaiʻi. Yet, as fierce controversy over the Akaka Bill continues to spread across the Internet and in print media, a new narrative has begun to emerge among the "ordinary" people—the Native Hawaiians whose everyday lives are impacted by federal and state decisions. The narrative continues into the early twenty-first century a story of land that began two centuries earlier, when the first malihini arrived in the archipelago.

The meanings and the uses—misuses—of land are central to the new narrative. With a similarity to the mo'olelo John and Eleanor shared, Hawaiian homesteads in particular come to stand for a badly applied policy, a continued deprivation and betrayal of the people, and the hypocrisy in a "benefit" accorded by the federal government.

At the same time, John often returned to his memories of Keaukaha to depict the core values of Native Hawaiian culture. Other members of his generation, caught in a net of insistent Americanization, tell a similar story—Eleanor, Etta, Mr. Ō'ili, and kūpuna whose reminiscences became part of a Hawaiian cultural renaissance.[11] The words in these stories carry a force, turning "living on the land" into a guide for preserving culture, even in the concrete space of a high-rise apartment in downtown Honolulu.[12] The "arts and skills" Eleanor described in the eulogy for her brother add another version of care for the land. Gathered together these form the basis for a new narrative, and an approach to reorganizing the relationship between the United States and Native Hawaiians that is only partially covered by the Akaka Bill or by bids for a return of the monarchy or the establishment of an independent nation-state. The approach anticipates the reconstruction of ahupua'a that will thrive on land still entwined with the United States, an empire whose possession of islands in the "American Lake" persists.[13]

The theory that stories, texts, and narratives have weight in the relations between peoples—the east and the west, the strong and the weak—appears in scholarly literature: Edward Said, for one, James Scott for another.[14] On the plane of everyday interactions, the "resistance" and rebalance of power a story can accomplish is equally critical. When the senior citizens in Waimānalo acted out the Bayonet Constitution, bringing rifles to bear on a weakened King Kalākaua, they appropriated history from the imperial authorities who had held onto it for two centuries. When Eleanor appeared in the District Court of Hilo to argue for custom over law in the meting out of punishment, she counted on her words to influence the judge's decision.

I went to court with her one afternoon, and observed the proceedings. Present in the official role of Hawaiian cultural expert, she pleaded for the cause of an adolescent boy. He had moved from household to household, committed small crimes, and was now threatened with prison. "His rehabilitation," she argued, would not be accomplished by placing him with hardened criminals, and she supplemented that conventional view with a specific plea: the boy, she said, should be placed in an 'ohana where, by living according to the ancestors, he would be "redeemed." The judge promised to consider her point. When we got back to her house, Eleanor expanded on a bigger plan. Given the overwhelming number of Hawaiian youth in prisons, she proposed a complete redrafting of sentencing rules.[15] Her idea, setting up houses for recalcitrant youth where elders would teach youngsters, was not going to fly in the state. But her passionate commitment to revising the justice system, like her proposals for a Hawaiian Cultural Center and her vision of a Peace Center, plays a part in the remedies advocated by the generation she repeatedly called on to "take a hand" in the future.

Had John lived into the twenty-first century, he would have seen that generation adamantly insert the "needs" of Native Hawaiians into discourse about the future of Hawai`i. Eleanor did live into the twenty-first century, and she observed a shift in the direction of concrete proposals for improving the lives of the people for whom she had always crusaded. The younger generation has "taken a hand," and in much the way John and Eleanor anticipated, through community associations, at statewide conferences, in staffing Hawaiian language immersion schools, and in cultivating land according to tradition—developing the taro patches that both sustain and symbolize a Hawaiian way of life. And neither the state nor the federal government is immune to the urgency of these movements.

The agency against which Eleanor brought her fiercest words, the Department of Hawaiian Home Lands, is bending to the demands of individual petitioners and lessees, and attending to the "children" who rightly inherit the land. Complaints like Eleanor's come to fruition in an increase of acreage allotted for homesteads, in a modification of the rules for acquiring land, and in a strengthening of kuleana to a constituency. The Office of Hawaiian Affairs, too, moves from being the target of suits to supporting motions for a change in the laws that regulate the public lands of Hawai`i. Under pressure, and in the face of increased Native Hawaiian oversight, OHA has promised to pay back the rent Eleanor claimed the people were owed.[16]

Whether or not the Akaka Bill will ever pass is less pertinent than the daily actions of individuals who take up the tasks set by kūpuna like John and Eleanor. The outcome may be a "reorganized relationship" between Native Hawaiians and the United States that goes beyond the stalemate created by disputes over *Akaka*. And the outcome will revise a long history in which Native Hawaiians have maintained the `āina under conditions of duress and displacement. In this projected relationship, lāhui will encompass generations who share a past and who increasingly exchange the stories that provide the force for collective action.

One afternoon in May 2010, about a year after he gave the graduation speech at Kailua High, Gordon talked with me about the meetings DHHL was holding in homesteads throughout the state. He attended the meetings in Waimānalo, and he listened to plans for "returning" acres to the Hawaiian people—the thousands of acres that constitute the land held in trust. In cases where the acreage could not be returned, the DHHL promised monetary compensation. Gordon was persuaded of the good intentions in the DHHL plan, if not certain of a timely implementation. He added the thread of thought upon which he based his graduation speech. Land was crucial, he said, but so was learning to care for it, by which he meant living in harmony on the ʻāina. While Gordon appreciated the material well-being an extension of acreage promised to Native Hawaiians, he also expressed concern about the righteous use of the resource—the "exercise of spirit" that would sustain the "generosity" of the land. He was still engaged with the Waimānalo men's group, and he placed a major responsibility on the shoulders of the homestead neighbors who attended his breakfast meetings.

Gordon's daughter lives in Waimānalo. He built her a large house on the plot that once held the house where she grew up, and where I first met the family. She is raising three girls in the homestead. Gordon's children—two sons in addition to the daughter—represent a new generation, whose choice of *being Hawaiian* occurs in a context in which local identity and talking pidgin play a role. The "crossing of boundaries" I described for John and Eleanor is different for the third generation, their moʻopuna.

In Keaukaha, Eleanor's grandchildren answered her call to action by enrolling in the Ka Haka ʻUla O Keʻelikōlani College of Hawaiian Language and the Hawaiian Studies Program at the University of Hawaiʻi, Hilo. Her moʻopuna will carry out two aspects of Eleanor's agenda: teaching the Hawaiian language to future generations, and appropriating elements of a profitable tourist industry for the sustenance of Native Hawaiians. This is the third generation in the ʻohana, and they can recite out loud the history of an armed takeover, speak the ʻōlelo makuahine in schoolyards, and act together to restore the lāhui. Through conserving the language and the values, they make living on the land a viable and vigorous option for all kānaka maoli. The new generation knows they, in the words of a kupuna, "are Hawaiian. Therefore it is good." They are part of the thousands of "unnamed" individuals crucial to the future of Hawaiʻi and preparing for that future through the particular, purposeful, and concrete practicing of arts and skills of old—adapted to the world John and Eleanor anticipated and did not live to experience. And as those individuals and their moʻopuna grow up, John wrote at the end of *Life Story of a Native Hawaiian*, "there will always be a story to tell."

Notes

1. I did not meet Albert. My first encounters and conversations with Eleanor occurred on Oʻahu, and he did not accompany her on those trips.

2. "The term `ohana was likewise a figure essentially belonging to a people who were taro planters. `Oha means 'to sprout,' or 'a sprout'; the 'buds' or off-shoots of the taro plant which furnished the staple of life for the Hawaiian are called oha"; E. S. Craighill Handy and Mary Kawena Pukui, *Polynesian Family System*, 3.

3. Mary Kawena Pukui, E. W. Haertig, and Catherine Lee, *Nānā I Ke Kumu* (I), 166.

4. Founded in 1882, Matson Navigation Company was a subsidiary of Alexander and Baldwin, a Big Five Company, until December 2011. http://www.staradvertiser.com/news/breaking/134862378.html?id=134862378, accessed 19 July 2012.

5. Indigenous concepts for differentiating Hawaiians are based on "rank, ancestry, birth-place, and ability.... At the same time, these indicators spring from an ever-encom-passing sense of spirituality, which simultaneously anchors Hawaiians to the `āina and connects them to the realm of pō where ancestors and spirits reside." Brandon C. Led-ward, "On Being Hawaiian Enough," 137.

6. "Foreign desires" is part of the title of Lilikalā Kame`eleihiwa's history of land policy in Hawai`i; "Look to the Source" is the subtitle of Pukui, Haertig, and Lee, *Nānā I Ke Kumu*.

7. Brandon C. Ledward uses the notion of "native hybridity" in his stimulating discus-sion of "diverse experiences of being Hawaiian," 137. It should be clear by now that I use *identity* throughout this book in the plural form strictly as a heuristic concept for capturing the "many social selves" each person has. In this vein, it is at best possible to talk about "identities," or, as William James, one of the often cited "fathers" of identity theory, stated: "He has as many social selves as there are distinct groups of persons about whose opinion he cares" (*The Principles of Psychology*, 294). In line with recent writings, I add the notion of fluidity and of continual negotiation of these "selves" over time. I benefited, too, from the critique of retrograde, essentialist, and often-na-tionalist concepts of cultural (social) identities that postcolonial theorists, including Stuart Hall, James Clifford, and Gayatri Chakravorty Spivak, developed in the 1980s and 1990s. As much as the "hybrid identities" in postmodern/colonial analysis are constructed as a concept for the postcolonial social selves that transgress the colonial past and the residues of tradition, they remain firmly rooted in modern Western iden-tity discourse and do not capture the ways John, Eleanor, and other Native Hawaiians I talked with think about their many social selves. As Chadwick Allen points out, most postmodern/colonial critics "fail to understand how discourses that intersect with the controversial blood/land/memory complex, including the discourse of treaties, might appear cogent for indigenous minority activists and writers"; *Blood Narrative*, 30. However, in contrast to Allen, I do not try to construct an "indigenous identity" out of those stories about "blood/land/memory." I thank Wolf-Dieter Narr for his critical remarks on identity.

8. See Pukui, Haertig, and Lee, *Nānā I Ke Kumu* (I), 171.

9. Ibid. (II), 48.

10. I thank an anonymous reviewer for this reference to *Place Names of Hawai`i*.

11. See Harden, *Voices of Wisdom*, and the oral histories collected through the University of Hawai`i Oral History Center.

12. See Jennifer Noelani Goodyear-Ka`ōpua, "Rebuilding the `Auwai"; Karen L. Ito, *Lady Friends*.

13. From Hal Friedman, *Creating an American Lake*.

14. While I credit the work of writers like Edward Said, whose claims about suppressed narratives are seminal, and James Scott, who persuasively argued for the importance of counter-hegemonic texts, I focus more intensively on the "ordinary talk" of individuals who gather around the calabash, sit on beaches, or carry their conversations into the

public settings of legislatures and town meetings. See Said, *Orientalism;* Scott, *Weapons of the Weak.* Tengan's *Native Men Remade* is an example of the new scholarly focus on everyday stories (mo'olelo) for contesting dominant narratives of colonization and nationhood.

15. "Imprisonment falls disproportionately on Native Hawaiians according to a recent study conducted by the Office of Hawaiian Affairs and the Justice Policy Institute (hereinafter OHA/JPI study). Native Hawaiians make up 24 percent of Hawai'i's adult population but 39 percent of the adult incarcerated population (Office of Hawaiian Affairs, Justice Policy Institute, University of Hawai'i and Georgetown University, 2010). Earlier data (2001) indicated that Native Hawaiian women were slightly more likely than their male counterparts to be overrepresented (44 percent of incarcerated women are Native Hawaiian, compared with 38 percent of incarcerated men in 2001; Office of Hawaiian Affairs, 2002)"; Meda Chesney-Lind and Brian Bilsky, "Native Hawaiian Youth in Hawai'i Detention Center: Colonialism and Carceral Control." See also Healani Sonoda, "A Nation Incarcerated."

16. In April 2012, Governor Neil Abercrombie signed into law a measure that settles OHA's unresolved claims to past-due income and proceeds from ceded lands. http://www.oha.org/page/public-land-trust-revenue-report, accessed 24 June 2012.

Glossary of Selected Terms

ahupua`a	division of land, by geographical features; a pie-shaped piece, running from mountain to sea
`āina	land, earth (that which feeds)
ali`i	chief, ruler, leader
hānai	to foster, adopt, feed
-keiki hānai	fostered, adopted child
hānau mua	oldest living member of a family, source of wisdom, keeper of tradition
haole	foreigner, now primarily a white person, Caucasian
ho`oponopono	setting right, resolving conflict
hui	association, group
kama`āina	child of the land
kanaka, kānaka (pl)	person, people; Hawaiian person [when capitalized]
-kanaka maoli	real or true person; Hawaiian
-kānaka `ōiwi	people of the bone; Hawaiian
kaona	hidden, subtle, implicit meaning
kuleana	responsibility, accountability, interest [by extension, a small plot of land]
kupuna, kūpuna (pl)	grandparent; member of grandparental generation
lāhui	people, collectivity, nation
laulima	working together, cooperating
luhi	burden, labor

maka'āinana	commoners [eyes of the land]
mālama	to care for
-mālama 'āina	care for the land, conserve
malihini	guest, visitor, stranger
mō'i	highest ranking ali'i
mo'olelo	story, tale, myth, legend, narrative
mo'opuna	grandchild, descendant
'ohana	family, extended family
'ōlelo	speech, language
-'ōlelo makuahine	native language, mother tongue
pono	harmony, righteousness, balance, well-being

Bibliography

Aikau, Hokulani K. *A Chosen People, A Promised Land: Mormonism and Race in Hawai`i.* Minneapolis, MN: University of Minnesota Press, 2012.

Ahuna, Eleanor Kalawai`akamali`iwahineli`ili`i Simeona. "Mama: Memories of Sarah (Ida) Kahauleilo Waipa Kealohapau`ole Pakele." In *Ho`okupu: An Offering of Literature by Native Hawaiian Women,* edited by Miyoko Sugano and Jackie Pualani Johnson, 12–17. Honolulu: Mutual Publishing, 2009.

Akoi, Rhea, ed. *Ku`u Home I Keaukaha: An Oral History.* Hilo, HI: Hui Ho`omau O Keaukaha Panaewa, 1989.

Aleinikoff, T. Alexander. *Semblances of Sovereignty: The Constitution, the State, and American Citizenship.* Cambridge, MA: Harvard University Press, 2002.

Allen, Chadwick. *Blood Narrative: Indigenous Identity in American Indian and Maori Literary and Activist Texts.* Durham, NC: Duke University Press, 2002.

Allen, Gwenfread. *Hawaii's War Years.* Honolulu: University of Hawai`i Press, 1950.

Ayau, Edward Halealoha, and Ty Kāwika Tengan. "Ka Huaka`i O Nā `Ōiwi: The Journey Home." In *The Dead and their Possessions: Repatriation in Principle, Policy and Practice,* edited by Cressida Forde, Jane Hubert, and Paul Turnbull, 171–189. New York: Routledge, 2002.

Bailey, Beth, and David Farber. *The First Strange Place: The Alchemy of Race and Sex in World War II Hawaii.* Baltimore: John Hopkins University Press, 1994.

Baker, Lee. "Missionary Positions." In *Globalization and Race: Transformations in the Cultural Production of Blackness,* edited by Kamari Maxine Clarke and Deborah A. Thomas, 37–54. Durham, NC: Duke University Press, 2006.

Bayart, Jean-Francois. *The Illusion of Cultural Identity.* Chicago, IL: University of Chicago Press, 2005.

Beechert, Edward D. *Working in Hawaii: A Labor History.* Honolulu: University of Hawai`i Press, 1985.

Bell, Roger. *Last Among Equals: Hawaiian Statehood and American Politics.* Honolulu University of Hawai`i Press, 1984.

Benham, Maenette K. P., and Ronald H. Heck. *Culture and Educational Policy in Hawai`i.: The Silencing of Native Voices.* Mahwah, NJ: Lawrence Erlbaum Associates, 1998.

Bernstein, Alison. *American Indians and World War II: Toward a New Era in Indian Affairs.* Norman: University of Oklahoma Press, 1991.

Boggs, Stephen T., Karen Ann Watson-Gegeo, and Georgia McMillen. *Speaking, Relating, and Learning: A Study of Hawaiian Children at Home and at School.* Norwood, NJ: Ablex Publishing Corp, 1985.

Brieske, Phillip Richard. "A Study of the Development of Public Elementary and Secondary Education in the Territory of Hawaii." MA thesis, University of Washington, 1961.

Brody, David. *Visualizing American Empire: Orientalism and Imperialism in the Philippines.* Chicago, IL: University of Chicago Press, 2010.

Brown, DeSoto. *Hawaii goes to War: Life in Hawaii from Pearl Harbor to Peace.* Honolulu: Editions Limited, 1989.

Budnick, Rich. *Hawaii's Forgotten History 1900–1999.* Honolulu: Aloha Press, 2005.

Burlin, Paul T. *Imperial Maine and Hawai'i: Interpretive Essays in the History of Nineteenth-Century American Expansion.* New York: Lexington Books, 2006.

Center for Oral History. Social Science Research Institute. University of Hawai`i at Manoa. An Era of Change. Oral Histories of Civilians in World War II Hawai`i. Honolulu, 1994.

Chapin, Helen Geracimos. *Shaping History: The Role of Newspapers in Hawai'i.* Honolulu: University of Hawai`i Press, 1996.

Chesney-Lind, Meda, and Brian Bilsky. "Native Hawaiian Youth in Hawai`i Detention Center: Colonialism and Carceral Control," *Hūlili: Multidisciplinary Research on Hawaiian Well-Being* 7 (2011): 1–26.

Chun-Hoon, Lowell. "Labor." In *The Value of Hawai`i: Knowing The Past, Shaping the Future,* edited by Craig Howes and Jonathan Kay Kamakawiwo`ole Osorio, 61–68. Honolulu: University of Hawai`i Press, 2010.

Clarkson, Gavin, "RECENT DEVELOPMENTS: NOT BECAUSE THEY ARE BROWN, BUT BECAUSE of EA: Rice v. Cayetano, 528 U.S. 495 (2000)," *Harvard Journal of Law & Public Policy* 24, no. 3 (2001): 921–963.

Clifford, James. *The Predicament of Culture: Twentieth-Century Ethnography, Literature, and Art.* Cambridge, MA: Harvard University Press, 1988.

Coan, Titus. *Life in Hawaii: An Autobiographical Sketch of Mission Life and Labors (1835–1881).* New York: Anson D.F. Randolph & Co, 1882.

Coffman, Tom. *Nation Within a Nation.* Kihei, HI: Koa Books, 2009.

Conn, Stetson, Rose C. Engelman, and Byron Fairchild. *Guarding the United States and its Outposts.* Center of Military History. United States Army. Washington, DC: US Government Printing Office, 2000.

Cook, Katherine M. *Public Education in Hawaii.* Bulletin No. 10. Washington, DC: United States Department of the Interior, 1935.

Corntassel, Jeff. "Toward Sustainable Self-Determination: Rethinking the Contemporary Indigenous-Rights Discourse," *Alternatives* 33 (2008): 105–132.

Corntassel, Jeff, and Cheryl Bryce. 2012. "Practicing Sustainable Self-Determination: Indigenous Approaches to Cultural Restoration and Revitalization," *The Brown Journal of World Affairs* xviii, no. 11 (2012): 151–162.

Cumings, Bruce. *Dominion from Sea to Sea: Pacific Ascendancy and American Power.* New Haven, CT: Yale University Press, 2009.

Davenport, William. "'The 'Hawaiian Cultural Revolution': Some Political and Economic Considerations," *American Anthropologist* 71, no. 1 (1969): 1–20.

Daws, Gavan. *Shoal of Time: A History of the Hawaiian Islands.* Honolulu: University of Hawai`i Press, 1968.

Day, Richard R. "The Ultimate Inequality: Linguistic Genocide." In *Language of Inequality,* edited by Nessa Wolfson and Joan Manes, 163–181. New York: Mouton, 1985.

Dening, Greg. *Beach Crossings: Voyages Across Times, Cultures, and Self.* Philadelphia, PA: University of Pennsylvania Press, 2004.

Dod, Karl C. *Corps of Engineers: The War Against Japan.* Washington, DC: Government Printing Office, 1966.

Dudley, W. C., and M. Lee. *Tsunami!* Honolulu: University of Hawai`i Press, 1988.

Du Puy, William Atherton. *Hawaii and Its Race Problem.* Washington, DC: US Government Printing Office, 1932.

Emery, Bryon Elwyn. "Intensification of settlement and land utilization since 1930 in Manoa Valley." MA thesis, Honolulu: University of Hawaii, 1956.

Evans, Rhonda. *A History of the Service of Ethnic Minorities in the U.S. Armed Forces.* Center for the Study of Sexual Minorities in the Military, University of California at Santa Barbara, 2003.

Everly, Hubert. "Education in Hawaii-Yesterday and Today." In *The Kamehameha Schools 75th Anniversary Lectures* [delivered by E. H. Bryan and others], 45–52. Honolulu: The Kamehameha Schools Press, 1965.

Ferguson, Kathy, and Phyllis Turnbull. "The Military." In *The Value of Hawai`i: Knowing the Past, Shaping the Future,* edited by Craig Howes and Jonathan Kay Kamakawiwo`ole Osorio, 47–52. Honolulu: University of Hawai`i Press, 2010.

Fitzgerald, Donald. "Pearl Harbor, the Army Corps of Engineers, and Punahou's Cereus Hedge," *The Hawaiian Journal of History* 25 (1991): 187–196.

Friedman, Hal M. *Creating an American Lake: United States Imperialism and Strategic Security in the Pacific Basin, 1945–1947.* Westport, CT: Greenwood Press, 2001.

Fuchs, Lawrence H. *Hawaii Pono (Hawaii The Excellent): An Ethnic and Political History.* Honolulu: Bess Press, 1961.

Geiger, Jeffrey. *Facing the Pacific: Polynesia and the U.S. Imperial Imagination.* Honolulu: University of Hawai`i Press, 2007.

Go, Julian. "The Provinciality of American Empire: 'Liberal Exceptionalism' and U.S. Colonial Rule, 1898–1912," *Comparative Studies in Society and History* 49, no. 1 (2007): 74–108.

Goodyear-Ka`ōpua, Jennifer Noelani. "Rebuilding the `Auwai: Connecting Ecology, Economy and Education in Hawaiian Schools," *AlterNative: An International Journal of Indigenous Peoples* 5, no. 2 (2009): 46–77.

Gough, Allison J. "Messing Up Another Country's Customs: The Exportation of American Racism During World War II." *World History Connected* (October 2007) at: http://www.historycooperative.org/journals/whc/5.1/gough.html.

Grimshaw, Patricia. *Paths of Duty: American Missionary Wives in Nineteenth Century Hawaii.* Honolulu: University of Hawai`i Press, 1989.

Hall, Lisa Kahaleole. "'Hawaiian at Heart' and Other Fictions," *The Contemporary Pacific* 17, no. 2 (2005): 404–413.

Halualani, Rona Tamiko. *In the Name of Hawaiians: Native Identities and Cultural Politics.* Minneapolis, MN: University of Minnesota Press, 2002.

Handy, E. S. Craighill, and Mary Kawena Pukui. *The Polynesian Family System in Ka-`u. Hawai`i.* Rutland, VT: Charles E.Tuttle Co., 1981.

Harland Bartholomew and Associates. *A General Plan for Waimanalo Valley, Island of Oahu, Territory of Hawaii.* Honolulu, Hawaii, 1959.

———. *An Action Program for Waimanalo Valley.* Honolulu, Hawaii, 1961.

Harden, M. J. *Voices of Wisdom: Hawaiian Elders Speak.* Kula, HI: Aka Press, 1999.

Hasager, Ulla. "Localizing the American Dream: Constructing Hawaiian Homelands." In *Siting Culture,* edited by Karen Fog Olwig and Kirsten Hastrup, 165–192. New York: Routledge, 1997.

Hawaiian Commission. *The Report of the Hawaiian Commission Appointed in Pursuance of the Join Resolution for Annexing the Hawaiian Islands to the United States.* Washington, DC: US Government Printing Office, 1898.

Hitch, Thomas H., and Robert M. Kamins. *Islands in Transition: The Past, Present, and Future of Hawaii's Economy.* Honolulu: First Hawaiian Bank, 1992.

Holman, Lucia Ruggles. *Journal of Lucia Ruggles Holman.* Special Publication 17. Honolulu: Bishop Museum Press, 1931.

Hoʻomanawanui, Kuʻualoha. "'This Land is Your Land, This Land was My Land.'" In *Asian Settler Colonialism, from Local Governance to the Habits of Everyday Life in Hawaiʻi* edited by Candace Fujikane and Jonathan Y. Okamura, 139–146. Honolulu: University of Hawaiʻi Press. 2008.

Hormann, Bernhard. "Integration in Hawaii's Schools," *Social Process in Hawaii* XXI (1957): 27–35.

———. "'Racial' Statistics in Hawaii," *Social Process in Hawaii* XII (1948): 27–35.

Howard, Alan. *Ain't No Big Thing: Coping Strategies in a Hawaiian-American Community.* Honolulu: University of Hawaiʻi Press, 1974.

Howard, Alan, et al. "Traditional and Modern Adoption Patterns in Hawaii." In *Adoption in Eastern Oceania,* edited by Vern Carroll, ASAO Monograph No. 1, 21–51. Honolulu: University of Hawaiʻi Press, 1970.

Howes, Craig, and Jonathan Kay Kamakawiwoʻole Osorio, eds. *The Value of Hawaiʻi: Knowing the Past, Shaping the Future.* Honolulu: University of Hawaiʻi Press, 2010.

Hunt, James R. *Education in the States: Historical Development and Outlook.* Washington, DC: National Education Association of the United States, 1969.

Imada, Adria L. "Hawaiians on Tour: Hula Circuits through the American Empire." *American Quarterly* 56, no. 1 (2004): 111–149.

Ito, Karen L. *Lady Friends: Hawaiian Ways and the Ties that Define.* Ithaca, NY: Cornell University Press, 1999.

Jackson, Frances. "Bombs in a National Park: Military Use of Hawaii National Park During World War II." *The Hawaiian Journal of History* 10 (1976): 102–107.

James, William. *The Principles of Psychology: In Two Volumes.* Vol. I. London: Macmillan and Co., 1891.

Johnson, Greg. *Sacred Claims: Repatriation and Living Tradition.* Charlottesville, VA: University of Virginia Press, 2007.

Jolly, Margaret, and Martha MacIntyre, eds. *Family and Gender in the Pacific: Domestic Contradictions and the Colonial Impact.* New York: Cambridge University Press, 1989.

Jones, Wilbur D., and Carroll R. Jones. *Hawaii Goes to War: The Aftermath of Pearl Harbor.* Shippensburg, PA: White Mane Books, 2001.

Kajihiro, Kyle. "The Militarizing of Hawaiʻi: Occupation, Accommodation, and Resistance." In *Asian Settler Colonialism: From Local Governance to the Habits of Everyday Life in Hawaiʻi,* edited by Candace Fujikane and Jonathan Y. Okamura, 170–194. Honolulu: University of Hawaiʻi Press, 2008.

———. "Resisting Militarization in Hawaiʻi." In *The Bases of Empire: The Global Struggle against U.S. Military Posts,* edited by Catherine Lutz, 299–331. New York: New York University Press, 2009.

Kamahele, Momiala. "ʻĪlioʻulaokalani: Defending Native Hawaiian Culture." In *Asian Settler Colonialism: From Local Governance to the Habits of Everyday Life in Hawaiʻi,* edited by Candace Fujikane and Jonathan Y. Okamura, 76–98. Honolulu: University of Hawaiʻi Press, 2008.

Kamakau, Samuel Mānaiakalani. *Ka Poʻe Kahiko: The People of Old.* Translated by Mary Kawena Pukui. Honolulu: Bishop Museum Press, 1964.

Kameʻeleihiwa, Lilikalā. *Native Land and Foreign Desires: Pehea Lā E Pono Ai?* Honolulu: Bishop Museum Press, 1992.

Kanahele, George Huʻeu Sanford. *Ku Kanaka: Stand Tall. A Search for Hawaiian Values.* Honolulu: University of Hawaiʻi Press, 1986.

Kanaʻiaupuni, S. K., N. Malone, and K. Ishiboshi. *Ka Huakaʻi: 2005 Native Hawaiian Educational Assessment.* Honolulu: Kamehameha Schools, Pauahi Publications, 2005.

Kaomea, Julie. "A Curriculum of Aloha? Colonialism and Tourism in Hawai`i's Elementary Textbooks." *Curriculum Inquiry* 30, no. 3 (2000): 319–344.

Kauanui, J. Kēhaulani. *Hawaiian Blood: Colonialism and the Politics of Sovereignty and Indigeneity.* Durham, NC: Duke University Press, 2008.

Kawaharada, Dennis. *Local Geography: Essays on Multicultural Hawaii.* Honolulu: Kalamakū Press, 2004.

Keahiolalo-Karasuda, RaeDeen. "A Genealogy of Punishment in Hawai`i: The Public Hanging of Chief Kamanawa II." *Hūlili: Multidisciplinary Research on Hawaiian Well-Being* 6 (2010): 147–167.

Kelly, Marion. "Some Thoughts on Education in Traditional Hawaiian Society." In *To Teach the Children: Historical Aspects of Education in Hawaii.* Honolulu: Bishop Museum Press, 1982.

Kent, Noel J. *Hawaii: Islands under the Influence.* Honolulu: University of Hawai`i Press, 1993.

King, Samuel P, and Randall W. Roth. *Broken Trust: Greed, Mismanagement & Political Manipulation at America's Largest Charitable Trust.* Honolulu: University of Hawai`i Press, 2006.

Kramer, Paul. *The Blood of Government: Race, Empire, the United States, and the Philippines.* Chapel Hill: University of North Carolina Press, 2006.

Kuykendall, Ralph Simpson. *The Hawaiian Kingdom: 1778–1854.* Honolulu: University of Hawai`i Press, 1938.

———. *The Hawaiian Kingdom: 1854–1874.* Honolulu: University of Hawai`i Press, 1953.

———. *The Hawaiian Kingdom: 1874–1893.* Honolulu: University of Hawai`i Press, 1967.

Kuykendall, Ralph S., and Herbert E. Gregory. *A History of Hawaii.* New York: The McMillan Company, 1926.

Ledward, Brandon C. "On Being Hawaiian Enough: Contesting American Racialization with Native Hybridity." *Hūlili: Multidisciplinary Research on Hawaiian Well-Being* 4 (2007): 107–140.

Levy, Neil M. "Native Hawaiian Land Rights." *California Law Review* 63, no. 4 (1975): 848–885.

Levy, Robert. *The Tahitians: Mind and Experience in the Society Islands.* Chicago, IL: University of Chicago Press, 1973.

Lind, Andrew W. *Hawaii's People,* 3rd ed. Honolulu: University of Hawai`i Press, 1967.

———. "Some Problems of Veteran Adjustment in Hawaii." *Social Process in Hawaii,* vol. XII (1948): 58–73.

———. "Trends in Post-War Race Relations in Hawaii." Rept. No. 25. *What People in Hawaii are Saying and Doing.* Romanzo Adams Social Research Laboratory. Honolulu: University of Hawai`i Press, 1959.

Linnekin, Jocelyn. *Children of the Land: Exchange and Status in a Hawaiian Community.* New Brunswick, NJ: Rutgers University Press, 1985.

Linnekin, Jocelyn, and Lin Poyer, eds. *Cultural Identity and Ethnicity in the Pacific.* Honolulu: University of Hawai`i Press, 1990.

Love, Eric T. L. *Race over Empire. Racism and U.S. Imperialism, 1865–1900.* Chapel Hill: University of North Carolina Press, 2004.

MacKenzie, Melody Kapilialoha. "Tribute: Chief Justice William S. Richardson (1919–2010): Ka Lama Ku O ka No`eau: The Standing Torch of Wisdom." *Hawaiian Law Review* 33, no. 3 (2010): 3–15.

Mannheim, Karl. "The Problem of Generations." In *Essays on the Sociology of Knowledge,* edited by Paul Kecskemeti, 276–322. New York: Oxford University Press, 1952.

Mānoa Valley Residents. *Mānoa: The Story of a Valley. The multicultural heritage of a Hono-lulu neighborhood.* Honolulu: Mutual Publishing Co., 1994.

Marcus, George E., and Michael M. J. Fischer. *Anthropology as Cultural Critique: An Experi-mental Moment in the Human Sciences.* Chicago, IL: University of Chicago Press, 1986.

Mattos, Helene Kahinupawaokalani, and Pamela H. Medeiros. "A Survey of Social and Economic Needs of Hawaiians on Hawaiian Homelands (Kewalo/Papakolea and Waimanalo)." MA thesis, School of Social Work, University of Hawaiʻi, 1977.

McGregor, Davianna Pōmaikaʻi. *Na Kuaʻāina: Living Hawaiian Culture.* Honolulu: Univer-sity of Hawaiʻi Press, 2007.

———. "ʻĀina Hoʻopulapula: Hawaiian Homesteading." *The Hawaiian Journal of History* 24 (1990): 1–38.

Merry, Sally Engle. *Colonizing Hawaiʻi: The Cultural Power of Law.* Princeton, NJ: Princeton University Press, 2000.

———. "Law and Identity in an American Colony." In *Law and Empire in the Pacific*, edited by Sally Engle Merry and Donald Brenneis, 123–152. Santa Fe, NM: School of Ameri-can Research Press, 2003.

Meyer, Manulani Aluli. "Our Own Liberation: Reflections on Hawaiian Epistemology." *The Contemporary Pacific* 13, no. 1 (2001): 124–148.

———. *Hoʻoulu: Our Time of Becoming: Collected Early Writings of Manulani Meyer.* Hono-lulu: ʻAi Pohaku Press, 2003.

Naya, Seiji. *Income Distribution and Poverty Alleviation for the Native Hawaiian Commu-nity.* Honolulu: East-West Center Working Papers, Economic series, No. 91 (2007).

Norbeck, Edward. *Pineapple Town: Hawaii.* Berkeley: University of California Press, 1959.

Nunes, Shiho S. "The Hawaii English Project." *Educational Perspectives. Journal of the Col-lege of Education, University of Hawaiʻi* 6, no. 3 (1967): 14–16.

Odo, Franklin. *No Sword to Bury: Japanese Americans in Hawaiʻi during World War II.* Philadelphia, PA: Temple University Press, 2004.

Office of Hawaiian Affairs. *Native Hawaiian Data Book.* Honolulu, 2002 and 2011 at: http://www.ohadatabook.com/DB2011.html.

Okamura, Jonathan Y. *Ethnicity and Inequality in Hawaiʻi.* Philadelphia, PA: Temple Uni-versity Press, 2008.

Okihiro, Gary Y. *Cane Fires: The Anti-Japanese Movement in Hawaii, 1865–1945.* Philadel-phia, PA: Temple University Press, 1992.

———. *Island World: A History of Hawaiʻi and the United States.* Berkeley: University of California Press, 2009.

Osorio, Jonathan Kay Kamakawiwoʻole. *Dismembering Lāhui: A History of the Hawaiian Nation to 1887.* Honolulu: University of Hawaiʻi Press, 2002.

———. "Living in Archives and Dreams: The Histories of Kuykendall and Daws." In *Texts and Contexts: Reflections in Pacific Islands Historiography*, edited by Doug Munro and Brij V. Lal, 191–201. Honolulu: University of Hawaiʻi Press, 2006.

———. "'What Kine Hawaiian Are You?' A Moʻolelo about Nationhood, Race, History, and the Contemporary Sovereignty Movement in Hawaiʻi." *The Contemporary Pacific* 13, no. 2 (2001): 359–379.

———. "Hawaiian Issues." In *The Value of Hawaiʻi: Knowing The Past, Shaping the Future*, edited by Craig Howes and Jonathan Kay Kamakawiwoʻole Osorio, 15–21. Honolulu: University of Hawaiʻi Press, 2010.

Otis, Alison T., William D. Honey, and Thomas C. Hogg. *Forest Service and the Civilian Conservation Corps, 1933–42.* Hawaii: United States Department of Agriculture, For-est Service, FS-395, 1986.

Parker, Linda S. *Native American Estate: The Struggle over Indian and Hawaiian Lands.* Honolulu: University of Hawai`i Press, 1989.

Porter, Bernard. *Empire and Superempire: Britain, America, and The World.* New Haven, CT: Yale University Press, 2006.

Prucha, Francis Paul. *The Great Father: The United States Government and the American Indians.* Vols. 1 and 2 unabridged. Lincoln, NE: University of Nebraska Press, 1995.

Pukui, Mary Kawena, E. W. Haertig, and Catherine Lee. *Nānā I Ke Kumu: Look to the Source.* 2 vols. Honolulu: Hui Hānai. An Auxiliary of the Queen Lili`uokalani Children's Center, 1972.

Rohrer, Judy. "'Got Race?' The Production of Haole and the Distortion of Indigeneity in the *Rice* Decision," *The Contemporary Pacific* 18, no. 1 (2006): 1-31.

———. *Haoles in Hawai`i.* Honolulu: University of Hawai`i Press, 2010.

Rosa, John P. "Local Story: The Massie Case Narrative and the Cultural Production of Local Identity in Hawai`i," *Amerasia Journal* 26, no. 2 (2000): 93–115.

———. "Race/Ethnicity." In *The Value of Hawai`i: Knowing the Past, Shaping the Future,* edited by Craig Howes and Jonathan Kay Kamakawiwo`ole Osorio, 53–59. Honolulu: University of Hawai`i Press, 2010.

Ruffner, Kevin C. "The Black Market in Postwar Berlin: Colonel Miller and an Army Scandal," *Prologue Magazine* 34, no. 3 (2002) at: http://www.archives.gov/publications/prologue/2002/fall/berlin-black-market-1.html.

Said, Edward. *Orientalism.* New York: Vintage Books, 1978.

Sahlins, Marshall. *Islands of History.* Chicago, IL: University of Chicago Press, 1985.

Sato, Charlene. "Linguistic Inequality in Hawaii: The Post-Creole Dilemma." In *Language of Inequality,* edited by Nessa Wolfson and Joan Manes, 255–272. New York: Mouton, 1985.

Schachter [Modell], Judith. *A Sealed and Secret Kinship. The Culture of Policies and Practices in American Adoption.* New York: Berghahn Books, 2002.

Schachter, Judith. "'A Relationship Endeared to the People': Adoption in Hawaiian Custom and Law," *Pacific Studies* 31, no. 3/4 (2008): 211–231.

———. "One Hundred Percent Hawaiian: Life Stories, Politics, and Anthropology," *Anthropology and Humanism* 35, no. 1 (2010): 81–97.

Schachter, Judith, and Albrecht Funk. "Sovereignty, Indigeneity, Identities: Perspectives from Hawai`i," *Social Identities* 18, no. 4 (2012): 399–416.

Schlesinger, Arthur, Jr. "The American Empire? Not So Fast," *World Policy Journal* XXII, no. 1 (2005): 43–46.

Schmitt, Robert C. *Demographic Statistics of Hawaii: 1778–1965.* Honolulu: University of Hawai`i Press, 1968.

———. "Some Construction and Housing Firsts," *The Hawaiian Journal of History* 15 (1981): 100–112.

Schrijvers, Peter. *The Crash of Ruin: American Combat Soldiers in Europe During World War II.* London: Macmillan Press, Ltd., 1998.

Scott, James. *Weapons of the Weak: Everyday Forms of Peasant Resistance.* New Haven, CT: Yale University Press, 1985.

Shoemaker, James H. "Hawaii emerges from the War," *Pacific Affairs* 19, no. 2 (1946): 182–192.

Shook, E. Victoria. *Ho`oponopono: Contemporary Uses of a Hawaiian Problem-Solving Process.* Honolulu: University of Hawai`i Press, 2002.

Silva, Noenoe. *Aloha Betrayed: Native Hawaiian Resistance to American Colonialism.* Durham, NC: Duke University Press, 2004.

Sonoda, Healani. "A Nation Incarcerated." In *Asian Settler Colonialism: From Local Governance to the Habits of Everyday Life in Hawai`i*, edited by Candace Fujikane and Jonathan Y. Okamura, 99–115. Honolulu: University of Hawai`i Press, 2008.

Spack, Ruth. *America's Second Tongue: American Indian Education and the Ownership of English, 1860–1900*. Lincoln, NE: University of Nebraska Press, 2002.

Spitz, Allan A. *Organization and Administration of the Hawaiian Homes Program*. University of Hawaii, Legislative Reference Bureau, 1963.

———. *Social Aspects of the Hawaiian Homes Program*. Report 1c, University of Hawaii, Legislative Reference Bureau, 1964.

Stannard, David E. *Before the Horror: The Population of Hawai`i on the Eve of Western Contact*. Honolulu: Social Science Research Institute (distributed by University of Hawai`i Press), 1989.

———. *Honor Killing: How the Infamous Massie Affair "Transformed" Hawai`i*. New York: Viking Press, 2005.

Steege, Paul. *Black Market, Cold War: Everyday Life in Berlin 1946–1949*. New York: Cambridge University Press, 2007.

Steinmetz, George. *The Devil's Handwriting: Precoloniality and the German Colonial State in Qingdao, Samoa, and Southwest Africa*. Chicago, IL: University of Chicago Press, 2007.

Stillman, Amy Ku`uleialoha. "'Nā Lei O Hawai'i'": On Hula Songs, Floral Emblems, Island Princesses, and *Wahi Pana*," *Hawaiian Journal of History* 28 (1994): 87–108.

———. "Of the People Who Love the Land: Vernacular History in the Poetry of Modern Hawaiian Hula," *Amerasia Journal* 28, no. 3 (2002): 85–108.

Stoler, Ann Laura. *Haunted by Empire: Geographies of Intimacy in North American History*. Durham, NC: Duke University Press, 2006.

———. "Tense and Tender Ties: The Politics of Comparison in North American History and (Post) Colonial Studies," *The Journal of American History* 88, no. 3 (2001): 892–865.

Stueber, Ralph K. "An Informal History of Schooling in Hawaii." In *To Teach The Children: Historical Aspects of Education in Hawai`i*. A Publication Accompanying the Exhibition Commemorating the 50th Anniversary of the College of Education and the 75th Anniversary of the University of Hawaii, 16–36. Honolulu: Bishop Museum Press, 1982.

Sullivan, Paul. "Customary Revolutions: The Law of Custom and the Conflict of Traditions in Hawai`i," *University of Hawaii Law Review* 20 (1998): 99–148.

Tachihata, Chieko. "The Sovereignty Movement in Hawai`i," *The Contemporary Pacific* 6, no. 1 (1994): 202–210.

Tagaki, Dana. "Native Hawaiians." In *Poverty in the United States: An Encyclopedia of History, Politics, and Policy*, edited by Gwendolyn Mink and Alice O'Connor, 493–496. Santa Barbara, CA: ABC-CLIO Inc., 2004.

Takaki, Ron. *Pau Hana: Plantation Life and Labor in Hawaii*. Honolulu: University of Hawai`i Press, 1983.

Talbott, E. Guy. "Making Americans in Hawaii," *The American Review of Reviews* LXXIII, no. 3 (1926): 280–285.

Tamura, Eileen H. "The English-Only Effort, the Anti-Japanese Campaign, and Language Acquisition in the Education of Japanese Americans in Hawaii, 1915–1940," *History of Education Quarterly* 33, no. 1 (1993): 37–58.

Taum, Ramsay Remigius Mahealani. "Tourism." In *The Value of Hawai`i: Knowing The Past, Shaping the Future*, edited by Craig Howes and Jonathan Kay Kamakawiwo`ole Osorio, 31–38. Honolulu: University of Hawai`i Press, 2010.

Tengan, Ty P. Kāwika. *Native Men Remade: Gender and Nation in Contemporary Hawai`i*. Durham, NC: Duke University Press, 2008.

———. "Re-membering Panalā`au: Masculinities, Nation, and Empire in Hawai`i and the Pacific," *The Contemporary Pacific* 20, no. 1 (2008): 27–53.

Tengan, Ty P. Kāwika, and Jesse Makani Markham. "Performing Polynesian Maculinities in American Football: From 'Rainbows to Warriors,'" *The International Journal of the History of Sport* 26, no. 16 (2009): 2412–2431.

Thomas, Nicholas. *Colonialism's Culture: Anthropology, Travel and Government*. Princeton, NJ: Princeton University Press, 1994.

Thrum, Thomas G. *The Hawaiian Annual for 1925. The Reference Book of Information and Statistics. Relating to the Territory of Hawaii, of Value to Merchants, Tourists and Others*. Honolulu, 1924.

Tibbetts, Katherine, Kū Kahakalau, and Zanette Johnson. "Education with Aloha and Student Assets," *Hūlili: Multidisciplinary Research on Hawaiian Well-Being* 4 (2007): 147–180.

Trask, Haunani-Kay. *From a Native Daughter*. Monroe, ME: Common Courage Press, 1993.

———. "Settlers of Color and 'Immigrant' Hegemony." In *Asian Settler Colonialism: From Local Governance to the Habits of Everyday Life in Hawai`i*, edited by Candace Fujikane and Jonathan Y. Okamura, 45–65. Honolulu: University of Hawai`i Press, 2008.

US Bureau of the Census. *U.S. Census of Population: 1950*. Vol. II: *Characteristics of The Population*. Part 51–54, Territories and Possessions. Washington, DC: US Government Printing Office, 1953.

Van Dyke, Jon. *Who Owns the Crown Lands of Hawai`i?* Honolulu: University of Hawai`i Press, 2007.

Walker, Isaiah Helekunihi. *Waves of Resistance: Surfing and History in Twentieth-Century Hawai`i*. Honolulu: University of Hawai`i Press, 2011.

Warner, Sam L. No`eau. "'Kuleana': The Right, Responsibility, and Authority of Indigenous Peoples to Speak and Make Decisions for Themselves in Language and Cultural Revitalization," *Anthropology and Education Quarterly* 30, no. 1 (1999): 68–93.

Watson, Trisha Kehaulani. "Civil Rights and Wrongs: Understanding Doe V. Kamehameha Schools," *Hūlili: Multidisciplinary Research on Hawaiian Well-Being* 3 (2006): 1–18.

Webb, Terry Douglas. "Mormonism and Tourist Art in Hawaii." PhD thesis, Arizona State University. Ann Arbor, MI: UMI, 1990.

Whitehead, John S. *Completing the Union: Alaska, Hawai`i, and the Battle For Statehood*. Albuquerque: University of New Mexico Press, 2004.

Young, G. Terry Kanalu. *Rethinking the Native Hawaiian Past*. New York: Garland Publishing, 1998.

Ziemke, Earl F. *The U.S. Army in the Occupation of Germany, 1944–1946*. Army Historical Series. Center of Military History, United States Army, Washington, DC: US Government Printing Office, 1990.

Index

Abercrombie, Neil, 176, 210n16
adoption, vii, 1, 12n1, 137–38, 140–42, 146, 149–51, 156n72, 166, 169–70, 195n38. *See also* hānai
ʻāina, 16–18, 20, 23, 28, 36, 44, 46, 71, 78, 79, 80n15, 128, 133, 137, 171–72, 183, 188, 199, 202, 206, 208, 209n5. *See also* land
    ahupuaʻa, 28, 34, 49n49, 56, 159, 163, 206
    mālama ʻāina 11, 16, 21, 23, 28, 31, 46, 130, 159, 187, 205
Akaka, Daniel, 40, 115n71
    Akaka Bill (Native Hawaiian Government Reorganization Bill), 185, 193, 197n90, 205–7
Allen, Gwenfread, 92, 113n12, 113n16, 113n22, 115n67, 124n7, 124n26
aloha, spirit of, 4, 12n2, 16, 21, 29, 35, 39, 45–46, 52, 80n15, 112, 130, 139, 144–45, 159, 187, 202
Alu Like, 38, 174, 177–78
American consumerism, 6, 41, 133, 153, 202
American imperialism, vii, 7, 14n21, 15n34, 17, 21, 60, 64, 72, 92, 99, 113n21, 11, 126, 160, 178, 203
American Indians. *See* Native Americans
Americanization, 9, 10, 12, 16, 27, 53, 58, 60, 64, 79, 82n60, 85, 102, 118, 132, 134, 147, 150, 206
annexation (Hawaiʻi), 14n21, 33, 45, 57–58, 60, 86
Apology (Public Law 103–150), 158, 184–85, 197n86. *See also* Clinton

Bailey, Beth, 93, 97
Benham, Maenette, 73

Big Five, 20–21, 60, 64, 75, 77, 98, 121–23, 199, 209n4
Bishop, Charles R., 57
Bishop, Princess Bernice Pauahi, 5, 66, 151
Bishop Estate, 37, 50n78
blood quantum rule, x, 2, 21–22, 48n18, 49n38, 146, 149–51, 167–70, 179, 183
boundary-crossing, 3–5, 41, 67, 134, 200–201, 208

Cayetano, Benjamin, 176, 197n94. *See also* Rice v. Cayetano
charter schools (Hawaiian), 70–71, 83n66
Civilian Conservation Corps, 11, 26, 43, 74–80, 83n80, 81, 85, 88, 89, 96, 111, 187, 202
Clinton, Bill, 110, 158, 173, 184–85, 188
Coan, Titus, 24, 54–56, 59, 78. *See also* missionaries
Cummins, John Adams, 160
Cummins, Thomas, 160–61

Dawes Act, 19–21, 34, 47nn9–10, 48n18
Dening, Greg, 4
Department of Education (Hawaiʻi), 63, 67, 69, 71
Department of Hawaiian Home Lands (DHHL), 4, 22–23, 28, 36, 42, 149, 163–72, 181–83, 186, 188–90, 207–8. *See also* Hawaiian Homes Commission
Department of Public Instruction (Territory of Hawaiʻi), 11, 53, 56, 58, 60, 63, 65, 75, 80n16, 81n23, 82n50
Dillingham Company, 121–22
Dole, Sanford, 60–61, 81n31, 82n60

Eisenhower, Dwight D., 105, 155n42
Enos, Eric, 56, 133

Everly, Hubert, 60

Farber, David, 93, 97
Fechner, Robert, 77

genealogy, 2, 13n6, 21, 26–28, 45, 147,
149, 151, 175, 183–84, 199, 204. *See also*
kinship
generation, ix, 6, 9–10, 13n8, 14n22,
15n33, 40, 53, 56, 65, 66, 68, 71, 73,
82n59, 110, 121, 134, 153, 159, 174, 178,
183, 193, 200, 202, 204, 206–8
General Allotment Act of 1887. *See* Dawes
Act
G.I. Bill (Servicemen's Readjustment Act
of 1944), 110, 154n26
Goodyear-Kaʻōpua, J. Noelani, 47n5 and
6, 71, 81n18
Great Depression, 9, 29–31, 74, 110, 128,
187

hānai, vii, 138–39, 142–53, 170–71, 201.
See also adoption
Handy, E. S. Craighill, 58, 209n2
Hālawa Housing, 127–31, 139, 155n55
haole, vii, 2, 18, 28, 32, 33, 57, 59, 67, 76,
81n17, 83n91, 89, 93, 95–96, 98, 101,
110, 114n61, 118, 131, 142, 179, 12
hapa haole 3, 4, 13n9
Harland Bartholomew and Associates,
162, 194n15
Hawaiʻi, 2, 6, 40, 43–44, 68
Kingdom of, 15n34, 45, 54, 57, 60,
137–38, 150, 160, 184, 196n86
sovereignty, x, 5–7, 14n22, 17, 31,
45–46, 159, 180–88, 191, 193,
200–203
State of, 5–6, 22, 68–69, 118–19,
156n75, 156n79, 162, 169, 174,
185, 195n55
Constitutional Convention
(1978), 173, 175, 185
legislature, 38, 45, 53, 69, 82n66,
171, 179, 183, 191, 193
Territory of, x, 9, 11, 30, 33, 47n11,
53, 58, 60, 64, 75, 87, 92, 93, 98,
113n21, 118–19, 124, 127, 156n79,
162
legislature, 18–19, 34, 131, 162
Organic Act of 1900, 21

Hawaiian Civic Clubs, 19, 41, 51n89
Hawaiian Homes Commission, 4, 6,
22, 24, 28, 36, 38–39, 120, 149, 161,
164, 180, 203. *See also* Department of
Hawaiian Home Lands (DHHL)
Hawaiian Homes Commission Act
(1921), 6, 11, 14n23, 16, 19–21, 29,
48n18, 159, 161, 176
Hawaiian Homestead(s) (homelands),
16–17, 23–32, 34, 36, 38, 46, 64, 73,
128, 135, 147, 159, 163, 172, 190, 200,
206
agricultural homesteads, 17, 18, 20,
23–24, 27–28, 36, 203
associations, 23, 41, 181–83, 190. *See
also* homestead hui
allotments, 17, 19, 20, 28–29, 47n9,
160
beneficiaries, 21–23, 170, 183
bureaucratic rules, 42, 149, 166,
167–72, 183, 207
designation of successor, 150–53,
168–71, 190
lease(s), 17, 20, 22, 48n25 and 28,
49n38, 120, 149–50, 160–61, 167–
68, 170–71, 186
homestead hui, 5, 23, 36–38, 41, 170,
172, 181
Keaukaha, 2, 11, 16–17, 20, 23–30,
35–37, 72, 86, 123, 126, 159–60,
172, 189, 206
meanings of, 16, 23, 30–32, 36, 130,
132, 147, 159, 172, 181, 190–92
Molokaʻi, 23–24, 28, 34, 49n50, 120
Panaʻewa, 17, 24, 28, 38–39, 159, 203
Papakōlea, 34, 66
rehabilitation, 17–19, 24, 37, 48n28,
188, 193, 206
residential homestead, 17, 23, 29–30,
36, 160, 161
reunions, 25, 35–36, 51n89, 130
Waimānalo, 2, 72, 88, 113n12, 160–
64, 174, 186–90, 193n9, 194n18,
202
Hawaiian language, 35, 41, 48n12, 65,
67–72, 134, 173–74, 191, 205, 207–8
Immersion program, 69–70
Hawaiian nationhood, 6, 15n34, 45–47,
57, 115n71, 137, 147, 152, 158, 159, 181,
184, 186, 188, 203–6. *See also* lāhui

Hawaiian Renaissance, 4, 10, 25, 31, 53, 67–69, 80n2, 82n60, 134, 151, 158, 159, 164, 173, 174, 206
Heck, Ronald, 73
Hilo, 11, 24, 30, 35, 36, 39–40, 50n89, 54, 87, 108, 123, 126, 127, 160
Holman, Lucia Ruggles, 54, 55. *See also* missionaries
Homestead Act of 1862, 19, 47n8
Honolulu, 20, 32–34, 49n60, 50n69, 66, 86–87, 90–92, 109, 112n4, 118–22, 127–31, 161–62
    Rapid Transit 95–98, 120
    Redevelopment Agency, 129–31
Ho`omanawanui, Ku`ualoha, 63
ho`oponopono, 141, 156n81

identity, constructions of, 2–4, 8, 13n10, 21–22, 28, 31, 79–80, 80n1, 146–47, 150–51, 153, 179, 199–200, 203, 205, 208, 209n5, 209n7. *See also* Native Hawaiian
Inouye, Dan, 40
Ito, Karen, 49n44, 81n25, 143, 145

Japanese, in Hawai`i, 24, 32, 33, 50n68, 64, 76, 82nn49–50, 93–95, 99–100, 107, 109–10, 115n67
Johnson, Lyndon, 173

Kaiser, Henry J., 162
Kalaniana`ole, Prince Jonah Kūhiō, 4, 13n13, 17–22, 29, 37, 47n20, 50n89, 167, 173, 183, 193
Kamakawiwo`ole, Israel, 159
Kame`eleihiwa, Lilikalā, 188
Kamehameha III, Kauikeaouli, 57, 81n18, 137, 160
Kamehameha Schools, ix, 5, 37, 50n78, 66, 72, 151–52
    John Doe v. Kamehameha Schools, 151–52
    Mohica-Cummings v. Kamehameha Schools, 151, 157n109
Kanahele, Dennis Pu`uhonua (Bumpy), 187
kanaka maoli/kānaka maoli, x, 10, 13n18, 17, 18, 21–23, 28, 46, 53, 61, 63, 80, 99, 11, 138, 146, 152, 173, 184,

    185, 188, 191, 193, 195n49, 202–4, 208
Kanaka`ole, Edith, 67, 71, 134, 177
kupuna/kūpuna, 3, 9–10, 13n18, 16, 35–36, 40, 43, 45, 67–68, 82n59, 118, 135, 153, 174–75, 190, 200, 208
Kawaharda, Dennis, 63
kinship, 4, 9–10, 12, 119, 137, 141, 146–50. *See also* genealogy; `ohana

laulima, 36, 46, 159, 163
lāhui, 6, 14n23, 46, 186, 190, 207, 208
land, chapter 1, 17–18, 23, 28, 31–32, 43, 47n11, 74–75, 128–29, 131–33, 149, 161, 175, 206. *See also* `āina; ahupua`a
learning, Hawaiian-style, 3, 8–9, 11, 14n29, 35, 39–40, 42, 57–59, 68, 70–71, 73–75, 86, 132, 135, 152, 201, 208
Lind, Andrew, 122
Lili`uokalani, Queen of Hawai`i, 12n3, 18, 52, 146–47, 156n100
local(s), 3, 34, 35, 50n79, 61, 67, 76, 96–98, 107, 110, 114n61, 114n62, 114n64, 208

Māhele (1848 land division), 47n11, 137–38
Mannheim, Karl, 9, 15n33
Markham, Jesse Makani, 64
martial law, 85, 90–91, 93, 96
Massie case, 33, 114n62
Mauna Kea, 43–44, 51n93
Mauna Loa, 43
McGregor, Davianna Pōmaika`i, 18, 48n12, 49n49, 51n95, 159
missionaries, 54–55, 59, 136–38. *See also* Coan; Holman
mo`olelo, ix, 7–8, 25, 53, 163, 204–5

Native Americans, 1, 20, 99–100, 112n18, 115n71, 177, 184–88, 196n63
Native Hawaiian, x, 6, 13n6, 18–21, 27, 38, 49n38, 53, 64, 158, 179, 202. *See also* identity, constructions of; kanaka maoli
    American citizen, 8, 19, 53–54, 59, 125, 135
    health, 41, 173–74, 178, 192, 195n51
    masculinity, 33, 64, 74, 102, 135, 154n36, 191, 210n15

military service, 46, 99–101, 102, 106, 111–12, 116n115, 124–25
poverty, 12, 18, 173–74, 188–89
racial definition, viii, 2, 21, 98–99, 107, 150, 177, 179. *See also* blood quantum rule; race
Study Commission, 173
terminology, x
Nisei, 64, 82n49, 93–95, 109–111

Office of Hawaiian Affairs (OHA), 13n6, 38, 68, 152, 175–77, 186, 190, 195n55, n56, 207, 210n15
ʻohana, 4–5, 16, 26–27, 34, 36, 58, 108, 112, 119–20, 132, 136, 138, 147, 150, 159, 169, 175, 179, 199, 201–2, 206, 208. *See also* genealogy; kinship.
Osorio, Jonathan Kay Kamakawiwoʻole, 7, 14n23, 204

Pearl Harbor (Puʻuloa), 11, 80, 87, 90–92, 94–95, 97, 109, 111, 114n65, 127. *See also* Hālawa Housing; World War II
Naval Shipyard, 6, 112, 124–27, 132, 136, 143, 153, 202
Pidgin (Hawaiian Creole English), ix–x, 8, 26, 53, 55–56, 58, 63, 65, 67, 69, 134, 208
Piianaia, Abraham, 147
plantations, plantation economy, 11, 18, 20–24, 29, 33, 35, 43, 50n79, 60–62, 75–78, 82n61, 83n91, 87–88, 96, 120–23, 127, 131, 154n19, 160–61
    pineapple industry, 20, 23, 28, 48n28, 120, 123, 126
    sugar industry, 88, 126, 127, 131, 154n34, 160–61, 163, 170, 183, 188, 193n9
Pōhakuloa Training Area, 43–44
public schools (Hawaiʻi), 11, 47, 52–54, 58–66, 68, 72–73, 82n49, 82n53
    absenteeism/drop out, 59, 73, 83n79, 173
    civilizing mission, 11, 54–55, 72, 99
    English as universal language, 8, 47, 55–59, 61, 65–69, 82n57
    moral discipline, 53–54, 56–57, 59, 64
Pukui, Mary Kawena, 58, 143, 177

Pūnana Leo Schools, 69
Punahou School, 66

race, 11–12, 18, 20–21, 33, 61–62, 64, 76–77, 81n45, 82n49, 87, 89, 93, 96–98, 106, 122, 151, 158, 167, 179, 183
Rice v. Cayetano, 47n9, 152
Richardson, William, 142
Roosevelt, Franklin D., 30, 34, 92–93, 95, 100, 103, 109–10, 114n41
Roosevelt, Theodore, 66

Sato, Charlene, 67, 82n57
Senior Citizen Clubs, 52–53, 174, 176–79, 206
Silva, Noenoe, 51n97, 55, 195n49
Standard English, ix, xi, 7–8, 14n30, 47, 53–58, 63, 65–67, 69, 82n57, 126, 134–35
sustenance (subsistence), 17–20, 22–23, 28–29, 31, 34, 37, 46, 56, 68, 70, 112, 119–20, 133–34, 147, 165, 169, 171–74, 186–88, 201, 208

Tagaki, Dana, 173
talk-story, 7–8, 15n34, 31–32, 67, 107, 112, 186, 192, 199–200, 208
Tengan, Ty P. Kāwika, 33, 64, 80n2, 102, 112, 113n18, 116n115, 154n36, 191
tourism, 30, 37, 39–40, 43–44, 75, 78–79, 111, 119–20, 129, 155n42, 160, 162, 181, 208
Truman, Harry S., 110–11, 124

United States
    Army Corps of Engineers, 87, 90, 92–93, 95, 113n21
    colonial policy, 2, 6–7, 11, 13n8, 14n21, 14n23, 15n34, 33, 54, 56, 63, 74, 80, 84n100, 150, 188, 192, 209n7
    Congress, 16–24, 28–29, 34, 47n7, 99, 106, 114n65, 119, 135, 154n33, 161, 167, 173, 184–88, 196n86, 205
    Department of the Interior, 25, 47n9, 61–62, 73, 82n49, 83n80
    Engineering Department (USED), 89, 92, 96, 123

government, 8, 12, 21, 40, 78, 88, 145,
161, 167, 184
law (legal system), viii, 1, 12, 15n34,
48n42, 57, 69, 90–95, 124, 135–38,
142, 146–53, 155n69, 156n75, 158,
166, 168, 170, 182–83, 204
military, 11, 33, 43–45, 75, 78–79,
86–95, 98–100, 104–7, 109–12,
124–25, 183, 194n15, 203
War department, 93, 100

Volcanoes National Park, 40, 42–44, 59,
74–80

Waihe'e, John David III, 171, 185–86,
196n80, 197n94
Wilson, Woodrow, 75, 161
World War II, chapter 3, 8, 11, 85, 99–112,
115n7, 201

Young, G. Terry Kanalu, 144

www.ingramcontent.com/pod-product-compliance
Lightning Source LLC
Chambersburg PA
CBHW060035030426
42334CB00019B/2337